WATER POLO COACHING SERIES
BOOK 1

BASICS OF SUCCESSFUL COACHING

BY: Dante Dettamanti

© 2008 by Dante Dettamanti. All rights reserve

DEDICATION

This coach's manual is dedicated to Bob Horn, legendary UCLA wimming and water Polo coach, who was probably the most influential person in my coaching career. He was responsible for putting college water polo on the map with his great teams of the 60's and 70's. Many of the players from those teams played on the 1968 and 1972 bronze medal USA Olympic teams. Coach Horn was the reason that I decided to attend UCLA as a graduate student in 1968-69. He took me under his wing and gave me the opportunity to coach at UCLA, Phillips 66 Water Polo Club, and Santa Monica Swim Club. He taught me the fundamentals of the game, how to coach the game, and allowed me to experience working with top collegiate and Olympic caliber athletes. I was one of his assistant coaches when UCLA won the first NCAA Championship ever held in 1969. Without his help and input I don't think that I would have achieved success as a water polo coach.

COVER: The photo on the cover was taken by Ron Robertson Jr. and shows former UC Santa Barbara water polo player Miles Price in the act of shooting a water polo ball.

ACKNOWLEDGMENTS

A water polo coach does not just arrive on the scene and know immediately how to coach. In order to be a successful coach, he/she has to gain from their experiences. It is a constant and on-going learning experience that includes learning from other coaches.
I want to acknowledge all of the coaches that I have come in contact with in the sport of water polo that have contributed to my success as a coach. Karl Bell was my first coach at Santa Maria High School, and organized the first water polo team in the city when I was a sophomore in high school. He taught me how to play the game of water polo. Jerry Hinsdale was my coach at UC Davis. He sparked my interest in coaching when my playing days were over, when he allowed me to serve as his student assistant coach in both swimming and water polo for two years.

Bob Horn, the legendary UCLA coach, was probably the most influential person in my coaching career. I was a graduate assistant coach at UCLA under Coach Horn when UCLA won the first ever NCAA Water Polo championships in 1969. At the same time I was also able to assist another legend in the coaching world, Monte Nitzkowski, USA Olympic Coach, who along with Bob Horn coached the Phillips 66 club team that produced many Olympians for the 1968 and 1972 USA Olympic team.

Along the way I was able to work with many of the coaching legends in the game of water polo, from the United States and around the world. At Stanford, I followed Art Lambert, two-time Olympic coach, who coached Stanford to it's first ever NCAA Championship. Even though he had moved on from Stanford, I learned a lot from him, through his players who were still on the team. His philosophy of using speed and the emphasis on the counterattack stayed with me throughout my career.

In the summer just prior to coaching at Stanford, I was able to assist Ted Newland, longtime coach at UC Irvine, at the 1977 World University Games. Coach Newland has more wins as a collegiate head coach than anyone in the nation. I learned a lot from him about practice organization and teaching the fundamentals; as well as from two-time USA Olympic Coach Bill Barnett, who I assisted for two years with the USA team at the 1990 World Championships.

I also value the help and advice that I received from Pete Cutino, Cal-Berkeley head coach, who supported me throughout my career at Stanford, especially in my formative first years as head coach. Pete Snyder, long time head coach at UC Santa Barbara, and I were co-coaches of the USA "B" team for four years in the early nineties. We had many great coaching experiences together, traveling around the world with the US team.

Over the years, I have also had the opportunity to work with and learn from top European coaches. Fritz Dennerline, Italian Olympic coach at the 1984 Olympic games, taught me about zone defenses. Alfred Balen, who coached the famous Spandau West Berlin club team that produced most of Germany's Olympians, taught me game strategies and how to double-team the center forward. I was also able to assist Ratko Rudic, three-time Olympic Gold medal winner with Yugoslavia and Italy, during his first year as USA Olympic coach. From Rudic I learned about the European game, defensive systems, and about extra man offense and defense.

I also gained a lot from reading books about coaches outside of water polo. Basketball is a team sport that has produced many outstanding coaches. Two of the legends of the game were John Wooden, from UCLA, where I learned about the value of team play and organizing practices; and Red Aurerbach, New York Knicks coach, where I learned that the fast break should be a way of life. One of the greatest football coaches of all time was Vince Lombardi of the Green Bay Packers. From him I learned about the importance of executing the fundamental of the game.

From Hall of Fame and Super Bowl Champion football coach Bill Walsh, who started his career at Stanford at the same time that I did, I learned the value of preparing a team in practice for anything they might encounter in a game. All of these lessons learned from these coaches went a long ways in shaping my coaching philosophy, as well as my coaching career.

ABOUT THE AUTHOR

Coach Dante Dettamanti has produced winning and championship water polo teams at all levels. He started as a graduate assistant coach at UCLA, under the legendary Bob Horn. While at UCLA, the school won the first ever NCAA Championship ever held in 1969. From there he went on to Occidental College, where he transformed a program that had been the league doormat, into league champions, in just two short years. After coaching at Oxy for 4 years, he went on to UC Santa Barbara and turned the water polo program around; again producing a league champion team and a NCAA top four finish in just three years time.

It was at Stanford University though, that Dettamanti came into his own as a winning coach. In 25 years at Stanford, his teams played in the NCAA Championship final game a total of 14 times, producing 8 NCAA Championships and 6 second place finishes. His teams have finished among the collegiate top four rankings a total of 23 times during his 26 year coaching career spanning four decades (the 70's, 80's, 90's and 2000's). He also is the only coach in NCAA history to win a championship in each of those four decades.

Dettamanti became only the second collegiate coach in NCAA history to record over 600 wins, along with UC Irvine's Ted Newland. His eight national championships ties the NCAA record for the most in NCAA history, along with the legendary Pete Cutino of Cal-Berkeley. His .800 winning percentage at Stanford also is an NCAA record. He has been named League "Coach of the Year" ten times and NCAA "Coach of the Year" six different times.

Dettamanti has also had great success at the International level. He coached the USA World University Games teams to Gold and Silver medals in 1979 and 1981; the highest finish ever for a USA National team. Dettamanti gained valuable International coaching experience as assistant USA National Team coach under Bill Barnett at the 1991 FINA World Championships; and as an assistant to top interntional coach Ratko Rudic at the 2001 World Championships..

Dettamanti has not only produced winning teams, but also top international players. Fourteen of his players have gone on to play for the USA Olympic Team, including three time Olympians Jody Campbell (80, 84, 88), Wolf Wigo (92, 96, 2000) and Tony Azevedo (2000, 04, 08). Several of his players have gone on to become successful coaches, including John Tanner, Stanford Women's Coach, Wolf Wigo, UCSB Men's and Women's Coach, and Jack Bowen, Menlo School Boy's Coach.

Coach Dettamanti continues to spread the word about the sport of water polo by giving coaching clinics around the world, writing articles on the "Water Polo Planet" website, and as an author of water polo books. He has written two books about the sport, "A Practical Guide to Coaching Water Polo" and a book for players, parents and fans of the game, "Understanding Water Polo".

TABLE OF CONTENTS
BOOK 1
BASICS OF SUCCESSFUL COACHING

Dedication

Acknowledgements

About the author

Introduction

Terminology

CHAPTER	PAGE
1. What it Takes to be a Successful Coach	16
The Keys To Successful Coaching	27
2. Developing a Coaching Philosophy	28
The Commandments of Water Polo	42
3. Coaching And Teaching Tips	43
4. Practice Organization, Skills and Drills	58
5. Game Tactics and Strategies	77
6. Training and Conditioning for Water Polo	108
7. Resistance Training for Water Polo	155
8. Exercise Myths That Coaches Need To Know The Truth About	187

INTRODUCTION

WATER POLO COACHING SERIES
BOOK ONE

BASICS OF SUCCESSFUL COACHING

BY

DANTE DETTAMANTI
STANFORD UNIVERSITY

The two books in the WATER POLO COACHING SERIES, Book One, THE BASICS OF SUCCESSFUL COACHING, and Book Two, FUNDAMENTALS OF PLAYING WATER POLO, are essentially the second edition of my first coaching book, A PRACTICAL GUIDE TO COACHING WATER POLO.

While the first edition has been very well received, I still felt that I could have done a better job of presenting the material in the manual. I wanted to make the material more understandable, especially the individual and team skills that were presented. I also wanted to make the manual more beneficial and useful to the water polo coach. The end result is a manual that is more professional; a manual that is more befitting to the sport of water polo.

In putting together the second edition, I found that in order to present new and updated material, and at the same time organize it in a presentable and more understandable form, would require more pages than could effectively be placed in one book. Consequently I have had to divide the manual into two separate books. The result is two manuals as part of a WATER POLO COACHING SERIES. BOOK ONE of the series presents the techniques of coaching, with an emphasis on how to teach and coach the sport of waterpolo; while BOOK TWO presents the fundamentals of playing the game of water polo.

In most coaching manuals that I have read about water polo, as well as other sports, about ninety percent of the material presented has to do with the X's and 0's and skills of playing the game (what to coach); while a small amount of material is actually presented on how to coach the sport. Learning "how" to coach is the area of coaching water polo that I feel is the most neglected in this country; and the area where there is the most need for coaches to learn about.

Most water polo coaches in this country have played the game, and consequently understand how the game is played. Many, however, have not had any kind of formal training in actual coaching. Many have not had the opportunity to work under a "mentor" coach, or to be an assistant coach at any level. Because of the great need for water polo coaches for both men and women in this country, many coaches are thrust into coaching positions without having any kind of coaching background what so-ever.

The need is so great for water polo coaches, especially at the high school level, that sometimes the only requirement for being a head coach is that the coach has played the game. In most foreign countries, coaches have to take coaching courses; and have to pass proficiency exams before they are allowed to coach. The United States has no such system. As a result, many coaches go into head coaching positions at the club or high school level without any kind of knowledge of "how" to coach their players.

Just because a coach has played the game, even at National or Olympic levels, doesn't mean that the coach knows how to coach. All it means is that he/she knows how to play the game. Having knowledge of how water polo is played is not enough if you cannot get that knowledge across to your players; and then get them to execute in a game what you have presented to them. There is a lot more to coaching than just standing in front of a chalk board and telling your players how to play the game, or perform a certain skill.

The best coaches know what material to present, they know how to present it so that players understand what the coach is saying, they know how to get their players to execute what the coach has presented, and they make effective use of their time in practice; so that the team doesn't waste time doing things that are not important, or not necessary. The most effective coaches are efficient in combining drills and conditioning together to train their players; and they don't waste a lot of time training the players with swimming that is not necessary for a water polo athlete.

It is amazing how much knowledge of water polo is wasted, or doesn't get across to the players because the coach doesn't know how to present the material; or know how to get his players to execute what is important in a game. A successful coach doesn't just need to know how to play the game, he/she needs to know how to teach young athletes how to play the game. Ninety percent of coaching takes place in practice. So, if you are not organized or efficient in your practice sessions, your players will go into games unprepared, and out of shape for the rigors of a water polo game.

One of the main reasons for writing this series is to help fill the gap in teaching coaches how to be effective and successful in coaching water polo. I am not saying that I know all of the answers, or that I didn't make mistakes along the way. It took me over 40 years to figure it all out. Some of it I figured out right away, and some of it took a lot longer. Even today, at 68 years old, I am still learning about coaching water polo.

In my first few years of coaching, I knew just enough to get by. Mainly because I played the game and learned from a mentor coach who knew the game and how to coach it. That was Bob Horn, the former UCLA swimming and water polo coach, winner of the first ever NCAA Championship in 1969. Coach Horn was a master at producing winning teams. I worked for him for two years as a graduate assistant, while I was studying for my Masters degree in Exercise Physiology.

Prior to that I was a student assistant coach for two years at my Alma Matter, UC Davis. In between I was able to learn a lot about leadership and teaching as a First Liutenant in the US Army Corps of Engineers. As an army airborne-ranger, I also learned the value of working together as a team to accomplish a goal.

While I credit my early success to what I learned from Coach Horn, I never stopped learning about coaching. Besides spending four years as an assistant coach before I ever became a head coach, along the way I was constantly analyzing, observing other coaches, reading about and listening to successful coaches in other sports, and learning from my own successes and failures. I took what I could use from other coaches and teams, and discarded what I couldn't use. If I did something as a coach and it worked, then I would continue using it. If it didn't work, I would try something else that did work. Along the way I became a better coach.

Writing this coaches manual has made me a better coach; because I had to think about and analyze everything that I was putting down on paper. I have always had a sense about what to do, and what not to do; but I still had to adjust my thinking many times along the way. A new coach does not just arrive on the scene knowing everything that there is to do, and doing the right thing every time. You have to grow into the job. If you refuse to adapt and make changes, or listen to others, then you are lost; and your team will also be lost.

Despite not being "fully formed" when I started coaching, I was still able to win at every level; partly because I utilized what I learned from other coaches, and reading about other successful teams and coaches, partly from applying sports science from my background in exercise physiology, partly by following my own instincts on what was going right or wrong, and partly because I had excellent players that I was able to effectively mold into a team.

Along the way I have learned what it takes to consistently win year after year. It took me 40 years to figure it out. All you have to do is read this manual and apply what you have learned to your coaching. I have already made all of the mistakes for you.

Book 1, "BASICS OF SUCCESSFUL COACHING" presents in detail what it takes to become a successful coach. A complete new Chapter 1 has been added on 'WHAT IT TAKES TO BE A SUCCESSFUL COACH"; and in addition to Chapter 2 on "DEVELOPING A COACHING PHILOSOPHY" presents the fundamental concepts that a person must follow that will allow him/her to have success in coaching water polo. These two chapters will also help you as a coach to develop your own personal philosophy of how you want your players to play the game.

The skills required to play the game of water polo are unique to the sport of water polo. If transfer of learning from the practice session to the game, or competitive situation, is to be maximized, the demands of the practice session should mimic as closely as possible the demands of the sport itself. How the coach presents the material in practice, and teaches the sports specific skills of water polo to his team, is critical to the success of that team.

A lot of the success of team sports has to do with the efficient organization of practice sessions in order to encompass all of the necessary skills to play the game of water polo. In Chapter 3 on "COACHING AND TEACHING TIPS", Chapter 4 on "PRACTICE ORGANIZATION, SKILLS AND DRILLS" and Chapter 5 on "GAME TACTICS AND STATEGIES", the coach will learn how to organize efficient and effective practice sessions, how to present the material, and how to teach the skills and tactics necessary to play the game of water polo.

While successful water polo coaches around the world are well versed in the tactics and skills required to play the game of water polo, many, including some Olympic and National Team coaches, are lacking in the knowledge to properly train their athletes to achieve maximum success. There are many misconceptions that coaches have about training water polo athletes. Many are based on a misunderstanding of physiological and psychological principals, and how to apply them to the requirements of the sport.

Because coaches have a tendency to keep "doing things the way that they have always been done", they can become "stuck in a coaching rut" of doing everything the same way year after year. Coaches need to start questioning some of the coaching "methods" that seem to have been successful in the past, or training "methods" that are religiously followed by water polo coaches, without questioning whether they work or not.

It is time for water polo coaches to start "thinking outside the box" and coming up with new and more productive and effective methods of training our athletes. I will present new material in this manual which will at least get coaches started in this thinking process of "why do we do things the way we do"? Following are some of the training methods that are common in our sport, but need to be questioned.

- Why do we have our athletes lift weights?
- Why do we have our athletes swim thousands of yards every day in practice, when the longest distance that they have to swim at any one time in a game is only about 20-25 yards?
- Why do we require our players to go out for the swim team?
- Why do we require our athletes to train twice a day during the competitive season?
- Why do we require our athletes to perform static stretching exercises on the pool deck before they get into the water?

Do you as a coach really know WHY you do these things, or are you simply doing things this way because they have "always been done this way", and "everybody does it this way"?

I want to alert all of the coaches that read this manual, that some of the conclusions that I come to in answering the questions presented above, do not follow mainstream thinking in the sport of water polo. Some might even consider these conclusions to be a little controversial. Hopefully I can get coaches to at least start questioning and thinking about many of the ways that we train our water polo athletes, that at the outset seem counterproductive to the success of our teams. It is then up to you, as a coach, to evaluate the material presented and make your own decisions on how you want to train your team.

One of the purposes of this manual is to investigate some of the "common" training practices in the sport of water polo, as presented above. There are quite a few "coaching practices" that will be covered in this manual that are commonly accepted in training water polo players; but are severely in need of change. This is mainly because they are time-consuming, unproductive, unnecessary, and end up taking valuable time away from what players should be doing, and that is learning to play the game of water polo.

One of the areas that we have to look at is the excessive swimming that we do in water polo. Excess mileage that is performed at slower than "game speed", and that is completely unnecessary for a sport that is basically a sprint sport. We are the only sport that requires our athletes to swim laps for anywhere from 25-50 percent of a practice session, the only sport that has the players perform morning sessions that are "swim only", and involve nothing but lap swimming, the only sport that puts the athletes through torturous 6-7 hour daily sessions during the first week of practice that we call "hell week".

Then to add insult to injury, a lot of the swimming that we have our athletes perform is completely uneccessary and wasteful long distance, or slow swimming, that does nothing to train the water polo athlete. Slogging out a lot of long slow swimming is a practice that is done by water polo coaches from around the world, and at all levels.

Then in this country we take it one step further. At the high school level we also require our athletes to be on the swim team during the water polo off-season. Instead of the water polo coach providing year around water polo specific training for the athlete, we have the swim coach do our training for us. The problem is that it is the wrong kind of swim training that does not always apply to water polo. Is this really necessary for playing water polo? Believe me, there are a lot of successful Olympic water polo athletes from foreign countries that have never been on a swim team!

Training our athletes in this way would be like a basketball coach telling the players to run about six miles during the first 45 minutes of a basketball practice, before they practice any kind of basketball; and then requiring all of the players on the team to go out for the cross-country running team durng the off-season.It is time for water polo coaches to stop this sort of unproductive training, and start to make the most effective use of our time to teach the skills, tactics and strategies of playing water polo.

The correct methods of training the water polo athlete, based on a practical application of science, are presented in Chapter 6 on "TRAINING AND CONDITIONING FOR WATER POLO". A complete analysis of the energy requirements of playing water polo are presented, along with the training methods that will effectively train your players for the requirements of playing the game. This chapter has been expanded to include new material and research into the latest swim training techniques, along with a complete analysis of the eggbeater kick and training the legs for water polo. A completely new method of training for water polo, called "ultra-short" training, is also introduced in this chapter.

A perponderance of evidence in the past ten years has brought into question the effectiveness of using dry-land strength training to increase the performance level of the competitive athlete in any sport, not just water polo. Several questions have to be answered in regards to strength training. Is the strength aquired from simply performing the sports activity itself, at a high intensity, enough to obtain maximum performance; or is additional strength obtained from dry-land training needed? An even more important aspect of strength training questions if the strength acquired from dry-land training is even transferable to the complex movements required to perform most sports activities?

In regards to performing a sport in the water (swimming and water polo), how much strength is actually required to propel a body through the water; especially when a good portion of the force applied by the arms and legs is dissipated into a medium (water) that moves when you push on it? Are there other factors involved that are more important than strength, when performing the water polo skills of swimming and the eggbeater kick.

Strength training is just one aspect of training that will be covered in Chapter 7 on "RESISTANCE TRAINING FOR WATER POLO. This chapter presents the latest up-dated material on how to train the various muscles of the body that are specific to water polo, and whether this is best accomplished in the water or on dry-land. Also covered in this chapter is the use of resistance band training to strengthen the "rotator-cuff" muscles of the shoulder that are important in preventing shoulder injuries.

There also are all kinds of myths in the world of sports and exercise. Water polo is no exception. Many well-meaning persons spread these myths because they don't know any better, and are just doing what they were taught by others. Ignorance, however, is no excuse in this day in age of computers and the internet! Information about research that has been done and opinions from experts in the field are there at your fingertips. All you have you do is take the time to question and look for it. Many of the myths and misconceptions in water polo, including some of the swim and strength training methods presented in Chapter 6 and 7 on "Training and Conditioning" and "Strength Training" are presented in Chapter 8, EXERCISE MYTHS THAT COACHES NEED TO KNOW ABOUT.

As a coach, you have two choices, educate yourself with the knowledge aquired from this manual, and from other sources: and then make an accurate training decision based on that knowledge, and the knowledge acquired from your own experiences. Or you can simply follow a checklist of drills and techniques that other coaches, even perhaps your own coach, have performed in the past, ignore the information contained in this book that is based on experience and science; and just keep guessing and following your instincts, hoping that someday your team will be successful.

Remember that "COACHING IS A LOT MORE THAN JUST KNOWING THE X's AND O's." I hope that you will take this statement to heart; and that through this two-part series, you will allow me to be the "mentor" coach that you may have never had. My desire for those of you who read these two manuals is to take the information that I have presented, and hopefully use it to help you coach your own successful water polo team.

Good luck and good coaching!

                                                      Dante Dettamanti

NUMBERING SYSTEM AND TERMINOLOGY

This NUMBERING SYSTEM for front court offense and defense, as well as for extra-man offense and defense, is commonly used in the United States at most all levels of play. A specific number, 1 through 6, is issued to each position in the water. This allows for easier in-pool communication between players as well as between coaches and players. See Diagrams A-1 and A-2 below for the numbering system and names that will be used in the coaching series for both even strength and man-advantage positions. Offensive players are marked with a "O" and defensive players are marked with an "X."

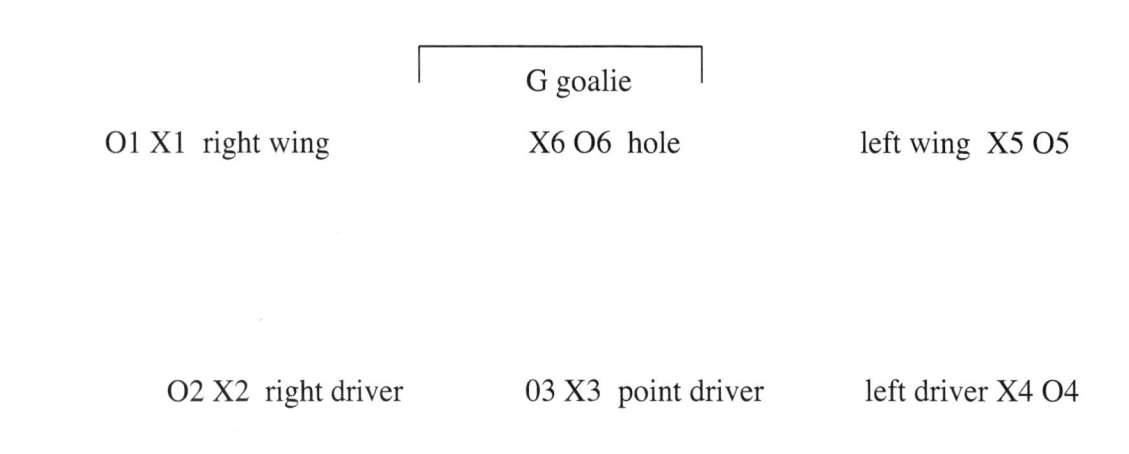

| G goalie |

O1 X1 right wing   X6 O6 hole   left wing X5 O5

O2 X2 right driver   O3 X3 point driver   left driver X4 O4

Diagram A-1 Front court offensive and defensive positions

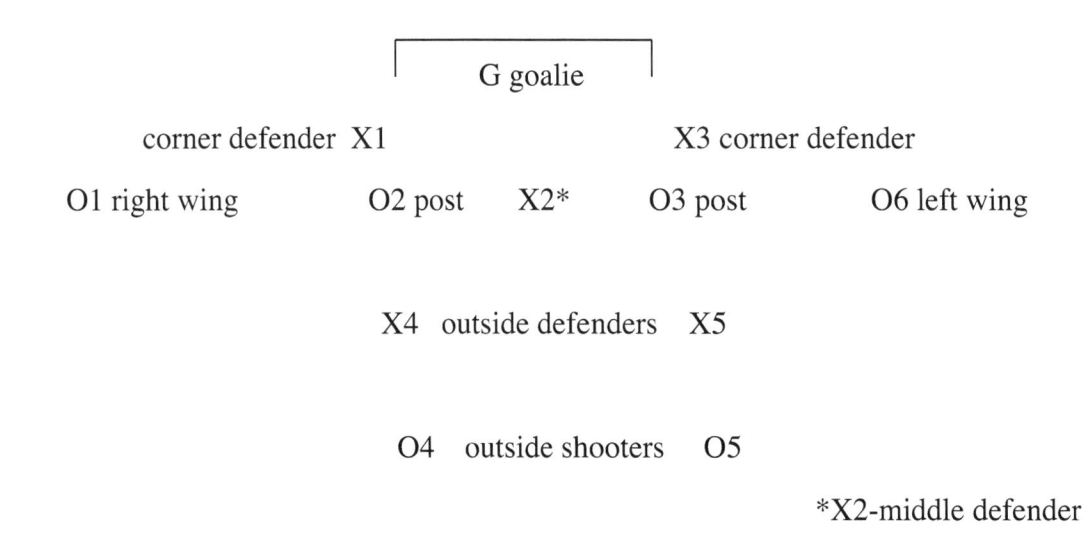

| G goalie |

corner defender X1   X3 corner defender

O1 right wing   O2 post   X2*   O3 post   O6 left wing

X4   outside defenders   X5

O4   outside shooters   O5

*X2-middle defender

Diagram A-2 Extra-man offensive and defensive positions

TERMINOLOGY

All of the gender references in the series refer to both male and female coaches, as well as to female and male players; even though most of the actual listed references are written as "he" rather than he/she or "she". This is mainly done for ease and efficiency of writing, and is not meant to infer that all water polo coaches and players are male. The information about coaching in the series is meant for both male and female coaches, while the skills and drills shown are to be performed by both female and male water polo athletes.

The same holds true for a majority of the photos of players performing water polo skills. Because I had available photos of mostly male players that I coached, or who posed for many of the skills shown in the series, I decided to use only photos of male players. These skills shown in these manuals are meant for use by players of all age levels; although the skills shown, for the most part, are not meant for the very basic beginner levels of water polo. Beginner skills are presented in other water polo books that are written by other authors. It is up to the coach who is reading the manual to decide how much his/her players, and at what age they are capable of absorbing.

Most of the terminology used in the books is self explanitory, or commonly used in the water polo world. There may be some confusion in the use of "extra-man" and "man-up". Extra-man is used when describing the 6 on 5 extra-man situation when a defensive player has been excluded; while man-up is used during the counterattack when a team has a one man-advantage over the defensive team. This occurs when one player has broken free of his defender during the counterattack, commonly referred to as the "free-man".

This can be anything from "one on nobody" when the first player is going against the goalie without a defender, 2 against 1, and all the way up to 6 against 5 one man advantage. Also during the counterattack, the "lead-break" is the person who is the first person down at the opposite end of the pool, guarded or unguarded. "Inside-water" is when a player has gained inside position in front of the goal, with no defender between the player and the goalie.

CHAPTER 1
WHAT IT TAKES TO BE A SUCCESSFUL COACH

A successful coach has to be good leader as well as a good teacher. Being a coach is teaching skills, attitudes and goals to players on the team. A coach must keep in mind that water polo is a game that requires the players to learn certain individual and team skills. The job of the coach is to teach the players how to apply these skills in a coordinated effort towards a common goal, to prepare the players physically to handle the rigors of the game, and to create a mental attitude that will help to overcome the efforts of the other team.

As a coach, you must know where you are going and how you are going to get there. You have to coach with enthusiasm and with confidence in your technical ability, you have to create an attitude that hard work pays off, and you have to pay attention to detail and make sure that players do things correctly. What you teach is important, but you still have to get the players to buy into your philosophy of the game; and to perform they way that you want them to perfrom. This might be difficult at first, especially for new coaches. But, as you gain more experience and success as a coach, the players will see that your system and methods work, and will be more willing to accept what you are trying to get across to them.

"How" you coach is just as important as "what" material you present. Your method(s) of presenting essential material to your players is critical to the success of your team. If you are presenting the wrong material, or not presenting it correctly, then there is not a chance of having a successful team. The players will just end up confused and unaware of what they are supposed to be doing do. Don't blame the players when this happens. It is the coach's responsibility to present the material so that the players understand and execute it correctly in a game. When they don't understand, it is the coach's fault, not the players.

WHAT IT TAKES TO BE A SUCCESSFUL COACH

Following are what I feel are some of the basic and fundamental concepts that a person must follow that will allow him/her to be a successful coach:

BE ORGANIZED

Before a coach steps on to the pool deck, he must know WHAT HAS TO BE DONE, and possess the capabilities and convictions to get it done. The coach also must determine WHEN THINGS HAVE TO BE DONE and WHY THEY HAVE TO BE DONE. Several factors affect this, but none is more important than your own personal beliefs. These beliefs comprise your coaching philosophy. This personal philosophy is something that the coach will impart on his players. It is important that a coach presents his philosophy to his players in a well organized and effective manner. (See Chapter 2 on "Philosopy").

HAVE A PHILOSOPHY THAT YOU BELIEVE IN

Your coaching philosophy is derived from your background as a player and coach, your education, the knowledge that you have learned from mentor coaches, from your experiences in the game, and from your own ideas and beliefs. It has a lot to do with how a coach wants his team to play the game of water polo; and what kind of image he wants the team to project.

It is derived from a process of thinking about critical issues, and developing rational reasons for holding one particular belief over another. A coach must constantly analyze what he is doing, and why he is doing it. Don't just do something because that is the way your coach did it, it is something that has always been done that way, or is something that was presented at a coach's clinic by another successful coach.

A coach needs to identify the important parts of the game that he will emphasize and teach to his players; and that will give his team the best chance to win. He has to identify the fundamentals, tactics and strategies that are important to success in water polo. What can we do as a team that will give us the best chance to win? You sometimes hear coaches say, "play the game right." What is right for you, or what is right for your team, may be different for different coaches, and for different groups of players. This then becomes your philosophy of how to play the game.

The coach then needs to identify a way that he wants his players to do things, how he wants them to act, and how he wants them to treat their teammates and others around them. This becomes the mental part of a coach's philosophy; the standards that he sets for how he wants the players to behave.

BE A GOOD LEADER

In addition to expertise and knowledge of the game, and knowing how and when to apply that knowledge, a good leader must have certain personal habits and characteristics that contribute to his/her effectiveness as a coach. These include the following:

*BEING YOURSELF- Stay within the framework of your personality and be authentic. Your style will work for you when you take advantage of your strengths, and strive to overcome your weaknesses. Don't try to copy the style of other successful coaches. They are what they are and you are what you are. If you're faking it by trying to be someone else, or something that you are not; you'll be found out.

*BEING PREPARED- No coach can control the outcome of a contest or competition, but you can control how you prepare for it. Work hard to prepare the team in practice for expected situations, events you know will happen. Equally important, plan and prepare for the unexpected. "What happens when what's supposed to happen, doesn't happen" is the question that you must always ask yourself and prepare for?

*PAYING ATTENTION TO DETAIL- Address all aspects of your team's efforts to prepare mentally, physically, fundamentally, and strategically, in as thorough a manner as possible. Pay attention to detail and make sure that players execute the fundamentals of the game correctly. Do not make the mistake of burying yourself in every small detail; but make sure that everything that is important is covered.

*EXPANDING YOUR KNOWLEDGE- The greater your expertise, the greater will be your potential to teach; and the stronger and more productive you will be as a leader. "The more you know, the higher you will go". You need to understand all aspects of the game, and of coaching the game of water polo.

Expand your knowledge by seeking out and learning from other coaches and mentors, and from other sources of information such as clinics, books, and publications from experts in the field. There never has been a coach or leader who has arrived on the scene fully formed; who has figured everything out by himself. We learn from others, whether it is consciously or sub-consciously. A good coach is always learning and never stops learning.

*BEING POSITIVE- Spend more time teaching what to do, than what not to do. Spend more time teaching and encouraging individuals, than criticizing them; and more time building up, rather than tearing down. For some reason, it is easier to criticize than to be positive; but it is something that a good leader has to learn to do. There is a constructive place for censure and highlighting negative aspects of a situation; but be careful in that it is not done simply to vent your frustrations. Balance the negative with the positive.

*BEING FIRM AND FAIR- Be clear in your own mind as to what you stand for, and then set standards of behavior for the team. Everyone on the team should be clear on what is expected in terms of behavior. It is up to the coach to discipline players in a fair manner that is the same for everyone, even the so-called star players on the team.

*BEING FLEXIBLE- Consistency is important in your approach; but there are times that it is necessary to change what you are doing. Don't stubbornly stick to something that you are doing, if it isn't working. Constantly evaluate what you are doing and why you are doing it. If you can't answer to yourself or explain it to your team, then re-evaluate, take suggestions from others, and then make up your own mind on what changes, if any, need to be made.

*BEING PERSISTANT- The leader who will not be denied, who has expertise coupled with strength of will, is going to prevail. Great coaches will simply not quit when it comes to installing their own system, and to push forward with their own plan. A coach should have an inner compulsion or drive; to get it done the way that he/she wants it done. Keep sending the same message over and over again to your team, until it sticks. Have a passion for the game, and for teaching the game the way that you feel it should be played.

*BEING AN ENTHUSIASTIC TEACHER- The dictionary defines "to coach" as "to give instruction or advice, to teach, to impart knowledge or skill". Strive to be the best teacher possible. Successful teaching requires reception, retention, and comprehension of the message that you are trying to get across. Have enthusiasm for the subject matter, and a passion for teaching the game the way that you feel it should be played. Without enthusiasm for what you are presenting, you cannot expect the players to be enthusiastic about the sport. Without enthusiasm, you take a risk that your team will become bored and tune you out.

COMMUNICATION

The ability to communicate to your team is critical to being a good teacher. Communication is the ability to organize and successfully convey your thoughts and ideas. Just presenting facts is not communication. Getting your point across to the players has to do with not only how much information you give them, but how much information they can absorb. Eighty percent, or more, of what your players hear will be forgotten within forty-eight hours.

Giving players too much information can be detrimental to learning. This is called "over coaching." It is better to give the players a little less information, and have the assurance that they have learned something; rather than giving them too much, and not being certain how much they have actually absorbed.

LEARN TO LISTEN

A big part of communication is listening to others. A coach that is not willing to listen, and keeps making the same mistakes, will find that success is much harder to come by. A coach should always be willing to listen to assistant coaches and to his players. They are the ones that have to live with your decisions, and are personally involved in the pool. Besides players and assistant coaches, have a team captain that can be a sounding board for decisions that you will make, or that you are about to make. In the end the final decision will be yours to make.

SIMPLICITY AND REPITITION

Remember this concept by the acronym KISS, "Keep it Simple Stupid". A coach should not be interested in trying to prove to his players that he is a genius, or show how much he knows. Before you put in a complex offense or defense, you have to know the learning capabilities of your players. Start and stay with an easy, simple approach to water polo. Don't get complicated, and present only enough material that they can absorb; and then repeat over and over again until they understand what to do. A basic principle of information retention is that you will retain almost 70% of what you listen to, if it is repeated six times or more. Even more can be retained if the person has to repeatedly and physically perform what is being presented by the coach.

Tips for presenting information to your team.
1. Keep it simple. Use straight-forward language; no need to get fancy.
2. Be concise and brief and not long-winded.
3. Organize your message in logical and sequential building blocks.
4. Be observant; know if you are connecting.

SET A STANDARD OF EXCELLENCE.

Set standards for how you want the game to be played, and how you want the players to act. Eliminate and correct mistakes. Instill in players the need for improvement, a drive to get better and better. Here's what's wrong and this is how to do it right! The coach can emphasize improvement as a way to win games, rather than just emphasizing winning in itself. This takes the pressure off players, and gives them a way to help the team win games by improving themselves as players. One way to do this is to set both team and individual goals at the beginning of the season; so that the players have realistic benchmarks to shoot for.

How players treat each other and react to people outside the team can also be incorporated in your "standard of excellence". Things like team play and team unity, respect for others (including your opponents), good sportsmanship, winning and losing with dignity, etc can be part of the standard of excellence that you impart on the team.

CREATE AN ATTITUDE

Just as important to a coach, than creating an offensive and a defensive philosophy, is creating an attitude. An attitude gives the team an identity that distinguishes them from other teams, and is something that can give your team both a physical and mental advantage over our opponents. It is something that your opponent has to worry about every time that they play you. An example of an "attitude" that we tried to create at Stanford was that "we are in better shape than the other team" and we can "outswim them".

Our goal was to wear down opponents throughout the game by out-swimming them on the counterattack. In crunch time in the fourth quarter, we knew that the game was ours. Once our players realized that we could win games by being in better shape than our opponents, it was easier to get them to work hard in practice. This gave us a tremendous physical, as well as psychological advantage over other teams in close games, especially in the important fourth quarter, or in overtime.

TEACH A "TEAM FIRST", NOT "ME FIRST" PHILOSOPHY

Besides the physical part of the game, a coach must also teach a philosophy that stresses the mental aspects of the game. The physical part is how you want your players to play the game. The mental part is how you want them to act and interact as members of the team. "Team play" is a key ingredient to the success of a team. Team play means unselfish play. Unselfish play means that a player will sacrifice his own personal goals in order to help out a teammate. The measure of a great team is that willingness to sacrifice for the team.

BE A GOOD PRACTICE COACH

Conducting practice sessions is the single most important aspect of coaching. Most of the time that you spend with your team is during practice. Most of the coaching that you do takes place in practice. It is during practice sessions that the coach instills the fundamentals of the game, installs his system of play, prepares for an upcoming opponent, and conditions the players to be able to effectively handle the rigors of the game.

How effective you are in organizing and presenting you practice sessions, goes a long way to determining the success and/or failure of your team. Your coaching philosophy defines you as a coach; but how you implement your philosophy in practices determines whether you are a successful coach or not.

PREPARE IN PRACTICE FOR WHAT YOU WANT YOUR PLAYERS TO DO IN THE GAME.

There is a saying in sports, that when something good seems to happen to a team, " We would rather be lucky than good." Good things don't happen because you are lucky. They happen because your team is prepared for every situation.

There is an even more realistic saying that says "Luck is when preparation meets opportunity". If your team is properly prepared in practice, they will be ready when the opportunity presents itself in a game. Luck is a phenomena that the coach cannot do anything about. Preparation, on the other hand, is definitely something that the coach has complete control over.

One of the key responsibilities of the coach is to prepare his team for upcoming games. Game preparation is done in practice. Ninety percent of a coach's work should be accomplished by game time. The players should be prepared ahead of time, for any situation that they might encounter in the game.

During the game, the coaches primary responsibility is to make substitutions when necessary, decide what offense or defense a team will run, and make minor adjustments in the game plan and tactics; depending on what the other team may do. It should be easy for the players to change what they are doing, if they have been prepared properly.

How well have you prepared your team? If you have done your job properly, the team should be able to coach themselves; if for some reason the car carrying you and your assistant coach broke down on the way to the game. That would truly show how effective your preparation for the game was. If you can honestly say that "yes, my team could play the game, even if I and my assistant were not present"; then you have done a good job of preparing them in practice.

DON'T WASTE TIME DOING THINGS THAT ARE NOT IMPORTANT

Besides being organized in your mind as to what has to be done, why it has to be done, and how it has to be done, a good coach has to be organized in regard to the most efficient and productive use of time. Wasting time on things that are not important, especially during practice sessions, can undermine all the planning and preparation that goes into getting ready to play the game. The more efficient a coach is during practice sessions, in a limited amount of time, the more information he/she can get across to the players; and in addition perform the conditioning and training necessary to prepare the players to play the game.

Make efficient use of your time by combining water polo drills with conditioning. Every possible minute should be spent in the water and involve as many players as possible. The session should be completely water polo related. Players should constantly be kept moving, and not just sitting around waiting to participate. Use as many goals as you have room for, so that all players can be involved at the same time in drills. If only half of your players are involved in a drill, have the other half do some kind of conditioning at the side of the pool, like legwork with weighted balls. It is important to keep everyone doing something productive during practice, rather than hanging on to the wall and just watching everyone else perform; or talking with their buddies.

CONDITION YOUR PLAYERS TO BE ABLE TO UNDERGO THE RIGORS OF THE GAME AND PRACTICE.

Besides teaching the fundamentals to his team, a coach needs to condition and train his players to handle the rigors of the game; one of the most physically demanding team sports in the world. It is up to the coach to get his players in shape to play the game; and to be able move up and down the pool over and over again at a fast pace, especially during the counterattack.

The counterattack can be effective in wearing down your opponents, but only if your team is in shape to do so for the whole game. Players who are properly prepared physically, don't wear out during the game; because they will be in great shape from counterattacking and swimming hard every day in practice.

An important concept in training water polo players is to train "specific to the game". When conditioning the team using drills and swimming, make sure that the type of swimming or movements that you do are specific to the sport of water polo. Water polo is an anaerobic sport consisting of a series of short sprints. The players need to be trained as close to anaerobic game conditions as possible.

The basic idea of conditioning for water polo, is that the team spends as little time as possible doing straight conditioning (swimming), and spend as much time as possible working on individual fundamentals and learning how to play the game. To do this effectively, keep the swimming short and intense, and close as possible to what a player actually does in a game.

The coach must, at the same time, incorporate conditioning into every part of the practice session. Combining swimming with shooting, drills, counterattack and scrimmaging is much more effective for water polo than just swimming laps. Make every part of the practice as rigorous as you can, and you will be rewarded with a team that will out-swim and wear down your opponents.

INSIST ON THE CORRECT EXECUTION OF THE BASIC FUNDAMENTALS OF THE GAME.

A coach cannot allow his players to execute the fundamentals of the game incorrectly. I always felt that players had to be called to task every time they came up short, rather then acting as if the transgression didn't happen. It is your job as coach to teach the basic fundamentals of the game, and to make sure that are executed properly. It is up to the players to learn how to execute them properly.

In water polo, every game situation calls for the execution of a fundamental part of the game. If players learn the proper way to handle these situations in practice, they will be able to execute them in the game; no matter what the opponent does tactically. A coach has to have patience, and allow time for the players to learn what he is trying to get across. If they are not getting the point, you might have to try another approach.

BE DEMANDING WITHOUT BEING OVER-BEARING.
When you critique players, make sure that they understand the importance of doing things right; and that you are correcting them because you want them to improve as players. Use past mistakes as an example of what someone did wrong, without piling it on. Focus on the "here and now". This is what you did wrong, and this is how you do it right!

THE SECRETS OF BEING A CONSISTENT WINNER

The biggest secret of being a consistent winner is that "there are no secrets to winning". The methods of winning consistently are right there for everyone to use. This is not "rocket science". If it was, I would be the last person to be telling you the secrets of winning. The hard part is separating the "right stuff" from the all of the extraneous and worthless stuff that is circulating out there in the world of coaching.

More than anything else, being an "effective" coach is the "secret" to being a consistent winner. More than knowledge of the game, "effectively" transferring your knowledge to your players; and getting them to execute that knowledge in a competitive game, is the "key to success" in coaching your team. A coach can't just throw everything that he knows at the players, and hope that something sticks. A coach has to have an idea of not only how much information he must present to his team, and what information he must present; but most importantly, how to effectively present the "relevant" information.

HOW EFFECTIVE IS YOUR COACHING?
There are hundreds of water polo coaches around the country, and around the world, who have an excellent knowledge of the game of water polo; and yet are not producing successful and winning teams. Understanding the game is not enough for success in coaching. The most important factor is getting your players to understand the game; and then getting them to perform in the way that you want them to perform.

If somewhere along the line, the coach's knowledge is not being translated into winning water polo, then the coach has to ask himself, "how effective is my coaching"? In other words, how much of the coach's knowledge is being transferred to the players and into winning games; and if it is not being transferred, why isn't it?

BECOME AN EFFECTIVE COACH
Following the points outlined above in this chapter will go a long way toward making you a successful coach. They are all important; but some are more critical than others in order to make a coach "effective", as well as successful. It is difficult to separate the two; because you cannot be successful unless you are effective. The most important elements of becoming an "effective" coach are outlined below.

IDENTIFY WHAT IS IMPORTANT
The first think that a coach has to do is to identify the most important parts of the game; and then prioritize them in order of importance. A coach cannot waste time on presenting information, or working on aspects of the game that are not important, or are of minor importance. Work on the most important aspects of the game first; and then if you have time, work on other less important parts of the game.

Pool time is very limited to most water polo coaches; so a coach who understands how to make effective use of the short time that he has, will be way ahead of the game. An effective coach must recognize what is a waste of time, and what needs to be worked on, depending on the skill level and needs of the team.

There are several ways to identify what is important, and what your team needs to work on. The best way is to work back from your first game, to your first practice. Identify what you feel the team needs to know in order to play their first game. Part of this is based on what your team already knows, and what they have learned during the summer before the fall season; and part of it comes from your personal philosophy on how you want the game played. What kinds of defense do your players need to know, what kind of offense do they need, and what kind of individual skills do they need in order to effectively implement the defense and offense.

In addition to that, the coach has to emphasize parts of the game that reflect his personal philosophy. For me, that would be conditioning, counterattack, 6 on 5 offense and defense, and team defense. These parts of the game also have to be worked on every day, prior to the first game of the season. It is up to the coach to figure out the best way to put everything together in an efficient and effective manner. After that, he can continue to work on those parts of the game, add more material based on the how the team did in their first game, and also work on what needs to be done to prepare for the next game.

PRESENTING INFORMATION- COACH BY DOING, NOT BY TALKING
One of the biggest mistakes that a coach can make is to give long chalk talks to the players before practice, or before games; thinking that they are going to remember everything that the coach says. TALKING is not coaching! The most effective way for players to learn something, is not by doing what the coach says in a chalk talk; but by actually doing what he wants in the water.

So, introduce what you want them to do by making a few simple, short points. Then have them get in the water and do it; making corrections as you go along. The effective coach does most of his coaching with the players in the water, and not at the chalkboard! For games, prepare the team in practice, only hit the high points during the pre-game chalk talk, and do not ask them to do something during the game that they have not practiced or prepared for.

An effective coach must present only a small amount of the most important information, knowing that the players can only absorb so much. Most information presented during chalk talks is wasted; because the players can only absorb so much information before they start losing interest, and stop paying attention. The same goes for time-outs and in-between quarters.

Keep it short, keep it simple, and only present a few key points that they will remember. Tell them what you want them to do, and do not re-hash what they have just done wrong. I tell young coaches who want to give out too much information during the heat of battle, "Make many points, and they will remember none of them; make two points and they will remember both of them".

IT IS TOO LATE TO TEACH ONCE THE GAME HAS STARTED

Teach the players "how to play the game" during practice, and not during the game. If they don't know what they are doing before the game starts, it is too late to teach them once the game is underway. I relate the quote that I read from the highly respected and successful NFL Coach Tony Dungee. " The good teacher talks while he is teaching; he doesn't talk during the exam". In other words, teach them in the classroom (practice). Once the exam (game) has started, there is nothing that you can do about it.

You can try to teach them something during the game; but don't expect them to execute what you told them, especially if they haven't practiced it. Stick to what you worked on in practice, perhaps making minor adjustments, or corrections, if the players are not executing correctly. Other than that, leave them alone. The coach who feels that he has to control and direct every movement, and every player during a game, has not done a very good job of preparing his players during practice.

EFFECTIVE CONDITIONING

Effective conditioning is part of effective coaching; and should not take a long time to perform, if done correctly. Utilize short, high intensity repeat water polo type swims, instead of slower longer distance swims that take longer to perform, and that do not help the players to get in "water polo shape". The key to conditioning is to spend just enough time that is necessary to train the players; leaving the rest of the practice for working on game related activities.

Effective conditioning, in addition to short sprint training, also involves combining conditioning with skill drills, doing a lot of counterattack work, and keeping the players moving during the entire practice. The most effective conditioning during practice is actually playing the game by scrimmaging. Wasting time by overtraining your players, is just as ineffective as wasting time in practicing unnecessary skills.

GAME CARRYOVER

How many times have you had your players perform a drill that involves a certain skill, only to have them perform that skill incorrectly in a game? Part of effective coaching is to get your players to perform in a game, what they learned in practice. This is called "practice to game carryover". The most "carryover" will be accomplished by practicing the skill as close a possible to the way that it is performed in a game; and then when the players have learned that skill, incorporating it as quickly as possible into a six on six game situation.

The coach shouldn't get too technical; but he must insist that the skill be performed correctly. Present different game situations that involve the particular skill; and perform them over and over again until the players can execute it in a game situation, without consciously having to think about doing it.

In the end, what separates the successful winning coach from the unsuccessful losing coach, is the ability to spend just the right amount of time (no more, or no less) performing the most important and critical aspects of the game; and effectively presenting the material in a way that will give the team the best chance to win. In other words, in order to be a "SUCCESSFUL WINNING COACH", he/she must become an "EFFECTIVE" coach.

SUMMARY

Success as a coach is often measured in terms of wins and losses. However, the great coaches don't go out there with the single idea of winning every game. If I had to summarize in one sentence what it takes to be successful as a coach, it would be:

"The great coaches teach the game and how it is supposed to be played; as well as prepare their team to play the game".

One of the most successful coaches in the history of the NFL, Hall of Fame 49er and Stanford football coach Bill Walsh said, "The great coaches seek solutions that will increase their team's chances of success in a competitive environment. THE SCORE WILL TAKE CARE OF ITSELF". Which, incidentally is the title of the last book that he wrote.

On the next page is a summary of what I feel are the basic fundamentals necessary to become a successful water polo coach. Most of them will be covered in detail in further chapters in the manual.

THE KEYS TO SUCCESSFUL COACHING

1. Develop a coaching philosophy that reflects how you want the game to be played.

2. A coach must decide what the most important fundamentals of the game are that will give his team the best chance for success.

3. Coach your players to practice and play with intensity and enthusiasm.

4. Create a team attitude, a part of the game that sets your team apart from other teams.

5. Coach with enthusiasm and with confidence in your technical abilities.

6. Teach your players that unselfish individual play is for the good of the team, and will give the team the best chance to win.

7. Constantly evaluate what you are doing and why you are doing it. Don't be afraid to make changes in what you are doing, if necessary.

8. A coach must teach the fundamentals of the game in an efficient manner, without wasting extraneous time on things that don't matter.

9. Instill in your players the need for improvement, a drive to get better and better.

10. Teach by doing, not by talking. Do most of your teaching in the pool, not at the chalkboard.

11. A coach must teach the basics of the game in a clear, concise, and simple manner that the players can understand and be able to execute.

12. Remember, it's not how much you say, but how much the players understand and absorb that is important.

13. A coach must prepare his players for games by covering all situations in practice that they will encounter in a game.

14. A coach must condition and train his players in order to be able to handle the rigors of the game of water polo.

15. Be efficient in your practices by combining different elements of the game together in drills and scrimmages. Include conditioning in everything that you do.

16. Pay attention to detail and make sure that players execute the fundamentals of the game correctly.

17. Teach your players about the importance of doing things the right way, and doing them the same way every time.

18. Set individual and team goals as a way to motivate your players.

CHAPTER 2

DEVELOPING A COACHING PHILOSOPHY

Before a coach sets foot on the pool deck for his first practice session, he/she must identify and describe his own coaching philosophy. This personal philosophy is something that a coach will impart on his players, and has a lot to do with how he wants his team to play the game of water polo.

As a coach you must keep in mind that water polo is a game that requires the players to learn certain individual and team skills. The job of the coach is to teach the players how to apply these skills in a coordinated effort, and towards a common goal; and to prepare the players both physically and mentally, so that they can overcome the efforts of the other team. The coach also needs to identify the important parts of the game that he will emphasize and teach to his players. This has to do with both the physical and mental parts of the game, how you want the game to be played and how you want your players to act and interact as part of a team.

You sometimes hear coaches say, "play the game right." What is right for you, or what is right for your team, may be different for different coaches and for different groups of players. What kind of image do you want your team to project? What can we do as a team that will give us the best chance to win? These are things a coach must ask himself when developing a philosophy that he can impart on his team, and hope to achieve success.

MY PHILOSOPHY OF COACHING

The topics that are covered in this chapter are a reflection of my own personal "coaching philosophy" that has taken me years to develop. There never has been a coach or leader that has arrived "fully formed"; who has figured it all out by themselves. The philosophy that you will form yourself, is developed from your own experiences as a player and coach; and also from observing and learning from others, whether consciously or sub-consciously. You never know when something that you have observed in the past, that has been sitting somewhere in the back of your mind, will re-surface as part of your philosophy of coaching.

My philosophy has been influenced by my educational background in exercise physiology and engineering, my years as an officer in the US Army, by teammates and coaches when I was a player, by coaches that I have worked with and worked for over the years, by players on my own teams, from teams that I have observed and competed against, and from reading and learning from coaches outside of the water polo community.

I have absorbed the good ideas, learned from the bad ones, applied some of my own concepts, and then came up with a philosophy that would give my teams the best chance of success; a philosophy that would increase our probability of winning in a very competitive environment. Coaches reading this section can take what they want out of it; and hopefully it will help them to develop their own personal "coaching philosophy".

CREATING AN ATTITUDE

Just as important to a coach as creating a philosophy, is creating an attitude. At Stanford, our attitude gave our team an identity that distinguished our team from other teams. It is something that gave our team both a physical and mental advantage over our opponents; something that the teams we played against had to worry about every time that they played us. It also gave us the confidence in knowing that there was something that we could do better than the other team; and when it came down to "crunch time", it would help us win the game.

The attitude that we tried to create was that "we are in better shape than the other team" and we can beat them by "out-swimming" them. Our goal was to wear down opponents throughout the game by swimming hard, and by counterattacking them at every opportunity. In the critical fourth quarter we knew that the game was ours. Once our players realized that we could win games by being in better shape than our opponents, it was easier to get them to work hard in practice.

This gave us a tremendous physical advantage as well as a psychological advantage over other teams. The counterattack became a trademark of the Stanford water polo team. Coaches from other teams would exclaim after a game, "don't you guys ever slow down". Years after I finished coaching, I had players from other teams come up to me and tell me that they hated playing against our team because of our counterattack.

ENCOURAGE FAST AND AGGRESSIVE PLAY

My teams counterattacked every time the ball changed hands. When teams played us, they knew that when they turned the ball over, they would have to worry about our counterattack. This made teams very tentative when they were on offense. We didn't just counterattack some of the time; we counterattacked all of the time. It became a "way of life" for our team. The players like to play this kind of game because it permits greater freedom and more initiative. It is also more fun to play. In addition, it is better strategy to prepare a team to play fast. A fast team can play a slow game; but it is difficult for a slow team to adjust to a fast game.

GETTING THE TEAM IN SHAPE

It is up to the coach to get the players in shape to play the game, and especially to be able to counterattack on every turnover. The counterattack can be very effective in wearing down your opponents; but only if your team is in shape to do so for the entire game. It didn't just happen that we were in better shape than our opponents. We had to work at it! The objective of our training sessions was to "keep the players moving at all times". We didn't wear ourselves out in games, because we were in great shape from swimming and moving and doing counterattack drills every day in practice.

Conditioning was included during every part of the practice session. Every team trains hard, but I like to think that our conditioning was more effective; because everything that we did in practice involved some kind of conditioning. Also, the conditioning that we did was specific to water polo, not just swimming laps. Combining swimming with shooting, drills, counterattack and scrimmaging is much more effective for water polo.

SWIM FAST IN PRACTICE, SWIM FAST IN GAMES
Part of my philosophy about conditioning for water polo came from my background and study of Exercise Physiology. I learned that if you want to repeatedly swim fast in a game, that you have to do the same in practice. I started the season every year by telling my players that we would swim less mileage in practice than any other team we played against. However, everything that we swam would have to be fast. I am not a big fan of long, slow swimming. I purposely designed our swim sets so that they covered shorter distances that simulated the swimming that occurs during a game; and also gave the players enough rest between swims, so that they could swim fast on every repeat.

PRACTICE HARD, PLAY HARD
In a close hard fought game, when both teams were tired at the end of the game, or in overtime, I felt that we had a good chance of winning; because the players were used to playing in stressful and fatigue situations in practice. The key is to have your players go hard in practice, even though they are tired. I found that players tend to loaf and pace themselves during long practices; so I purposely kept our practice sessions shorter so that they could practice with intensity throughout the whole practice session.

YOU PLAY LIKE YOU PRACTICE
Part of my philosophy is that you play in games the way that you play in practice. A player can't just slop through practice after practice, and then produce a miracle on game day. If you as a coach allow players to take bad shots in practice, they will also take bad shots in the game. If your team can't get back on defense in practice, they won't get back in games either. A player can only prepare himself for the demands of the game by playing with the same game enthusiasm and intensity in practice.

SPRINTS AT THE END
When players were tired at the end of practice, we would do more hard and short swims. My philosophy, which I emphasized at all times, was that the hard swimming that you do at the end of practice when you are fatigued, gets you in the best shape. I would challenge the players to sprint as hard as they could, emphasizing that this would really help them in the 4th quarter; or in overtime when the other team was really tired. On some days we would have a sprint contest to see who the fastest sprinter was; or reward the fastest swimmer after each sprint with an early exit from practice.

REST YOUR PLAYERS
I knew from experience just how much I could demand from my players, and how hard to push them. A good coach also knows when to rest his players. A coach can't expect good performance in games from tired players. Learn to recognize the obvious signs of fatigue in your players, and give them the necessary rest; so that they can give their best in games.

Resting (tapering) the players can be done every week, every month, or only once at the end of season, depending on how hard the players have been training, and the importance of each game played during the season. If it will be a difficult game that is classified as a "must win", and the team needs to be at their peak in order to win the game, then the coach has to taper the team. Taper consists of cutting down on the intensity and length of practice sessions for several days prior to the game. Increasing carbohydrates in the diet in order to increase energy producing glycogen in the muscles, is also necessary for a good taper, and to insure optimum performance.

PUT THE PRESSURE ON (DEFENSIVE)

Another "attitude" that we tried to create was to always put the pressure on the other team, and never make it easy for them to move the ball down the pool. We did this by pressing man-to-man all over the pool. We challenged every pass, played the passing lanes and fronted the hole, making it difficult for the other team to move the ball down the pool and into scoring position. Putting pressure on the other team takes advantage of the 30-second shot clock, and the limited time that they have to get a shot on goal.

Because pressure will delay the ball from getting into the scoring area, teams will run out of time to run their offense. Many times they will not get a shot off before they have to give up the ball as the shot clock expires. At times the pressure will result in a steal and a turnover; thus helping to fuel our counterattack. When the ball would turn over, our positioning in front of the offensive players would many times give us a man advantage in the other direction.

DEFENSE WINS GAMES

Defense is the key to winning water polo games. Stressing the defensive part of the game should be an important part of a coach's philosophy. When a team is prepared and committed to playing defense every time they jump into the pool, that team has an opportunity to win any game, even if the other team is more talented.

Anyone can play defense. All it takes is the three D's of desire, discipline, and dedication; the desire to stop the other team from scoring, the discipline to follow the defensive game plan, and dedication to the defensive part of the game. It is up to the coach to instill this defensive philosophy, and the importance of defense, to the entire team. Players have to understand that stopping the other team from scoring, and keeping the score low, gives the team a better chance to win the game. A low scoring game can be won by anybody. You don't have to be better than the other team. You just have to play better defense!

EXTRA-MAN MAKES THE DIFFERENCE

Another phase of the game that needs to be practiced and emphasized every day is extra-man offense and defense. The success of the extra-man usually determines which team will win a close game. However, just having a man advantage does not guarantee a goal will be scored. Time is a factor, and the players need to concentrate, make good passes, and find the player with the best chance to score.

Extra man defense needs to be emphasized equally as much as the offense. Stopping a team from scoring, when they have an extra man, can render a psychological blow that they may not recover from. The most important statistic that you should keep track of, is how many times you score on your extra man opportunities, and how many times you stop the other team from scoring on their opportunities.

MENTAL PHILOSOPHY

Besides the physical part of the game, a coach must also develop a philosophy that stresses the mental aspects of the game. The physical part is how you want your players to play the game. The mental part is how you want them to act and interact as members of the team; and how you want them to act towards the opposition, and other people that they come into contact with.

TEAM PLAY

"Team play" is a key ingredient to the success of a team. Water polo is a team game. We can't succeed unless we do it as a team. Team play means that an individual will sacrifice himself for the team. Team play means unselfish play. Unselfish play means that a player will pass up a shot to give a teammate a better shot. The coach has to stress to the players that "the pass leading to the shot is more important than the shot itself". Without the pass there is no goal.

A situation can occur where there are two players in front of the goal, and one has the ball and an open shot on goal. The player with the ball draws the goalie to his side with a fake, then passes to his teammate for the easy goal on the other side of the pool. This, to me, is the essence of team play; a player giving up his chance to score so that his teammate can score. A selfish player would have kept the ball and taken the shot himself, without even looking at his teammate. This attitude has to be coached and encouraged; because it is human nature to always think of yourself first.

TAKING CREDIT FOR THE GOAL

An individual who scores a goal shouldn't take credit for what the team has accomplished. All the person that scored has done was finish the play with a goal; not taking into account everything that his teammates did to help set up the goal. The person who just scored should point his finger at his teammate to acknowledge and thank him for the pass that gave him the chance to score.

PLAYING DEFENSE IS TEAM PLAY

Team play means that everyone must play defense. Scoring goals is not the only thing in water polo. Team play must be built in practice with an emphasis that includes playing defense. A coach should emphasis the defensive concept every day in practice, and credit must be given to the players who are making good defensive plays. Player must realize that if they play good defense, they will be rewarded with a starting position on the team. It is up to the coach to follow through on these kinds of promises. A player who scores two goals, but gives up four, is of no value to the team.

Another aspect of defensive team play includes helping out a teammate. As a defender you must guard your man, but at the same time be looking around to help out a teammate. Help in from the wing when your teammate has been beaten on a drive, drop back on 2-meters to help out the hole-guard, switch with a teammate when there is a mismatch with the man that he is guarding, and cover up for a teammate who is taking a shot, or gets burned on the counterattack.

THINK DEFENSE WHEN YOU ARE ON OFFENSE
One of the hardest things for players to comprehend, is to start thinking about helping a teammate defensively, while his team is still on offense. Players always have to be anticipating that their team will eventually loose the ball; and they must be ready to go back on defense, sometimes even before the ball is turned over. Players must always be on the alert for these kinds of situations; and be ready to help the player that has been burned; usually the player passing the ball, or the player shooting the ball.

IF YOU ARE NOT INVOLVED, GET BACK!
Offensive players who are not directly involved with the offense, or are on the other side of the pool away from the ball, are in the best position to help out a teammate who has been "burned." This situation comes up a lot, especially when the shot clock is about to expire. With only a few seconds left on the shoot clock, everyone but the player shooting the ball should be heading back on defense. Defensive players who are leaving early to go on the counterattack, especially have to be covered.

ASSISTS
At the very least, the assist in water polo, the pass leading to a shot on goal and a score, should carry just as much weight on the statistics sheet as a goal scored. Some teams don't even record assists. Not acknowledging assists puts more emphasis on the goal, than the pass that was made to make the goal possible. The coach should stress assists as much as goals.

The sport of ice hockey has the right idea in awarding points for assists as well as goals. They both carry the same weight in hockey. Even though they are not part of the official stats in water polo, there is no reason why the coach can't keep track of assists in a game, and reward players accordingly.

IT DOESN'T MATTER WHO SCORES A GOAL, AS LONG AS IT GETS SCORED
A coach should not make a big deal out of how many goals a player scores. The most important aspect of scoring is that his team scores more goals than the other team. It shouldn't matter who scored the goals, as long as they get scored. Emphasizing how many goals are scored by an individual player takes away from the team aspect of water polo.

If you as the coach stress individual scoring, then your players will never help a teammate to score a goal. They will be more concerned with how many goals they score, rather than if the team wins or loses. To emphasize this point in my final year of coaching at the high school level, except for the official score sheet, I did not keep a record of individual goals scored. Make sure your players understand that as long as the team wins the game, it doesn't matter who scores the goals.

COMMUNICATION

Communicating with teammates is an important ingredient of team play. On offense, a player should call out where the ball should be passed, or where his teammates should be positioned, or warn a teammate who is being blind-sided. On defense, help direct teammates to the correct defensive positions, and call out different defensive switches and assignments. The first player back on defense has to "direct traffic"; telling his teammates where to go, and who to guard.

It is especially important for the goalkeeper to take charge and direct the players in front of him, directing defenders to the ball, calling out the defense they are in, calling back defenders into a zone, or who he wants to crash on the 2-meter player. Directing defenders on where the goalie wants them positioned, is especially important when the other team is on the counterattack.

I used to tell my players, "Don't be a sheep and just follow the rest of the flock. Take charge and be the king of the sheep." This came from an old "Far Side" cartoon. The players used to get a chuckle out of this saying; but they understood that I wanted them to be leaders in the pool, and not just followers.

TEAM UNITY

Team unity means that players can count on each other in every phase of the game. Players have to have the attitude that they can't let their buddies down. The measure of a great team is that willingness to sacrifice for the team. Everyone must understand what their role is on the team, and must do their part for the team to succeed.

They must be aware that if they let down at any time, they are hurting the team. Everybody is in this together. No one individual can take credit for winning a game, nor should one individual be blamed for a loss. "Victory is produced and belongs to all. Likewise, failure belongs to everyone".

Players have to support each other in everything that the team does. This includes little things like taking out the goals, and putting on pool covers at the end of practice. When practice is over, no one wants to stay around and put in pool covers. Everyone wants to shower and head home for dinner. I had a rule that no one went to the showers until all of the end-of-practice chores were completed. Sometimes I literally had to go into a shower room and grab a player "by the ear" and yank him back out to the pool to finish the job at hand.

That player would also get a reprimand about "we are all in this together" and by leaving early you are "letting down your teammates". Taking a shower early, before the rest of the team, may seem like a trivial matter; but I felt that it was critical to nip these kinds of things in the bud, in the interest of team unity. If the team can't count on a player to help put in pool covers, how can we count on him to help his teammates during a game.

RESPECT OTHERS

Respect each other. The way that the members of your team, and the coaches, interact with other people that they come in contact with, reflects on the school, the coach, and the players themselves. Try to get your players to treat people that they come into daily contact with respect, both at the pool and in their everyday life.

This includes teachers, parents, coaches, teammates, opponents, referees, and everyone from the pool manager to the waiter at a restaurant. Young players should especially be polite and respectful to their elders and people of authority. In the Italian club system, at every level of play, all team members will greet the coach and shake hands with him upon arriving at the pool for practice.

The coach must also respect everyone on the team, including the last man on the bench. He should praise correct performance and effort; and critique the mistakes of all of the players equally, including the best players on the team. The coach must care about the last man on the team as much as he cares about the stars on the team. This includes making sure that every player gets an equal opportunity to play during practice sessions.

If you can't use a player, then you shouldn't have him wasting his time sitting around doing nothing during practice. If you choose a player to be on the team, then use him! If not, then don't choose him in the first place. Substitutes must be made to feel that they are an important part of the team. Give the subs a role to play when they enter the game, and acknowledge their contribution to the team's success. Do not give false praise, as the players will see right through it. For example, "The manager did a great job handing out water to the team. We couldn't have won the game without him!"

HAZING DOES NOT BELONG ON A TEAM
A coach should not allow or tolerate a "caste" system, in which younger players are treated differently from older players. Definitely do not allow hazing of underclass players, simply because they are young. They are part of the team and contribute, or will contribute, to the success of the team, just as everyone else does. Hazing includes demeaning "team initiation" ceremonies, as well as having rookies do all of the team chores; like putting in and taking out goals, and carrying balls and hats to the games.

Divide up team chores equally among the team members, or have the whole team help with tasks after practice. A great way to assign team chores is to have passing contests, sprint swim contests, and end of practice scrimmages. The losing players, or team, have to perform a task that has already been decided before you start the contest. It is amazing how hard a group of players will work just to get out of a task, like putting in pool covers.

These kinds of competitions can get very intense, but can actually help the team as a whole; in that it simulates the kinds of situations in practice that they will come across in real games. How your players handle these kinds of "pressure" situations in practice, can tell you a lot about your team and individual members of the team, before you even play your first game.

DON'T FORGET THAT YOU ARE TEAMMATES
Don't let players yell at each other, especially veterans yelling at young players. If a player makes a mistake, it is up to the coach to critique him, not his teammates. Older players should be mentors, and help out the new players, not criticize or yell at them. A life lesson learned among teammates is tolerance to one another.

We should go out of our way to respect and satisfy each and every person on the team. Some coaches even go so far as to assign an older player to a younger player as a "mentor". This is a great way to pass on individual skills and team behavior that an older player gains from being on the team for a longer period of time.

HOW TO HANDLE A PROBLEM ATHLETE

It doesn't happen very often, but every once in a while a team has an individual that puts himself ahead of the team. This is a player who becomes so self-centered, self-important and selfish that he thinks that he is more important than the team. He starts acting like a big shot; as if he is solely responsible for what the team has accomplished, and has taken over ownership of the group's achievements. When it gets to the point when the actions of this individual are starting to affect team cohesion, and starting to become detrimental to the success of the team; it is time for the coach to take charge and take care of the problem.

First, the coach has to recognize when someone is a negative presence, a malcontent within the team. He must then sit down and talk with the individual to help him understand the problem, to understand how his actions are affecting the team, and to help get his perspective back in balance. After communicating the problem to the individual, either the problem goes away, or the individual has to go away. This is the time when the coach has to have a "hard" inside edge. He has to make and carry out a harsh decision to punish the player, in a manner that is fast, firm and fair.

Depending on the severity of the actions of the individual, it may even go so far as having to remove the player from the team. It makes the decision even tougher when it involves one of the better players on the team, perhaps even the leading scorer. In a situation like this, for the good of team pride and unity, and to be fair to everyone, the punishment has to be carried out regardless of the stature of the player involved.

The coach may be even greatly surprised to see that the team will be more cohesive, and many times play better without the malcontent, even if he is the best player. It will certainly help improve the team "chemistry" and provide some "peace of mind" for the coach, as well as the players. There is a saying that describes this situation in a nutshell, "Good talent with a bad attitude equals bad talent".

GOOD SPORTSMANSHIP

I want my players to show good sportsmanship towards their opponents. Fear no opponents, but have respect for them. I do not allow my players to taunt other players; and I do not allow excessive celebration and showboating after scoring a goal. My feeling is that you have just scored; you don't need to call more attention to yourself. Educate your players on the bench to the fact that it is unsportsmanlike conduct to yell intimidating remarks to the other team, or to the officials.

HOW GOOD IS THE OTHER TEAM

Never play down the abilities of the other team, or players from the other team. It can sometimes have a detrimental effect on the outcome of the game. If the players on your team think that the other team isn't very good, they will usually play down to their level. As soon as you tell a team that the goalie from the other team isn't very good, he will have the game of his life, and your team will not be able to buy a goal. If you are playing a team that is much weaker than your team, try to find something about them that your team must overcome in order to win the game. On the other hand, the players on your team will see through it if you build up a weak team as the "greatest thing since sliced bread". Give your team something to focus on during the game, rather than the shortcomings of the other team.

FOCUS ON YOUR TEAM

When you are playing against a team, or a player, that is stronger than your team, don't dwell on how strong they are, or on how good a particular player is. Prepare your team by trying to take away some of the other teams strengths. Make the weaker players on a team beat you, not the strongest player. Always focus on what you want your team to do, and how you want to play a particular player. Sometimes the simple solution is to put your best defender on the other teams best player, and let the chips fall where they may. Concentrating too much on another player can sometimes work against you, if other players on a team can also hurt you; or if the other team has prepared for a situation like this.

IMPART A PHILOSOPHY ON YOUR PLAYERS

There are many attributes that make an athlete stand out ahead of all the others. Some of these attributes are part of a player's personal make-up, and some have to be imparted to the players by the coach. It is not just a player's obvious physical talents, but what a person makes of his talents. It is the little things in his psychological make-up that allows him to become a better player than everyone else.

Things like competitive attitude, willingness to prepare physically and mentally to play the game, the desire to improve and learn, passion for the game, unselfish attitude, knowledge of the game, and leadership qualities, are examples of the traits of a good/great player that can be emphasized by a coach to his players. Following are some of the qualities that can separate the best from the rest:

IT DOESN'T HURT TO HAVE AN EGO

Don't let anybody tell you that a big ego is a bad thing. All the great players that I have ever coached have all had ego to spare. A big ego is pride, self-confidence, self-esteem and self-assurance that the person can do the job, and do it better than everyone else. Ego is a powerful and productive engine. It often translates into a fierce desire to do your best, and an inner confidence that serves you well when things get tough.

Psychologists suggest that there is a strong link between ego and competitiveness. Three water polo players that I have coached, Jody Campbell, Wolf Wigo and Tony Azevedo, all played on three USA Olympic teams, and were among the most competitive athletes that I have ever known. I would also put Craig Klass, a member of two USA Olympic teams, into this same category. They all had that inner-drive to be the best water polo players in the world; and they were!

None of these four outstanding players ever let their egos turn into egotism. Egotism is when ego turns into something else entirely. It's an inflated ego that causes the athlete to become arrogant and enamored with his self-importance. The problem athlete that becomes a detriment to the team (as described above), is the kind of athlete that has allowed his ego to turn into egotism.

MAKE THINGS HAPPEN

I always felt that a player could overcome deficiencies in his play by playing aggressively. There are two kinds of athletes, those that make things happen, and those that let things happen to them. I would rather have a player who is over-aggressive, than one who is passive and doesn't do anything. The latter player is just "taking up water".

It is up to the coach to instill in the player the desire to play aggressively. One way a coach can do this is to encourage smart and aggressive play, without hand-cuffing him with too many restrictions. A player cannot be afraid to do something aggressively, or he will not do so. It is much easier for the coach to control an over-aggressive action with coaching, than to get a passive player to become more aggressive. Sometimes it is just not in a player's personality to play aggressively.

LEARN PROPER TECHNIQUE

A player can have all of the intensity in the world; but he will end up running into a bullet if he doesn't learn proper technique. Technique is the responsibility of the coach and what he teaches during practice. It is also the responsibility of the player, through his ability to learn as much as possible about the game, and execution in game situations. Stress to your players that they need to be a practice player first, and learn to properly and quickly execute the fundamentals of the game.

SELF-DISCIPLINE

It is up to the coach to instill discipline on the team, and at the same time players have to have the self-discipline of doing the right things that will make them successful water polo payers. If the team is to be successful, the players need to be disciplined in their play and in their personal life. DISCIPLINE IS DOING WHAT YOU HAVE TO DO, DOING IT AS WELL AS YOU CAN, DOING IT THE SAME WAY EVERY TIME, AND DOING IT THE RIGHT WAY EVERY TIME.

It is not enough to talk about being disciplined; players need to implement it in the pool and in their daily lives. Discipline on offense has to do with things like taking the right shot at the right time, and making the correct and safe pass every time. Discipline on defense has to do with playing team defense, pressing your man every time, helping a teammate, not committing unnecessary fouls, playing in the passing lanes and staying within the defensive system.

Discipline away from the pool has to do with keeping yourself in shape year around, constantly working on your own to improve yourself, keeping up your school studies; and doing things in your personal life that will keep you from becoming as good a player as you can be, like proper diet, adequate sleep, no drugs and alcohol, etc.

PLAY YOUR BEST

One of the philosophies of the great UCLA basketball coach John Wooden, was that no matter what the outcome of the game, a player could feel good about his performance, if he felt that he played the absolute best that he could play. If his team won the game, but the player did not play well, then he needed to work harder and improve his performance for the next game. If his team lost, then the player could at least feel that he did everything that he could do to help his team win.

Players need to understand that playing well includes all parts of the game, not just scoring. Players can contribute to a win even if they don't score a goal; if they can help their team win by performing all the other aspects (like defense) of the game well.

PLAY WITH PASSION

Not only must a player have a passion for the game, but must also play with passion. The worst thing that a player can do is to try and play the game, and not like what he is doing. Maybe he is playing because his parents played, or maybe he is just trying to earn a scholarship, or be accepted into a good college. When you see a player like this, it is obvious that he doesn't really want to be there. If you don't love the game, and you don't love playing the game, then you shouldn't be there! Don't play the game to please someone else; play the game to please yourself.

Tony Azevedo, perhaps the greatest player to ever play the game of water polo in this country, has a passion for the game; and a passion for playing the game that is infectious, and rubs off on everyone around him. Not only does he help his teammates with his play, but also with his exuberance and attitude toward the game of water polo.

GET THE MOST OUT OF YOUR PHYSICAL TALENTS

Impress on your players the fact that everyone has physical abilities to start with. It is the players that do the most with their abilities that succeed in their sport. Learning to work hard, and spending the time to improve and develop their playing skills, will separate them from the rest of the players. This is especially true if players are willing to do extra work outside of the pool, and apart from the required practice sessions. Simply doing the minimum that is necessary to play the game, will not elevate them above others who play the game.

The great athletes are constantly striving to improve and learn all they can. They never stop learning, perfecting, and molding their skills. They understand the connection between hard work and achieving their potential. We all understand this; you do and I do. Everybody who is serious about the game knows what it takes. The difference is how much are you willing to give to get there. Former Indiana basketball coach Bobby Knight's quote is very apropos here:

"The will to win is not nearly as important as the will to prepare to win".

OVERCOMING ADVERSITY- STOP FEELING SORRY FOR YOUR SELF

Everyone encounters adversity. Players must discipline themselves to do the best that they can under the circumstances. Don't whine, don't complain, learn how to except criticism without making excuses. Don't sit back and pout when you miss a shot, while your teammates are covering up for you on defense. Forget the missed shot and get back on defense! Players need to be mentally tough and be able to handle losing a game, or overcoming adversity during the game.

Field players have to be like goalies under these adverse situations. If the goalie gets scored on, he has to forget about it and keep playing. If you make a mistake in a game, move on and play the rest of the game well; just as the goalie has to block the next shot taken against him after he has been scored on. Players need to overcome losing a game by not feeling down or feeling sorry for themselves; but learning from the experience and coming back and trying to win the next game.

OVERCOMING THE BAD CALL

Players need to understand that no matter how good a referee might be, he is only human; and may make a bad call once in a while. Players have to overcome the bad call by playing better, not by falling apart. I have seen teams lose games that they shouldn't have, because they could not handle a referee's bad calls.

I did not allow players to criticize bad calls in practice, and I certainly did not allow it in games. It is the head coach's job to criticize a call by the referee, not the assistant coaches or the players. Sometimes I would make bad calls in practice on purpose, or not make a call at all, to see how the players would handle the situation. A player who cannot handle a bad call in practice, certainly cannot handle one in a game.

NEVER BLAME THE OFFICIALS

Even though you might think that you lost a game because of a bad call, never let the players hear you say this. They will use this as an excuse, and not make the adjustments necessary in order to win the next game. A coach can use this as a learning experience by telling the players that they should have not put themselves in a position where the referee's call could lose the game for them.

AWAY GAMES

You can always expect referee calls that seem to go against your team, especially when you are playing a game away from home. Part of the seemingly "bad calls" are because of your player's unfamiliarity with local officials, and the way that they call the game in that particular area. A coach should warn his players to expect bad calls away from home, and not let the calls affect the way that they play the game.

Traveling overseas with a team is a great experience that gives the players a chance to have fun, gain experience, and at the same time learn to overcome adversity at every port of call. When they go overseas, the players have to overcome jet lag, lack of sleep, bad food, no hamburgers, cold water, local referees, etc., and still compete and win water polo games. I would caution players to handle these problems without complaining. Players have to be able to learn how to "roll with the punches" or they won't survive.

Traveling to another country is also an opportunity for your players to learn about another culture that is different from theirs. It is also a good learning experience for your players for when they have to travel to another area to play a game or tournament, even within the boundaries of their own state and beyond.

PLAY WITH DIGNITY

Learn how to be a gracious winner and win or lose with dignity. A player should not act any differently, whether his team has won or lost a game. Hold your head up high after a loss and don't gloat after a win. Don't make excuses or blame someone else for losing a game, especially one of your own teammates. Never blame one player for a loss, even though he might have made a crucial mistake at the end of a game.

The point that the coach is trying to get across is that "we are all in this together." We win as a team and we lose as a team. The team, together, puts themselves in a position to win or lose the game. No one individual can win or lose the game, without help from his teammates.

TEACHING LIFE'S LESSONS

For some coaches, teaching life's lessons to their team is an important part of their coaching philosophy. In many ways the coach is like a second father to many of the players. He is certainly a confident person to whom the players can look up too. Many times they can talk to the coach about things that they don't feel comfortable talking to their parents about. Besides the discussions a coach might have with an individual player, other aspects of the game that a coach teaches his player can help them learn about many of life's lessons.

A good coach teaches his players about working hard, achieving goals, teamwork, unselfish play, helping teammates, playing your best, communication, team unity, overcoming adversity, respect for others, win and lose with dignity, good sportsmanship, and discipline. These are examples of life's lessons that a coach can impart on his players in the course of coaching the game of water polo. The beauty of athletic competition is the life's experiences that a person can experience while playing a game. Many of these lessons will carry on to a successful and productive adult life.

THOUGHT IS BORN OF FAILURE

One of the keys to success as a coach, is to constantly evaluate what you are doing, and why you are doing it. If you try something in practice, or in a game, and it doesn't work for you; evaluate why it failed. Only by failing at something will you know that you have to try something else that works. This can be any situation from a drill that doesn't work, to how you approach different players on your team. Always be evaluating your situation, and be willing to make changes to what you are doing, if necessary.

But don't make changes just to be making changes. Sometimes you can over-analyze things to the point, where you are making so many changes that it keeps the team from progressing. This is called "paralysis by analysis." Sometimes you have to just let things play out, and the problem will solve itself; or the problem may not have a solution at all, and no amount of analysis will solve it.

I have taken everything that I learned over the years and used what I felt was important to the success of my teams. I constantly analyzed everything that I was doing, and why I was doing it. If I didn't believe in it, or if it wasn't working, I dumped it. If I couldn't answer why I was doing something, I also dumped it.

A coach should have a reason for everything he does, and not just do something because someone else is doing it, or your former coach did it that way. Use what works for you and fit it to your own individual COACHING PHILOSOPHY.

Listed on the next page are important fundamentals of playing water polo that I try to emphasize to the players on my team. These are the basic rules and fundamentals that show them the way that I feel the game should be played.

THE COMMANDMENTS OF WATER POLO

Following are important fundamentals of playing the game of water polo that are essential to success as a player and as a team, and which reflects my own basic coaching philosophy:

1. Learn the basic fundamentals of the game and learn to execute them properly.
2. Practice hard and play hard. Learn to practice and play the game with enthusiasm and intensity.
3. The will to win is not nearly as important as the will to prepare to win
4. Speed and quickness are important physical aspects of the game. Learn how to swim fast in games by swimming fast in practice.
5. Get into the best condition possible to play the game, by playing and swimming as hard as you can for the entire practice.
6. A strong eggbeater kick is necessary for success in playing water polo.
7. Playing good defense is a key to winning water polo.
8. Take pride in making a good pass every time.
9. The pass leading to the shot is more important than the shot itself
10. Counterattack at every opportunity.
11. Anticipation and reaction are important ingredients for a successful counterattack. Learn to out-react your opponent.
12. The success of the extra-man offense and man-down defense usually determines which team will win a close game.
13. Avoid turnovers while on offense and create turnovers with a pressure defense.
14. Knowing that you can count on your teammates, and that they can count on you, helps to promote team unity.
15. Team play is unselfish play. Passing up your chance to score to set up a teammate to score, and covering up for a teammate on defense are examples of this.
16. Learn how to overcome adversity and discipline yourself to do the best that you can under the circumstances.
17. Fear no opponent, but have respect for him.
18. Get the most out of your physical talent by playing your best every time you jump into the pool.

CHAPTER 3

COACHING AND TEACHING TIPS

There are many coaches that are knowledgeable about the game of water polo. More important than knowledge of the game, is the ability to get that knowledge across to the team; and to can get them to execute it on a consistent basis. A big key to success is to know what parts of the game that you are going to emphasize to your players. Once you decide what you are going to teach your team, then you have to get your players to understand and execute what you are teaching. This takes communication with your players.

Communication is not always simple to do. Just presenting facts is not communication. A good communicator has to know how to get his message across to his team. Just because you are giving them information, doesn't mean that they are receiving it. This chapter will present tips on how to commumicate and get relevant information across to your team.

DECIDING WHAT YOU ARE GOING TO TEACH

The first step in coaching, before anything else, is to decide what parts of the game to emphasize and teach the players, so that the team has the best chance of winning? Front-court offense, counterattack, defense, extra man, speed, strength, legs, game situations and tactics are all important aspects of the game of water polo. Which should you as the coach emphasize the most?

Deciding what is most important has a lot to do with the coach's philosophy of the game, the kind of personel on the team, the experience level of the players, and the weak and strong points of the team based on past perfromance. Should you emphasize all of the above, or just some of the above? Should you adapt the players to your game, or adapt your game to the kind of players that you have? These are questions that you have to answer before you start.

When I first started coaching at Stanford, I usually had smaller, but quicker and faster players; so I adopted a style of play that emphasized speed. To me this was the best way to utilize my players, and a way that we could score goals that the other team could not defend. I would sit down at the beginning of the season and list all of the things that I felt we needed to be able to do to be able to play the game. This was based on my philosophy and the strengths and weaknesess and playing level of the team.

I then would prioritize and start working on the most important parts first; eventually covering everything prior to the first game. A key to success is to make sure that the most important parts of the game are emphasized; and to make sure that you teach the players how to play the game, and not waste time on teaching skills and doing things that are not important.

TEACH THE BASIC FUNDAMENTALS

It is your job as coach to teach the basic fundamentals of the game, and it is up to the players to learn to execute them properly. In water polo, as in other team sports, there are different kinds of fundamentals. There are the basic fundamentals that every player must learn from the very first day that he/she jumps into the pool. These are fundamentals like swimming head up, passing and catching the ball, learning how to eggbeater, learning how to shoot the ball, etc.

Vince Lombardi, the great Hall of Fame football coach of the Green Bay Packers believed strongly in the correct execution of the basic fundamentals of the game. His philosophy was that you didn't need fancy plays to beat the other team. He believed that if you executed the basics of blocking and tackling better then the other team, that you would win the game. He worked on these skills, over and over again in practice, until the players could execute them in their sleep.

Once the players master the basic fundamentals, the second step is to teach the fundamentals of playing the game of water polo. These are the individual skills necessary to play the game; skills like learning how to pass under pressure, learning how to press without fouling, learning how to guard 2-meters, learning how to release for the ball, etc.

A third step is to put all of the basic fundamentals, and the individual skills together; and then apply them to game situations. It is not enough just to teach the basic fundamentals and skills, and then leave it at that; hoping that players can utilize them and put them together in the game. The fundamentals have to be put together by the coach, in a structured manner that is withing the concept of the team of six players and goalie working together as a cohesive unit.

Water polo is a game of ever changing situations. Players must learn the basics of what to do in each situation, and how to play together in each situation that they encounter. These fundamentals are commonly called "tactics". Every situation that is encountered in a game is unique on to itself. Consequently, every possible game situation (tactics) must be practiced until the players understand what to do in that situation.

Basically, players are applying the individual fundamentals of playing water polo to the changing tactical situations of a water polo game. If players learn the proper way to handle these situations in practice, they will be able to execute them in the game, no matter what the opponent does.

GETTING YOUR POINT ACROSS

Getting your point across to the players has to do with not only how much information you give them, but how much information they can absorb. One of the basic principals of communication is the principal of "information limitation". The human attention and memory system functions as a bottleneck to learning. Even though there is unlimited amount of information to which we can attend to, we are limited in the amount we can actually process and absorb.

Age is a factor in how much information you give out. The younger the players, the less attention span they have. For youngsters just starting out in the game, keep it simple and have fun. You will keep them involved in the sport much longer if you do. Our capacity to process information is further diminished during times of stress and fatigue. Because of fatigue, teach a new concept early in practice; rather than later when the players are tired.

OVER-COACHING

Giving players too much information can be detrimental to learning. This is called "over coaching." It is better to give the players a little less, and have the assurance that they have learned something; than to give them too much and not be certain how much they have actually absorbed. It really is a waste of time to give out too much information. This applies to chalk talks, scouting reports, player critiques, pre-game and post game talks, time outs, and in between quarters and half time.

Young coaches (and some older experienced coaches too!) like to show how much they know about water polo, and say much more than is needed. Use straight-forward language that the players can understand. There is no need to get fancy or long-winded. The younger the players, the more simple and to the point the coach has to be.

I have watched coaches that stand on the side of the pool and talk to ten-year olds for 10 minutes about a drill they are about to perform. Meanwhile the players are sitting in the cold water, shivering, and not listening to a thing the coach says. He probably lost them after the first minute. Youngsters in cold water do not need long chalk talks. Nobody does! Not even older players in warm water.

Keep it short, clear and concise. Organize what you are going to say in a logical sequence that builds into your final message. Observe the people that you are talking to, and know if you are connecting with them. Be enthusiastic about the subject matter that you are presenting to the players. If you are not enthusiastic, or get long-winded in your presentation, they will get bored and tune you out.

After you have given the players a short introduction about what you are going to do, get them into the pool and set them up to perform the drill or skill that you have just talked about. Giving them a long and detailed outline on exactly what you are going to do is not necessary. They are not going to get it right the first time anyway, no matter how long you talk. Coach as you go along, while they are in the water and performing the drill; making changes and corrections as you go along.

INTRODUCING A NEW CONCEPT

Introducing a new concept should be done early in the daily training session, before fatigue sets in and the players have lost their capacity to learn. If you are introducing a new concept to the team at a practice session, stress one or two points only during your chalk talk. You don't have to go over every detail during the chalk talk; they won't remember it all anyway. Go over one or two major points and then correct mistakes as you go along.

PREPARE FOR EVERY SITUATION IN PRACTICE

The coach has to prepare his team in practice, for every situation that they could encounter during a game, offensively, defensively and tactically. Offensively they must be prepared for any kind of defense that they will encounter; defensively they must be ready to play any kind of defense, and to change from one to another during a game.

Tactically they must be ready and be prepared for every kind of game or time management situation; including end of quarter, end of game and end of shot clock situations, protecting a lead, playing from behind, etc.

Special plays for different situations must also be practiced. How does the coach know if he has prepared his players properly? If he has prepared them well, they will be ready for anything that comes up in a game. All the coach has to do is give a few words of direction as a reminder, and the players should be able to execute what the coach has prepared them to do.

USE OF SMALL DRY ERASE OR MAGNETIC WHITE BOARDS

You probably have seen coaches use these during games to diagram a play or game situation during a time out or in between quarters. I feel that these types of white boards are completely unnecessary, especially if the coach has done a good job of preparing his players in practice. If the coach has to draw up a play during a game, then he has not prepared them properly. If they have practiced the play, then they should only need a few words, as a reminder from the coach, to execute that play.

If a new play is necessary, then not only has the coach not prepared them for every situation; but he shouldn't expect the players to execute a completely new play that they have never practiced or seen before. Besides that, how many players in the water can actually see what the coach on the deck is diagramming on his small 10" x 12" white board?

Watch the players the next time you see a coach diagraming a play on an eraser board during a game. See how many players are even watching and paying attention! Coaches use these boards as a crutch to avoid having to explain the play verbally. Then when the players have trouble executing the drawn-up play, the coach can blame the players; instead of the fact that he had not prepared them properly in the first place.

Coaches! Throw those small eraser boards away! You don't need them. Learn to express yourself verbally to the team. But even more important than that, prepare the team in practice for every situation; so that you don't need to use a board to diagram every play or every situation that comes up.

PLAYER CRITIQUE

A coach cannot allow his players to execute the fundamentals of the game incorrectly. I always felt that players had to be called to task every time they came up short, rather then acting as if the transgression didn't happen. You have to have patience and allow time for the players to learn what you are getting across. If they are not getting the point, you might have to try another approach.

When you critique players, make sure that they understand the importance of doing things right, and that you are correcting them because you want them to improve as players. Make sure that they know that you like them, and that you are criticizing their play, and not them personally.

MISTAKES AS A TEACHING TOOL

It is only natural that players will make mistakes in practice, especially when they are learning a new concept. Correcting the mistakes that players make in practice can be an effective teaching tool. Mistakes in games can also be an effective teaching tool. Use these mistakes as a way for the players to learn how to do it right.

When you criticize and then give feedback, focus on the here and now. Try not to conjure up images of poor play from the past. This will be perceived as "pilling it on", and will create a sense of brow-beating that will cause the coach to lose respect and credibility.

When a player does something incorrectly, he should be told what he has done wrong, and shown or told how to do it right. Having a player repeat something a second time, but in the correct way, can help both the player and the team to not make the same mistake again. Make sure that the rest of the team is listening and watching, so that they will not repeat the same mistake.

CRITICISM AND POSITIVE REINFORCEMENT

One thing that is difficult for all coaches to do is to critique a player, and at the same time try to stay as positive as possible. Positive reinforcement is a powerful instrument for improving performance; but it is not easy to do all of the time. For some reason it is easier to be negative than it is to give praise. A coach has to find the right mixture of constructive criticism and positive reinforcement for optimum results.

A good mixture of praise and criticism is to say something positive first, about what the player has done well; followed by a critique on what the player has done wrong. That being said, a coach can't always sugarcoat everything that the players do with positive reinforcement. The player's will recognize when a coach is not sincere about his praise, and is only doing it to make them feel good. Praise can be overdone, the same way that constant criticism can be overdone.

Good plays should receive positive recognition, and bad ones should receive criticism. When a coach is happy with the team's performance, the team deserves to be praised. When a coach is legitimately angry, it is appropriate to express that anger, as long as it is done in a constructive way that helps the players to correct what they have done wrong; and as long as the players have been told ahead of time what it is that will draw criticism from the coach. It is very important to set clear expectations ahead of time of what will incur the coach's wrath.

The players have to understand that the coach will not get angry with a lack of ability, an inability to understand the coach (that's the coach's fault not the players), or with most mistakes when they are made the first few times. The coach reserves the right to get upset about things like a lack of effort, a lack of respect, a lack of interest, and the mistakes that come from them; and the same mistakes that are made over and over again.

A coach needs to get to know his players and how they will respond to criticism. Two players on the same team may make the same mistake; but one will need criticism and the other will need encouragement. Find out what makes each player "tick" and change your approach accordingly. I found this to be one of the most difficult situations to handle as a coach.

However you handle the situation, be sure to be firm and stay consistent. If you say something, make sure that you follow through. Treating them all fairly is more important than how you treat them individually. Remember, you are not out there to please everyone. Your job is to get the most out of your player's abilities.

GAME SLIPPAGE
There is always a certain amount of "game slippage" in every game. "Game slippage" is the difference in what you practice and what you actually do in the game. A coach can avoid this by correcting mistakes in practice, and by having the players do things correctly. Doing something right in a drill does not always carry over to a scrimmage or game.

Once players have learned how to perform a particular skill during a drill, it must immediately be incorporated into a full speed game situation; and then repeated over and over again. Once a player can do the skill at full speed, and in a game situation, without having to think about it every time; it will lessen the "slippage" that occurs from practice to a game.

LET THE TEAM KNOW WHAT YOU EXPECT OF THEM
At the beginning of the season, the coach should sit down with the team, and with individual players as well, and let them know what you expect of them, both individually and collectively. Spell out what you want from the players in a clear, specific and comprehensive manner. Be direct and to the point. Cover everything about your philosophy and how you want them to play the game, how you want them to perform, and how you want them to act toward each other, their opponents and everyone else that they come in contact with.

This is a good time to go over team rules (if you have any), dress codes, etc. and anything else that involves being a member of your team. Players will thrive in an environment where they know exactly what is expected of them, and what the consequences are if they fail to abide by the parameters that you set for them.

SETTING GOALS
One of the keys to motivating players is to set realistic goals for individuals and for the team to achieve. A coach should meet with each one of his players before the start of the season for an evaluation meeting. The coach has to communicate to the player the things that the player does well and the things that he needs to improve on.

This is also a good time to go over what the coach expects from the player, and what his role on the team will be. Team goals can provide motivation for the players, and also give the players an idea of what the coach considers important for the team to be successful. Examples of offensive team goals that the coach can set, include how many goals your team should average per game, how many should come from your front-court offense, how many from your counterattack, and how many from your extra man offense.

On the extra man you can set a goal to draw a certain number of ejections per game; but more importantly, what percentage of extra man opportunities can you convert into goals. Examples of defensive goals are only allowing so many goals by your opponents per game, or holding the other team to a low percentage of conversions on the extra man.

REALISTIC GOALS

Some team goals will let the team know where you expect them to place among the other teams they are competing against. Goals such as winning a national, league or sectional championship, qualifying for the post season, placing among the top half of the league, or simply winning more games than the previous year, are examples of various goals that you might set for your team. These goals need to be realistic and attainable goals. You have to set these goals high enough, so that they present a challenge to the team; but at the same time, not so high that they don't have a chance to accomplish them.

SETTING TEAM RULES

It is up to the individual coach as to whether he/she will set team rules. Whatever rules are set for the team must be clearly communicated at the beginning of the season. Most of them have to do with behavior of individuals, both away from the pool and at the pool. Some may have to do with academics; such as requiring a certain GPA to play water polo.

Some coaches will have the seniors on the team set the rules and punishment for infractions of the rules; or it can be a combination of rules that are set with the coach and seniors on the team, or only from the coach himself. Involving the seniors makes them feel that they are team leaders and are responsible for the success and failure of the team. Punishment for rule infractions can be set ahead of time; or made up as you go along, depending on the severity of the infraction and the circumstances surrounding the infraction.

Some coaches do not feel comfortable setting rules ahead of time, and instead have a general rule that concerns "actions that are detrimental to the success of the team". This usually depends on the age and maturity of your team. Older and more mature athletes can usually handle less absolute rules than younger players.

Rules of this type can be made up to correct a problem that may come up during the coarse of the season. For instance, if you are having a problem with players coming late to practice, then initiate a rule that players who come late without notifying the coach first, will have to swim at the end of practice. Examples of the types of rules for different situations are as follows:

1. Game rules- Any player that commits an act of aggression during a game for which the punishment is suspension for a game, will be suspended an additional game by the coach.

2. Practice rules-
   a. Players must notify the coach by e-mail or cell phone ahead of time if they are going to be late or miss practice.
   b. No talking while the coach is talking
   c. No shooting of the ball after the whistle blows to end a drill, or when the goalie is not looking.
   d. Players cannot sit on a ball or hang on to the wall during practice.
3. Travel rules- Make the players sign a code of conduct when they are on team trips. Many schools have these as standard forms, or you can make up your own. Be sure to include something about alcohol and drugs and destroying property in hotels, etc.
4. Behavior away from pool- Most of these kinds of rules have to do with alcohol, drugs, and academics. Make sure that you have a strict policy on this sort of violation.

GAME PREPARATION

The great Hall of Fame and 49er football coach Bill Walsh prepared his team by scripting ahead of time, the first twenty-five plays of every game. He was the first football coach in the nation to do this. It has now become common practice. His philosophy was that 20% of the final score of a game is due to luck, such as a referee's bad call, a tricky bounce of the ball, an injury, or some other happenstance. Accept the fact that you can't control that 20%.

However, the rest of the 80% can be under your control, with comprehensive planning and preparation. Regardless of the level of talent, the coach has to maximize the 80% when it matters most, on game day. Your job as a coach is to get more out of your 80% than the opposing coach gets out of his 80%.

HAVE A PLAN AND REHEARSE IT
One of the key responsibilities of the coach is to prepare his team for upcoming games. Game preparation is done in practice. You must prepare the team for all possible situations. Games are won by preparing in advance for whatever might happen. This is called contingency planning, and it is similar to what the fire department does before they send out the firefighters to fight a fire; and it is what an army does before it send it's soldiers to battle.

They have to prepare for anything that might happen in the heat of battle. Without a contingency plan they would perish. Having a well thought out game plan that prepares your team for every situation will give the team an excellent chance to win.

Not only must you have a plan, but also prepare for what happens if the plan fails. What happens if you prepare your team for your opponent's zone defense, and they come out in a hard press. Both the coach and the players should know what to do in that situation; because you have played against a press in practice. You shouldn't need to draw up an offense on a clip-board to show your team what to do. A little reminder from the coach about how to beat the press, and away you go!

SPECIAL PLAYS- SPECIAL TEAMS

Everything must be covered; nothing can be left to chance. Teams have to be prepared to play whatever defense or offense the coach decides to play; and then be able to change the defense or offense during the game at a moments notice. Coaches should have special plays for after a time out or game situation, for the front-court offense, front-court defense, and extra-man offense and defense. If the opposing coach calls a time out and sends in a special play, the coach should have a defense to counter that play.

You might want to call a time out and execute a special play yourself. All of these plays have to have been rehearsed in practice. so that the players will know what to do with just a few words from the coach. Having well thought out plays that are designed for every situation that might come up, not only helps the players to execute them; but also helps the coach to come up with a play or plan during times of great stress. It is not always easy to make a rational decision during the stress of the game. By analyzing, planning and rehearsing in advance, the coach can come up with the best decision for the situation at hand.

A coach can even have certain players designated to go in on "special teams", similar to what they do in football. I usually had players designated for "after time-out" special teams for the 6 on 5 offense, and 5 on 6 defense. They had played together in practice and knew what to do. I simply had to call out "6 on 5 special team" and give them a play that they had already rehearsed.

We also had a 5-man defensive unit that we inserted into the game to defend the other teams 6 on 5 after-time-out play. If the coach has to diagram a "new" play on a clip-board during a time out, one that that the players have never seen before; don't expect them to execute it. Have a plan for every situation and prepare for it in practice.

SCOUTING REPORT

A scouting report should be presented to the team early in the week before the game. It should be in precise and condensed spoken form, not written. I have observed coaches that present a twelve page scouting report to the team that goes into minute detail about the upcoming opponent. How much of the twelve pages do you think the team will remember, and more importantly, how much will they execute in the heat of battle?

A coach does not have to go into too much detail. This is another example of giving the players too much information. The result will be confusion and uncertainty; not want you want in order to win the game. Condense and simplify! Go over what your team will do against the other team. This is your game plan. Then practice what you will do in the game. This will help assure that they execute the game plan during the course of the game. I don't like to tell a player, or the team, to do something in a game that we have never done before. If I have to do that, I feel that I have made a coaching error.

WHAT ARE WE LOOKING FOR WHEN WE SCOUT A TEAM?

A coach needs to scout the opponent's general tendencies, and prepare for those tendencies. However, it is better to focus on what your team can do, rather than be preoccupied with every detail of what your opponent might do. Don't do so much to prepare that you change what you are used to doing. You can confuse your players by giving them so many new things that they cannot execute.

Following is the kind of information that I want to know about a team that we are preparing to play:

1. What kind of defense do they play- hard Press and front, zone, gap?
2. What is there offense against a press, zone or gap?
3. Any weakness that we can exploit? Weak players that we can drop off of?
4. Strong players that we have to be aware of (2-meter players, shooters, etc.).
5. 6 on 5 offense- positions of strongest shooters, tendencies (post or outside shooters), special plays.
6. 5 on 6 defense- corner coverage, press outside shooters, weakness we can exploit?
7. Goalie- strengths and weaknesses
8. Team and individual speed- how is their counterattack, how well do they defend the counter?

Your team should already know what to do in most of the above situations, if you have prepared them all season long. As a reminder, go over the other team's tendencies and pay attention to what your team should do to overcome them. Make your team aware of strong and weak players, and what they should do against them. Don't make out the best player on their team as a "superstar"; but go over how you want to play him. Many times it can be as simple as pressing the strong player, and dropping off the weak player.

A big mistake that coaches make is to characterize the goalie from the opposing team as being "great" or "weak". The players should not have to change the way they shoot the ball depending on the abilities of the goalie. Prepare your players to take good high percentage shots. They will go against any goalie. Good shot selection is more important than the ability of the opposing goalie.

Shooters will lose their "edge" when shooting against a goalie that the coach has told them is weak. They will start forcing shots that they normally don't take in hopes of getting an "easy" score. Inevitably the "weak" goalie will have the game of his life against your team, and your players will hit every crossbar; or throw the ball over the goal on every shot.

PRE-GAME CHALK TALK

In the chalk talk before the game, the coach should summarize the game plan that has already been practiced prior to the game. Keep it short and to the point. Hit the high points! It is important that the coach not give out too much information that will only serve to confuse the players. Tell them what you want them to do, not what you don't want them to do. Invariably they will remember what you said; but will forget that you used the word "don't". They will then end up doing what you "didn't" want them to do. Human communication is funny that way.

If you are going to have your assistant coach make a few points, make sure he understands what you are trying to get across to your players. Ask him to keep it short, concise, and to the point. An assistant coach that is overly ambitious will try to show that he knows the game; but many times he can counter what you are trying to do, and further confuse the players. Sometimes it is best to only have only the head coach speak to the team before a game. Let the assistant coach speak to individuals, or about a part of the game that he may be responsible for.

MOTIVATION TO WIN

It is not always up to the coach to motivate the players to win every game. The coach should talk to the players about the importance of the game, and give them a reason to win that particular game. The coach cannot give an inspiring Knute Rockney locker room (win one for the Gipper!) emotional speech before every game to motivate the team to win. Those kinds of speeches get a little old after a while and lose their effectiveness.

It is up to the players to motivate themselves to win games. If they can't do this on their own, then they have to question their reasons for being in a competitive sport. Just the opposite is true when your team is playing in a very important game, or championship game. The players will be so psyched up that it could affect their play in the game. In this situation the coach does not need a rah-rah emotional speech, but needs to try and calm the players down by remaining calm himself.

GAME MANAGEMENT

Just as important as planning and executing practice sessions, is how the coach manages the game. This includes how he will handle every part of the game itself, including warm-up, starting line-ups, substitution, time-outs, changing offense and defense, how to handle situations that might come up, etc. All of these things have to be thought about ahead of every game, and correctly executed during the game. After gaining some experience in game management, it will become second nature to a coach, so that he doesn't have to think about it.

WHO STARTS?

I didn't always start all of the best players; but looked for balance, the ability to play defense and the ability to play together, as factors in who started the game. I would try to get equal playing time for about nine to ten field players. It is difficult to get more than that into a game that only lasts a little over an hour. Players have to learn that they have to earn their position on the team.

It is amazing how big a deal "playing time" and playing in the "starting" lineup is to players. My policy was that it was not important who started the game, but who was in the game at the end, in a critical situation. Sometimes substitutes get more playing time than starters. A coach should always explain to the players why they are not starting, and what they have to do to become starters.

CHANGING YOUR LINE-UP

A coach can change starting line-ups from game to game in order to reward good performance in practice, or in the previous game. Be sure that you inform the team at the beginning of the season that this is the way that you will operate. Substitutes will work harder if they know that they will be rewarded with a starting position.

On the other hand, a starter can become complacent in his position and sometimes needs to be "benched" in order to give him a wake up call, and get him to start playing the way he is capable of playing. Before the coach announces the starting line-up to the team, it is important that he has a private meeting with a player who is being benched. The player in question has to be told why he is not starting and what he has to do to earn his position back.

SUBSTITUTIONS
I would sometimes bring in a player off the bench to spark the team when needed; or to play a key role on offense or defense. Substitutions many times have to do with your team needs at the time, especially late in the game. If you need goals, then you have to put in your best scorers. If you need to prevent goals, then you need defensive players in the game. Sometimes you might need to have your fastest swimmers in the pool, and sometimes your smartest players. In a close game you want players in the game that you can count on to make good decisions, especially in pressure situations. You should know your players well enough to know who should be in the game in certain situations.

Young coaches may have to write down the substitution patterns that they intend to use in a game; but also be prepared for unexpected situations that come up when a player is having a bad day, or is injured. Players have to know that they cannot question every time the coach takes them out during the game. During the "heat of battle" is not always a good time to explain to a player why he is out of the game. After the game the coach should go out of his way to find the player affected and explain the situation to him.

ROLE OF SUBSTITUTES
The coach needs to impart on the substitutes the idea that they have a very important role to fill when they enter the game, that they are an important part of the team, and that the team can't win without them. Substitutes should know that their job is not just too score goals; but also to play defense, make good passes, and make good decisions.

The coach may want to give a substitute a specific role, such as guarding a player from the other team, controlling the ball in the front court offense, playing a specific position on offense or defense, or something that caters to his specific talents or skills. Perhaps a player on the bench is your best outside shooter, and you need a goal at that particular time. Have him go in with the purpose of drawing a foul outside 5 meters, and then taking the subsequent shot.

SUBSTITUTE FOR LACK OF EFFORT, NOT FOR A MISTAKE
Never substitute a player for making a mistake. I will sub for lack of effort, but not for making a mistake. If it is obvious that a player is having a bad game, then give him some time to work his way out of it. If that doesn't work, then sub him out and talk to him; or have your assistant coach talk to him about how he is playing. If he feels that he can turn his game around, then re-insert him into the game.

If you give up on a player too soon, he will never gain the confidence to become a better player. If a player is tired, he should ask to be taken out. I would rather have a fresh player that we can count on, than a tired player who cannot cover up. If a player needs to rest, but cannot come out, he should rest on offense, not on defense.

TIME-OUTS

Have a specific purpose in mind when calling time-outs. If you just want to change the players for extra-man or defensive and offensive purposes, then just call a short coaches 20- second time-out (college level rules) and make your changes. If you want to set up a special play, if the team is not executing the game plan, if you want to change what you are doing, if what you are doing is not working, if you want to change the momentum of the game, or if your team needs a rest; then call a regular two-minute time-out; and bring them over to the side of the pool for a short talk.

Know what you want to say before you talk to the team. While the team is swimming over to the side of the pool, consult with your assistant, give the players a few seconds to recover, and then demand their undivided attention. Speak clearly and concisely and make only one or two points. Do more than that and you will lose them. If you need them to concentrate on only one thing, then that is all you should cover. Summarize in a word or phrase to reinforce the message and then ask, "Do you understand? Are there any questions?"

Tell them what you want them to do; but don't dwell on what they have just done wrong. I learned this the hard way in a game. I called a time out and was going on and on about what they had just done wrong. One of my players interrupted me with "what do you want us to do now, coach"?

TIME OUTS FOR SUBSTITUTION- 6 ON 5

The coach may want to call a time-out to set-up a critical 6 on 5 situation when his team needs a goal, when the kick-out occurs in the back-court, when there is not enough time to swim down and set up, or when the best 6 on 5 combination is not in the water at that particular time. As mentioned above, the coach should have a pre-arranged group of players who have practiced together, and that will give his team the best chance to score. They should know who they are and how to execute any plays that the coach calls for.

INSTANT TIME OUT!

At the college level in this country, and in some international competitions, coaches are given an air horn to use in order to call a time out, in case the crowd noise is so loud that the referee cannot hear the coach's voice. The coach can take advantage of the air horn, and call an "instant" time out in a critical situation where his team may be about to lose the ball. In a closely contested game, where perhaps your team is leading by a goal, with little time left in the game; the opposing team takes a shot and the ball rebounds into the water right in front of one of your players, who is immediately surrounded by three players from the other team.

In this situation, where your player can easily lose the ball and give the opposing team another shot on goal; the coach can blow the air horn to call an instant time out, thus averting the loss of the ball to the other team. Players in the water can also call an instant time out, if they find themselves in a similar situation where they are about to lose the ball. Make sure that all of your players know what to do in these kinds of situations. Even more important, make sure everyone knows how many time-outs the team has left in the game.

WHO'S DOING THE TALKING?

Former USA National Team and Olympic gold medal coach Ratko Rudic had a policy of only having the head coach speak to the players before, and even during the game; in order not to confuse the players. Many head coaches will consult with their assistants before they speak to the team during a time out, or in between quarters; but only the head coach should address the team. This is a good policy to follow in order to avoid giving mixed messages to the team.

The role of the assistant coach is to advise the head coach during the coarse of the game, and also to help out individual players; but not at the same time that the head coach is addressing the team. If the head coach has complete confidence in the assistant coach, and that they are "on the same page" fundamentally and tactically, then he can allow the assistant to speak to the team when called upon.

WARM-UP

How much control should a coach exert over the team warm-up prior to the game? It depends how much you trust your team to warm up properly. Experienced players should know what they need to do in order to warm up; so you can give them a little more leeway. If you need to make sure that they are ready to go at the start up the game, you or your assistant coach should monitor the warm up. Team captains or volunteer assistants can also run the warm-up drills, with direction and guidance from the head coach.

SPLIT THE TEAM FOR WARM-UPS

I like to divide the team in half, with the starters and first few substitutes doing their swimming warm up; while the other half warm up their arms and then takes shoots at the back-up goalie. In the second part of the warm-up the roles are reversed; with the starting group shooting at the starting goalie, and the second group doing their warm-up swim.

The warm-up swim consists of slow to intermediate swim speeds for about 400-500 yards, using the freestyle stroke, backstroke, breaststroke and eggbeater kicks. At the end of the swim, each player should do a few quick start and stop swims with a scissor kick to get started, with a few jumps thrown in.

Leg warm-up should also be done prior to passing and shooting; or can be done at the same time that the players are doing warm-up passing. The reason for dividing the team into two groups is to be able to get in more shots on goal for each individual; rather than having one player wait in line for the whole team to shoot.

SPRINTS

Just prior to the start of the game (5 minutes), have your captain bring the team together for head-up sprints. Four 25-yard sprints with 10-15 seconds rest between each one should be sufficient. This allows the players to swim hard, get a second wind before the game starts, and then be ready to swim fast immediately at the start of the game.

The reason for a poor or slow start to the game may be in your warm up. A fast start is critical to the success of the team. Against a team that is not ready to swim fast, your team might be able to get the early lead with a few quick goals. This can be a potential psychological advantage for your team, that the other team might not recover from.

EMOTIONAL CONTROL

A coach has to control his emotions during the game, especially when talking to the team. It is hard to coach when you are angry or upset. This is probably one of the most difficult things that a person has to learn as a coach, especially if he is an emotional person and angers easily. You have to show some emotion, and at times you might have to get angry with your players; but if you are out of control, don't expect your players to be in control, or listen to what you have to say.

POST-GAME TALK

After the game is over, the coach doesn't need to say a lot to the team. This is not the time to analyze the game in detail. Do that at the next practice after the game, when you've had a chance to go over the game film. Emotions are too high or low for the players to get anything out of an after-game talk. Just say a few words of congratulations if you won the game, or a few words of encouragement if you lost. If they won, the players want to get showered and changed, and then go out and celebrate with their friends and families.

After a loss is not a good time to get on them either. They are already feeling down from losing; you don't need to get them down anymore than they already are. Wait and talk to them when your emotions, and the player's emotions, are both under control; and after you have had a chance to evaluate the game or look at game films.

CHAPTER 4

PRACTICE ORGANIZATION, SKILLS AND DRILLS

"CONDUCTING PRACTICE SESSIONS IS THE SINGLE MOST IMPORTANT ASPECT OF SUCCESSFUL COACHING".

Most of time that a coach spends with his team is during practice. This is where you do most of your teaching, and the players learn how to play the game. How effective you are in organizing and presenting you practice sessions, goes a long way in determining the success and/or failure of your team. Most of a coach's time and effort should go into preparing and conducting practice. Your coaching philosophy defines you as a coach; but how you implement your philosophy in practices determines whether you are a successful coach or not.

FIRST AND FOREMOST, THE COACH IS A TEACHER
The answer to success in coaching does not lie in some form of super-strategy, or some ultra-super plan. Success overall does rely on basic, sound teaching abilities. The ability to teach the fundamental skills (basic water polo) to the individual athlete is critical. A coach can have all of the water polo knowledge in the world; but if his/her knowledge is not getting across to the players, then all of that knowledge is wasted.

An effective coach/teacher gets his point across so that the players understand what he is saying; and more importantly, learn to implement what he is trying to get across. How you teach the skills and fundamentals of the game will not only define you as an "effective" coach, but will define the success or failure of your team. Do the job correctly in practice and the coach will be rewarded with a team that understands how to play the game; and correctly executes the learned skills and tactics in a competitive situation.

A coach cannot just "make a speech" or have the players "practice a skill", and expect that the players are going to do what he/she says, or do what they have practiced. There is often a huge gap between what is presented by the coach, what is practiced by the players, and what they actually do in a game. There has to be a "pathway" from the introduction of a skill or tactic, to the actual implementation of that skill or tactic in a game situation. The correct pathway from teacher (coach) to pupil (player), to implementation, has to be conducted according to principles of learning that have been studied by psychologists for years.

TEACHING-LEARNING PRINCIPLES

It is up to the coach to make sure that what he says, and what he does in practice, is first learned by the players, and then actually implemented in the game. The bottom line is that fundamental skills of the game cannot be just practiced or talked about; they have to be incorporated into game situations in practice.

How a person learns a skill, and then implements the skill in a game, depends on how the information is presented by the coach; and then absorbed by the players. It is important for the coach, as a teacher, to know and understand the principles of teaching/learning; in order to effectively get information across to players. Once a player learns a skill, he then has to learn when and how to use that skill during a game.

It is up to the coach to put players in practice situations where the player has to make a decision of when to use, or not use, a certain learned skill. Feedback from the coach is critical in these situations, especially when the player makes the wrong decision or executes incorrectly.

BASIC PRINCIPLES OF LEARNING

Coaches should always be on alert for teaching principles that accelerate the learning process. Following are some of the basic principles of learning and skill-conditioning that apply to water polo, as well as to other sports:

REPETITION- All skills or parts of the game, in order to be learned, must be correctly repeated over and over again, and under game conditions, until a player can perform the skill without having to think about it. Without sufficient training to produce an over-learned state, automatic and smooth movements will not result. Patterns of movements are what are represented in the brain as a result of training. If there are no patterns, then an individual has to respond consciously to exercise; that is, think about every movement. That is what happens with beginners.

Players have not learned a fundamental skill until it becomes second nature (a habit), and until they can perform it correctly, quickly and automatically while involved in game situations. The goal of a drill is to create a correct habit that can be produced without conscious thought, and under pressure. At first the drill must be broken down and practiced individually. Then, as quickly as possible, the skill should be incorporated into a full game-like situation, and performed under conditions that are as close to game conditions as possible.

PRACTICE MAKES PERFECT- Practice makes perfect, which may improve or worsen the present skill level of your players. Insist that your players understand that only "perfect practice makes perfect". Continuous learning and progress depend primarily on each player's interest, motivation, and attitude.

It is up to the coach to insure that players are in the right frame of mind to do things correctly. He can acomplish this by stressing how it will improve them as individuals, and aid in their contribution to the overall success of the team.

Individual and team competition, along with a "reward and punishment" system, is one way to make sure that players do things correctly; and also be assured of practice to game "carry over". Left on their own, many players tend to goof-off during drills. This can be avoided in individual drills, as well as team drills and scrimmage situations, by creating a competitive atmosphere for each drill and scrimmage. It also puts more "game like pressure" on the players, the kind of stress they will experience during competitive matches.

FEEDBACK
Feedback is necessary for effective learning. Mistakes made in practice provide an excellent teaching tool. Your player's mistakes should be used as feedback, or "status" reports on their progress. Feedback from a coach, or other player, that can be used to improve the quality of the skill efficiency, is equally important. Coaches should make every effort to provide feedback about what is being done right, as well as what is being done wrong. A tip for coaches: Give them information that they can use, not just emotion! Players should expect constructive criticism from coaches and should make every effort to accept and learn from such feedback.

SPECIFICITY- The performance capacities of movements such as sprint swimming and the eggbeater kick, are based on correct application and efficiency of mechanical skills. Performances and movements of these kinds of skills are neurologically determined. This requires much training of a specific nature, so that the exact movement involving the exact muscles and nerves, and the same intensity, is trained over and over again, until it can be repeated in an efficient manner.

DECISION MAKING- The more specific the practice and training drills can be to water polo (competitive settings and demands), the more effective they will be in enhancing competitive performances. If transfer of learning from the practice session to the game or competitive situations is to be maximized, the demands of the practice session should mimic as closely as possible the demands of the sport itself; not only in terms of the movement execution requirements, but also in terms of the perceptual and decision-making aspects of the performance.

This can be accomplished by the coach by presenting different situations to a player in practice; so that he can learn to make the correct decision on how to use a particular skill when confronted with these situations in a game. The purpose of varied practice activities and drills should be to allow the athlete to adapt to all conditions and performance variations that could arise in a competitive situation.

SKILL CONDITIONING- Skill conditioning consists of the neuromuscular coordination necessary to perform complex motor tasks associated with a given sport, i.e. dribbling a basketball and coordinating a dunk, stick-handling and shooting a puck in hockey, shooting a ball, taking and receiving passes, and swimming with a ball in water polo.

Even the kind of swimming that a water polo player utilizes requires different skills to perform. Skill conditioning differs from physical conditioning in many ways; but the biggest way it that whereas physical conditioning has a general application to the athlete, skill conditioning has a specific application to the performance of a certain aspect of a particular sport. Soccer skill conditioning, for instance, will only improve your skills in soccer. Performing skills outside of soccer will not help, and will likely hurt your soccer skills.

The physical conditioning of skill-dependent sports should use forms of training that allow the exact skill to be practiced, while undergoing physical stimulation that will cause the body to adapt and change. For maximum efficiency, a coach must determine the most important skills in his sport, especially those that players must improve to raise their level of performance; and then modify the conditioning program to emphasize those skills.

PHYSICAL CONDITIONING
Water polo is a sport that cannot be played properly unless the players are in the very best possible physical condition. It is possible to condition and improve players in certain aspects of the sport by performing conditioning activities in isolation, such as swim conditioning and strength training. However, in accordance to the principle of specificity, it is also important to develop water polo fitness in such a manner that the fitness is functionally appropriate to water polo. This will allow a player to effectively meet the demands of the game.

Isolated actvities such as swim conditioning can be used for evaluation and training purposes, because all the players have to swim the same set distance in a certain amount of time. However these activities should be used sparingly and for a short period of time each day, so as to not take away from the important skill learning and conditioning that is necessary to play the game of water polo.

The major determinates of this physical training is that it be as game-like as possible, and be of sufficient repetition and loading to cause specific training effects to occur. Thus, training programs should not consist of a number of unrelated activities; but should seek to combine activities that develop both skills and fitness at the same time. A way to become more efficient in training skills, and the physical part of a game, is to have the players perform drills that combine the two, much as the way they are performed in competition.

PART-WHOLE MEHOD- When teaching new skills, or altering established skills, it is common practice to break skills into component parts, and "build" the movement patterns. This "part-whole" approach is most effective when the skill to be learned is complex and has clearly defined natural breaks or components (e.g., a gymnastics routine, switching from a horizontal to a vertical position in the water). Such an approach to learning, however, may be of little to no value when the skill is essentially continuous, with no natural breaks (such as in running, swimming, shooting a ball).

Once the skill is learned with the defense involved, it must immediately be incorporated into a full court 6 on 6 game situation. Something will always come up in a game situation that you did not figure on when first learning the drill. Players must learn to react to different situations, rather than just perform pre-memorized skills and formations. They will improve and learn to play the game properly, based on the number of full court 6 on 6 situations that they are exposed to during practice and games; and whether they learn and remember these situations.

TRANSFER OF SKILLS- Skills from one sport do not transfer to another sport, even for similar skills. For instance, throwing a baseball, football and water polo ball require different skills, even though the action of throwing the ball is similar. Some sports are very skill oriented (golf and tennis), while some sports are very physical oriented (running a marathon). Most team sports, like water polo, are a mixture of the two; so most teams must practice improving both the physical and skill parts of their sport. This requires that coaches do not waste time training skills and conditioning that does not specifically apply to the skills and physical part of a game.

HOW TO AVOID BOREDOM AND CREATE GAME-LIKE PRESSURE SITUATIONS AT THE SAME TIME
No matter what you do as a coach, there will come a time during the season when boredom sets in. Try to do the boring repetitive skills early in the season when the players are still alert and anxious to learn. Later in the season you can work on game situations and prepare for the team that you are going to play that week, doing less of the repetitive and boring skill work. Creating competition among the members of the team will go a long ways to eliminating boredom.

Not only that, but competition in practice can create similar pressure situations that occur frequently in games. It is amazing how competitive players will become, and how hard they will work, just to get out of practice a few minutes early; or not have to stay after practice and take out goals and put in pool covers. Following are examples of competitive situations that the coach can create in practice:
1. Passing contests – Two players pass the ball back and forth. Gradually increase the distance the ball is thrown as the drill goes on. If any one of the two players drops the ball on the water, that team is eliminated from the contest. The first few pairs of players to be eliminated must put the goals into the pool.The last pair that is left does not have to stay after practice to take out the goals and cover the pool. In addition they have the honor of being declared the "best" passers on the team for the day.

2. Shooting contests – This is one of my favorites. Line up 6-8 players at the six-yard line (parallel to the goal), each one with a ball. On the whistle have the first player shoot at the goal, followed by the next player, and then the next, etc. The players keep shooting one at a time for a period of time, say 2 minutes. Before you start, set a number of goals that the players think they can score during the time allotted. If they score the set number, the goalie has to swim 200 yards butterfly. If they shoot less than the specified number, the whole team has to swim 200 yards butterfly.

3. Double hernia – This drill is described in Chapter 5 on "Conditioning and Training". It involves two players swimming the length of the pool. One takes a shot under pressure, and then they both swim back in the other direction for a one-on-nobody shot at the goalie. The premise here is that players should not miss a one-on-nobody against the goalie. Set a number of one-on-nobody goals that have to be made in a row, say 15 or 20. A miss by any one player starts the count over again. The drill goes on and on, until the required number of shots are made. This is a great drill to create a situation where the players have to depend on each other to succeed.

4. Penalty shots- At the end of practice, have a penalty shot contest. Every player on the team must take a shot, and the team must make a certain percentage of the shots (80%). Not making the percentage means extra swimming for everyone on the team, If they make the percentage, the goalie must do extra swimming. Not only is this a great drill to create some excitement and competition at the end of the workout; but it gives the coach a good idea of who can handle the pressure of taking a penalty shot in a game. This kind of thing is a great "team bonding" situation for the team to learn about relying on each other and that "we are all in this together as a team, win or lose".

5. Game competition- During scrimmages at the end of practice, set up games where score is kept. The winner gets out of practice early, or doesn't have to do any work at the end of practice. The coach can set the score beforehand, depending on the kind of teams he sets up. If the first unit is playing the second unit, then give the second team a lead that they have to protect. The coach can also set up equal teams; but set the score at zero-zero to start the game. Both teams should get equal time (by quarters) to score at both ends of the pool, and against both goalkeepers.

    The coach can also set up some kind of scoring criteria that emphasizes the parts of the game that he feels are important. For instance, give a point for every goal, two points for every assist, three points for every counterattack goal, or give one point for a normal goal and two points for a six-on five goal, or give one point for a normal goal and two points for a goal scored after being fouled outside 5-meters.

Reward a team that earns a kick-out with two extra man situations, instead of only one. If they score on both, they get to add both scores to their total. (The ball is live after the second attempt). In addition to offensive points, reward the defense by giving points for defensive skills that the coach wants to emphasize. For instance award a point for every steal or blocked shot. Play to 30-40 points. The winning team gets out and the losing team takes out goals and puts in pool covers.

6. Extra-man competition- Having the team perform multiple extra-man (6 on 5) situations in a row, can be one of the most boring parts of practice. In addition, it is not a good way to create stressful extra-man game situations; because there is no reward for a good defensive or offensive play. Similar to shooting competitions as described above, at the end of practice have each team do ten 6 on 5's each.

The coach can set up a system of offensive and defensive rewards that will emphasize different parts of extra-man offense and defense. Besides giving a point for each goal, the offense can earn extra points for a goal scored from a post-position, or a goal scored by shooting off of a pass. The defense can earn extra points for a blocked shot. Use a shot clock with 20 seconds on it, so they have the same amount of time to take the shot before the teams are even-up.

7. Four-man tournament- Create equal four-man teams and hold a mini-tournament. Three teams are the ideal number for a tournament. If you have more than twelve players, give each team one or two subs that must be rotated after every goal. In the last hour of practice you can have six games of ten minutes each, with each team playing the other teams twice each. Make sure that the teams change ends the second time that they play each other, so that they shoot at different goalkeepers each time.

A team gets 2 points for a win, 1 point for a tie, and zero for a loss. The first place team gets out early, the second place team takes out the goals and picks up balls, while the third place team has to put in pool covers. This is a great team conditioner, especially if the games are played in a 30-meter pool. It is better suited for a 25-meter or 25-yard pool, however.

8. Get out swims – Do sprints at the end of the practice. Start on the whistle and finish on the wall so that everyone gets an equal chance. Winner (or first two finishers) of each sprint gets out. Everyone else stays in and does more sprints.

9. One-man swim challenge- I learned this from my days as a swim coach. If your team is in the middle of a grueling swim set, lets say 30 X 50-yard repeats, stop after the 20th or 25th repeat, and announce to your team that if your best swimmer does a certain time on the next swim, the whole team gets out of doing the last three or five repeats. Make the time a challenging one; but one you feel that your best swimmer can do.

PRACTICE GAME SITUATIONS

Game situations that occur during the front-court offense and 6 on 5 offense, at first must be taught utilizing different defensive formations. Players must learn how to execute against every type of defense that they could possibly see. This is done by repetition, e.g. ten front court offenses or ten 6 on 5's in a row. Once they learn to perform against the expected defense, then they have to learn how to perform against the unexpected defense; similar to what would occur in a game.

Surprise the offense with unannounced defenses in practice, so they will know what to do when that defense come up in a game. Communicate to the defensive team ahead of time what defense you want them to run, without the offense having any prior knowledge. If you have practiced every situation before-hand, then they should know how to handle a different defense when it comes up in a game.

If the coach has to call a time out whenever a different defense is presented to the players in a game, then he has not prepared them properly in practice. At the very least, the team should know how to run an offense against a press, different zones, and different gap defenses, without additional instructions from the coach.

ADDING STRESS TO GAME SITUATIONS

The above-mentioned competitions, where players are rewarded for winning, are great ways to produce game-type of stress in practice. One type of stress that is difficult to produce in practice, is the situation where a referee makes a bad call during the course of the game; or makes a call that affects the outcome of the game. In the competitive scrimmages described above, where the players are desperately trying to win some offered reward, or avoid punishment, the coach can purposely make a bad call to see how the players react to the situation.

This can then be used by the coach as a learning situation, for the players to learn how to handle a bad call by a referee in a game. This all must be explained to the players after practice, especially if the call affected their reward of getting out of practice early. The coach can then call the game "even" and give them another way to end the practice, like taking 6 penalty shots for each team. This, by the way, also simulates a real game penalty shooting tie game situation.

TEN STEPS TO A SUCCESSFUL PRACTICE

1. KNOW WHERE YOU ARE GOING AND HOW YOU ARE GOING TO GET THERE.

   A coach has to figure out what needs to get done; and what are the most important parts of the game that need to be emphasized to enable his team to win. Much of this has to do with the coaches personal philosophy of how he wants the game played. Next, he must determine what fundamentals of the game the players need to learn in order to execute the parts of the game he deems most important.Then he must analyze the personnel on the team, determine their strengths and weaknesses, and what they need to learn in order to play the game well.

   Finally he has to prioritize the parts that need to be emphasized the most, and which ones that have to be emphasized the least. The coach must organize the practice so that the team spends more time on the most important points, but at the same time makes sure that everything is covered.

2. COMBINE AND CONDITION

   There are only so many hours per day that are available for practice each day, and the more effective a coach is in combining different parts of the game together, the more efficient the practices will be. Always try to include conditioning in every drill.

   For instance, instead of just picking up the ball and shooting it at the goal, incorporate other things into the drill. Add another player to the drill and have him pass the ball to the shooter. Make them both swim the length of the pool before they pass and shoot the ball. This adds conditioning and passing to the drill. Then add defensive players so that the players learn how to pass, shoot, and receive the ball under pressure. This is all water polo related; and it sure beats swimming laps for conditioning.

3. PRACTICE WITH INTENSITY.

   The players need to learn how to practice with the same intensity in practice that they do in a game. Players can't practice in a casual manner, and then suddenly turn it on in a game. The coach must make the practice demanding enough so that the players can prepare themselves for the demands of the game. At the same time the coach must not allow players to "take it easy" during practice, and must encourage them to work as hard as they can.

   Try to single out and praise players for working extra hard, especially on swim sets. A coach can reward the hardest workers by letting them out of practice a little early, or by allowing them to get out of the goal removal and pool cover work at the end of the workout.

4. MORE IS NOT NECESSARILY BETTER.
   Players play with more intensity when practices are shorter rather than longer. The longer the workout, the more the players tend to loaf and pace themselves; and not pay attention to what is going on. Two and one half hours is about the maximum time for a practice session. Two hours is ideal, especially at the high school level.

   If you are prepared as a coach, if your practices are run in an efficient manner, and you have prepared your athletes to work hard, then 2 hours to 2 1/2 hours at one time is all that you need to get everything accomplished. I always tell my players that we will have short practices; but I expect maximum intensity from them throughout the whole practice session. Practices at the end of the season or just prior to a game should be less than 2 hours in length.

5. WASTED TIME
   A lot of time in practice is wasted time and not very productive. If a coach can eliminate the unnecessary extra time from a training session, his team will get a lot more out of the session; and he can actually accomplish more in a shorter period of time. A coach who is organized, and knows what he is doing, will not waste time doing things that are not necessary; but are just done to fill up time.

   Wasted time is doing things like swimming long distances that are not related to water polo, doing drills that are not related to the game, performing individual skills without adding defensive players, learning skills that are not related to the game, performing unrelated activities (like running) that cannot be carried over to water polo, and just plain "goofing off" by the players.

6. DOUBLE SESSIONS
   Double workouts are only appropriate during the pre-season, when classes have not started yet; and the coach has to get a lot of information across to the team in a short period of time. If a coach is going to have morning conditioning sessions, he should at least make them water polo related. Get the water polo-type of swimming and leg-work out of the way in the morning, add some 6 on 5 work, and then spend the afternoon working on shooting, game related front court offense and defense, counterattack, scrimmages and tactical game situations.

   These extra morning sessions should not be more than 1 to 1 ½ hours in length. Shorten the afternoon workout from 2 to 2 1/2 hours for a maximum of 3 to 3 1/2 hours total in one day. Even 3 1/2 hours a day is stretching it when it comes to overworking the team, and at the same time fitting in academic requirements. Morning sessions can also be a good time to perform shoulder strength and stability exercises, or pool or dryland strength circuits, without interfering with water polo specific practice in the afternoon.

7. DEMAND CORRECT EXECUTION IN PRACTICE.
   The coach cannot let players execute fundamentals and drills incorrectly in practice, or they will execute them incorrectly in games. Practice is the time to correct mistakes, before they become a problem in a game. Teams can be consistent and disciplined in games, if they have had that lesson ingrained in them in practice. In correcting a mistake, the coach should wait until the play has run out and there is a break in the action.

   Make sure that everyone on the team is paying attention, including the players that are not directly involved or sitting on the sideline. These are great learning situations for everyone on the team, not just the player involved in the play. The players sitting on the side many times will treat the time when they are not directly involved as a big social-hour. Then when it becomes time for them to perform, they end up making the same mistakes that the coach had just corrected. Talk about wasting time!

8. CONSTRUCTIVE CRITICISM
   The players must be taught to expect constructive criticism, and that "it is all right to make mistakes." Just don't repeat the mistakes! The goal here is to eliminate mistakes in practice that will carry over to the game. Many coaches like to say something positive before they criticize a player. This can help in tempering the criticism; but is not always possible to do. It is your job as the coach to correct mistakes, and make sure that the players are doing things right. Remember to criticize the action, and not the player personally.

   The coach should try to make corrections during a lull in the action, so that it doesn't disrupt the flow of the practice. There are times when a mistake has to be corrected immediately, and the correct way to do it must be explained or demonstrated. If it is a critical enough situation, then stop the action and correct the mistake. If necessary, have the player involved perform the action over again, but in the correct manner. Again, make sure that everyone is paying attention.

9. WHEN TO STOP A DRILL
   If a drill is going poorly, it is probably better to cut it off than to keep going on and on until it is done correctly. Point out the problem and go on to something else. You might want to come back the next day with a different approach to the same drill. A great teaching tool is to find a player who is doing the drill correctly, and have him demonstrate it for the rest of the team.

10. FOCUS ON YOUR ATHLETES IN PRACTICE
    Before a tough competition, it is easy to oversell your opponent's abilities. Instead, work on skills that will help overcome the opponent's strong points. Prepare for a strong opponent by preparing for situations that might come up, but don't build up the opponent to the point where your players become intimidated by their "supposed" invincibility. Give your team confidence by preparing and using good tactics to overcome a strong opponent.

TIME MANAGEMENT- USE THE CLOCK

Teams should practice time management situations that have to do with both the shot clock and the game clock, as described in Chapter 5, "Game Tactics and Strategies". Teams need to know how to manage the clock, both when they have a lead, or are behind the other team. The situation also depends on how many goals a team is leading by, or losing by; and how much time is left in the game, quarter or shot clock. These situations can be set up by using both a shot clock and a game clock during practice, and by setting the score to create different scenarios.

I really don't know how a coach can run an effective practice without using a shot clock. If players are to learn how to handle time management situations, a shot clock in practice is imparative. This will pay dividends in a game when your players will know exactly what to do in every situation that they are confronted with. Otherwise they will be wandering aimlessly up and down the pool, wondering what to do. I want my players to know what to do without having to call a time-out in order to explain every situation.

ONE-WAY COUNTERS

Of all the hundreds of drills that I have used over the last 40 years, this is probably the drill that I have used the most. I have found it to be more useful for teaching game situations on offense, defense and the counterattack; more than any other drill that I have ever used. Start at one end of the pool with a 6 on 6 front-court offense and defense. The coach can create any kind of situation that he wants by 1) putting different times from 5 to 30 seconds on the shot clock, 2) changing the type of front-court defense that a team is playing at the start of the drill, and 3) changing the position of the ball.

On the shot on goal or turnover, both teams counterattack to the other end of the pool. It doesn't matter if a goal is scored, a shot is tipped out by the goalie, or the ball rebounds back into the field of play. Both teams counterattack on the shot, no matter what happens. Possession automatically goes to the defense. This teaches the players to react to the shot, without looking back to see if a goal was scored or not. This is called "going on anything".

If the counterattacking team does not get a shot at the other end, they must run a frontcourt offense, much as they would in a game. If they do score on the counterattack, then they get a corner throw and a chance to run a frontcourt offense, or run a "corner-throw special play".

At the end of each one-way counterattack, the coach can stop and discuss what went right or wrong with the drill. This creates a great learning situation; and gives the coach an opportunity to discuss the situation right after it happens, without having to interrupt play. The same team counters ten times in a row; then switches so that the other team counters ten times.

CREATE A FREE MAN ON THE COUNTERATACK

When both teams are set up in the front court, the coach can also start the one-way counterattack drill by calling out the hat number of an offensive player. Upon hearing his hat number, the player goes underwater for a few seconds while the other eleven players immediately go on the counterattack.

By calling out the numbers of different offensive players, the coach can create any kind of counterattack situation that he wants; everything from a one-on-nobody to a 6 against 5 man-up situation. Again, a critique of the execution of the counterattack can take place at the other end of the pool, after the completion of the one-way counter. Or, the coach can create another counterattack situation, by having both teams counterattack back in the other direction immediately after a turnover or a shot is taken. Again, "going on anything". Ideally, a different man up situation will be created in the other direction.

This is known as a "two-way" counter drill. It is excellent for teaching teams how to cover back when they have a man-up in one direction. It also teaches players how to "counter-the-counter" and take advantage of a team that losses the ball, or takes a bad shot during the first counterattack. Did I mention that this is also a great conditioning drill?

6 ON 5 ONE-WAY COUNTERS/SCRIMMAGES

A great way to practice the extra-man (6 on 5) is to run one-way or two-way counters, or full court scrimmages, where the coach, acting as a referee, kicks out players during the course of the drill, and from anywhere in the pool. The referee-coach can create game situations for both the 6 on 5 offense and defense by calling exclusions at different times during the drill or scrimmage. Again, a natural break in the action after the 6 on 5 is completed is a good time for the coach to critique the play.

This also teaches the players how to quickly get into the extra-man defense or offense that the coach has created. The coach can call kick-outs at 2-meters, on the perimeter, during the counterattack, and at either end of the pool. The coach can also call offensive fouls at any time, and try to create man-up situations on the subsequent counterattack. This is much better than just setting up ten 6 on 5's in a row in front of the goal; because it simulates actual game exclusions.

Once the shot is taken on the 6 on 5, both teams should counter to the other end of the pool. This will also teach the players to counterattack and try to get a free man when they are a man down. The coach should alert the players ahead of time that he may not be calling a legitimate kick-out; but that he is trying to create different 6 on 5 situations. He should try to make it as realistic as possible, calling something that at least closely resembles an exclusion foul.

DESIGNING A DRILL

The first thing that a coach must do in designing a drill is to break down whatever he wants to work on. It may be a new skill, a team weakness that you discovered from a previous game, something you feel the team needs to work on, or something that the opponent may do that the team needs to practice against. In choosing drills, ask yourself the specific purpose of the drill that you want to use. Does the drill relate directly to your offense or defense? Is the drill a better teaching devise then a six on six situation? Is the drill helping your team improve in some area of the game, or are you just fitting it in your practice plan because it is convient?

The coach shouldn't do a drill just to keep the players occupied; or do a drill that he reads about in a drill book, or a drill that his coach used to do when he was a player. Fit a drill into your team's specific needs. If the movement is a complex one, break down the skill into smaller parts, and work on those individually before you put them together as one. Some skills and movements cannot be broken down (swimming, shooting) and should be practiced by making small refinements or adjustments to the complete movement.

INCORPORATING DRILLS INTO THE GAME

Once the basic skill is learned, then defense or offense must be introduced into the drill, eventually incorporating it into a 6 on 6 game-situation. The sooner the better! Skills performed without defensive pressure can be very different then when performed with the defense present. Some drills do not have to be broken down, and can immediately be incorporated into a full 6 on 6 situation.

Water polo is a full court game that requires teams to move from one end of the pool to the other. Consequently, learned skills should be incorporated into full court 6 on 6 drills as soon as possible for maximum effect. Incorporating the skills into full court situations is an excellent way to give the players "choices", and to get them to "think" about how and when to effectively use the different skills that they have just learned.

GAME CARRY OVER

Ideally, everything that you do in practice is carried over to a game. This isn't always the case; but you can insure a high percentage of "practice retention" in the game by repeating a drill under game conditions, until the players perform it correctly, without thinking, and at game speed. The coach cannot let the players get away with doing something incorrectly in practice, or they will do it that way in a game. By correcting a mistake in practice, the coach may not have to correct it during a game.

WASTING TIME

Each practice should be carefully planned and organized to prevent wasting time. Not only must there be a specific purpose for every drill; but every drill must be placed in the most advantageous time during the practice period. A drill used at an improper time is just about as useless as a drill that has no concrete purpose at all. Every effort should be made to condition the players for game competition, and the drills should be devised and used to best advantage for that purpose. The coach should have a logical sequence that incorporates one drill into another, going from the basic skill drill, to a half court drill, and then finally to a full court drill,

Another place where time is wasted is when teams are changing from one drill to another. Players can be a little lazy in these periods between drills, and it is up to the coach to get them moving. I always had a team rule that players had to "swim freestyle", and not "lazy breaststroke", or kicking on a ball when going from one drill to another. Players love to shoot the ball at the goal every chance that they get; but this is another example of wasting time. Not only does the errant ball have to be retrieved; but everyone has to wait for that player to join the next drill. When the whistle blows to end a drill, no one can shoot the ball.

Sometimes a punishment for these kinds of infractions has to be incorporated, until the players learn how not to waste time. After a while these kinds of things just become second nature as the way that things are always done; and no further punushment will be required.

Another part of practice where time is being wasted, is when the goalie does not have an extra ball inside the goal to "feed" the counterattack. I always hated wasting time waiting for the goalie to climb out of the pool to retrieve the only ball that is available. The players have just busted their guts to swim down the pool, have created a "free" man, and lo and behold, no ball! This kind of thing drives me batty as a coach.

TEACH PLAYERS TO REACT
The eventual goal is to practice a particular skill at game speed, and under game conditions, so that the players can react to the situation without having to think about it. One of the hardest skills to teach a player is to "react" immediately to any kind of turnover when the ball changes hands. This is especially true in reacting to a shot that has just been taken. Teaching all of your players to react on every turnover can really put pressure on the other team; and can make a difference of a 2-3 goal swing in your teams favor at the end of the game.

The first instinct of the defender is to look back and see if the goal was scored or not. In order to break players of this habit, the coach has to do a lot of reaction drills, and make sure that the players react without looking back. This skill must be practiced over and over again, until it becomes an automatic reaction by all six players. The coach has to constantly stress the importance of immediately reacting to the shot or turnover, and what it can do to create a man-up situation on the subsequent counterattack.

Explain to the players about the advantage they can gain by out-reacting the other team. The number of goals that they can score will far out-weigh the few times that they might not get the offensive rebound off the bar of the goal. They also have to understand the importance of every player (6-man counter) reacting to the turnover, and just not a few of them.

If they have to look back, they can look after they have taken a few strokes, and have gained the offensive advantage going in the other direction. They can always come back and cover in case their team has not gained control of the rebound. If a goal has been scored, they have only wasted a few strokes by reacting. If the players still don't get it, the coach may have to incorporate some kind of swimming or push-up punishment for every time a player doesn't react.

To put more pressure on an individual to react, have the whole team swim or do push-ups when one player doesn't react. Not only will that player have to answer to the coach when he doesn't react, but to his peers as well. Sometimes this kind of "peer" pressure is the best kind of pressure. If the whole team benefits from a "reaction" in a game, then they all must "suffer" when one player does not react in practice.

PLANNING THE SEASON

The coach should have a general plan for the season, based on what he feels the team needs to work on. These are the skills and parts of the game that he feels are important, and that the team needs to be able to execute in order to succeed in the up-coming season. The best way to do this is to work back from the first game on the calendar, and list what skills, tactics and strategies you feel the players will need to successfully play the game.

The coach doesn't have to be too specific as to the exact timing, but should write down everything he feels is important, and then prioritize. Essential higher priority items should be worked on first; but eventually everything must be covered in a logical order, and the team must be prepared in time for the first game.

EARLY-SEASON

Early season is when the team works on the basic fundamentals of the game, and when the coach starts installing the team's basic offensive and defensive formations and systems. This is the time for the coach to start stressing his personal philosophy, goals for the team, and how he wants the game to be played. This is also the time for the coach to get the team in shape. How much conditioning depends on what kind of shape they are in when they arrive at practice on the first day.

Most players play all summer, and then take a few weeks off before the start of fall practice, so they shouldn't be in too bad of shape when they arrive. For most men's teams, games usually start about 3 weeks after the first day of practice; so there is not a lot of time to get the team in shape before the first competition. 2-a-day practices for the first week or two are usually done by most men's teams; with emphasis on quality sprint training.

Coaches have to be careful and not "pile it on" during the first few weeks of practice. There is nothing to be gained by going 6-8 hours a day of intense training during this time, in hopes of getting everyone back into shape fast. The result of this kind of training will be tired and hurt players, that because of fatigue will not have learned much about how you want them to play the game. As the first game approaches, the coach then has to make a decision on when to start resting his players; depending on how hard the players have been practicing, and the quality of competition in the first game.

Women's teams that don't compete in the Fall usually have more time to practice before the start of competition; so 2-a-day workouts are not necessary to prepare the team for a winter-spring schedule. Because of the extra time to prepare in the Fall, coaches can gradually get women's teams into high intensity training, rather than hitting them all at once with high intensity 2-a-day training as the men are required to do.

Coaches for both men and women should stress to the players the value of arriving in shape on the first day of practice; so that more time can be spent on water polo, and less on conditioning. This, however, may be a "lost cause" for most teams; because it is difficult for the players to train on their own during the vacation or holiday periods prior to the start of practice.

The best way to handle this situation is to get the players in great shape before they go home for vacation. Then when they return from vacation, they will still be in decent shape, despite having done very little during the holiday period.

MID-SEASON

The middle of the season is the time to make adjustments to the game, depending on the team's success or failure in previous games. Every game should be evaluated (on film if available), and the parts of the game that need to be worked on should be stressed during the weeks practice sessions. At the same time, the coach should keep working on the fundamentals of the game, and the way that he wants the team to play the game. Mid-season should involve more and more time on game situations and tactics, and preparing for specific opponents. Continue conditioning the players, with emphasis on game speed and the counterattack.

LATE-SEASON

The end of the season is the time to fine-tune the team's offense and defense, and to prepare for the post-season. Come up with a few variations that your opponents have not seen, and have not had time to prepare for. Shorter practices, more scrimmaging and less swimming is in order. Continue practicing game situations and 6 on 5 extra-man.

POST SEASON

Post season is the time that you rest your players, and work on specific parts of the game, like front court offense and defense, counterattack, and 6 on 5 situations. Much of this can be done in half-court situations, although the team can always do a few one-way counters, or spend some time on a full court scrimmage. The important thing here is rest. Weights (if you are doing them) and swimming laps should be eliminated, although a few sprints can be performed (along with counterattack drills) to keep the players up to game speed.

WEEKLY PLAN

The team's practice plan for each week will vary depending on several factors. The four most critical factors are: 1) who your opponent will be, (2) what time of the week your games are, (3) how difficult a game it will be, and (4) how important are the games for seeding or advancement into post-season competition. If every game that you play is important to advancement to post season competition, than you will have to rest your players before each game. The more difficult the game, the more you must rest the team. An opponent that your team can easily beat will allow you to play that game without "resting" or tapering.

WEEKEND GAMES

During the season, an ideal situation is one in which your games are at the end of the week. This will allow you to work the players very hard during the beginning of the week, and then taper down towards the end of the week. Early in the week, you can condition more, while working on the counterattack and front court situations; while the end of the week should be spent working more on half-court, 6 on 5, and game situations. As the week goes on there should be more scrimmaging and less swimming.

Make sure that you rest your goalies as well, so that they don't have tired legs for the game. If your opponent is one that you can easily beat, or if the result of this particular game does not figure in to whether you play in the postseason or not, then don't rest the team. If there is any doubt about the result of the game, rest your players!

MID-WEEK GAMES

The most difficult scenario is when you have two games during the week, i.e. one on Wednesday and one on Saturday. If the game on Saturday is the more difficult of the two, then you can work through the mid-week game. If they are both difficult, then you have to have two mini-tapers, one for each game. In this situation the hardest work days would be Monday and Thursday, with easy days on Tuesday and Friday, the days before each game on Wednesday and Saturday.

DURING HIGH SCHOOL AND COLLEGE COMPETITION, EVERY GAME COUNTS.

Teams who have to qualify for post-season play need to insure that they win enough games by resting their players each week. The overall record during the season usually determines their fate in the post-season. Every game becomes a critical one. Teams can no longer afford to work hard and "play through" games during the season, and then taper at the end of the season for the league tournament post-season play-offs.

At both the high school and college level, seeding is an important factor in winning tournaments, or post-season competition. Since seeding is based on your record, this is another good reason to rest your players each week. Of course, whether you rest your team or not, always depends on the quality of our competition during the course of the season.

A coach who tries to manipulate the seeding, and the choice of teams that his team will play, can find his team "left out in the cold" at the end of the season. Unless the team is so dominant that they shouldn't have any problem qualifying, then the coach must rest his team for every game, and win as many games possible. As a coach, you cannot control what other teams are doing, only what your team is doing. So make sure that your team is rested and playing well for every game.

DAILY WORKOUT SCHEDULE

How you schedule what you are going to do each day of the week depends on the following criteria:

    1. Time of the season.

    2. Who your opponent is and how important the game is. Work on opponent related drills later in the week and closer to game day.

    3. Swim less as the week goes on, especially if you need to rest the team.

    4. Work on game related passing and shooting every day.

    5. Work on half court offense and defense every day.

6. Teach a new concept early in the season and early in the daily practice session. When learning a new concept or skill, do your intense conditioning at the end of practice. Make sure that you incorporate a new concept into your full court 6 on 6 sessions as soon as possible.

7. Work on counterattack every day.

8. Work on 6 on 5 extra-man every day.

9. Scrimmage every day

A lot of the above scenarios can be combined in order to make practice more efficient. Conditioning can be incorporated into everything that you do, including 6 on 5 offense and defense. The one-way counterattack drill as described above is a combination of frontcourt offense, defense and the counterattack. Also, as described above, 6 on 5 can be also incorporated into one-way or 2-way counterattack drills.

TYPICAL DAILY SCHEDULE

A typical daily schedule for a 2 1/2 hour workout would be as follows:

>30 minutes warm-up and conditioning, including swimming, leg work and passing

>30-40 minutes of passing and shooting drills, individual offensive and defensive drills, 6 on 5 offensive and defensive drills.

>30 minutes of counterattack drills

>30-40 minutes of controlled scrimmage, game situations.

The total time for the workout decreases as the week goes on, assuming a weekend game that you have to win. The day before a game would be very easy, only 1 1/2 hours long; with more emphasis on front-court tactics, 6 on 5, shooting, and game situations. Swim conditioning is reduced as the week goes on, with more emphasis on shorter sprints and scrimmaging towards the end of the week.

WRITE IT DOWN

When a coach starts planning a daily practice session, he must write down what he plans to do for that practice, and how much time he wants to spend on each part. As he gains more experience in planning a practice, he can simply write down, or have in his mind, what he wants to work on.

The amount of time spent on each part will be more a matter of "feel", than by a prescribed time that has been written down. Whichever way he does it, the coach has to be flexable; and be willing to make changes if things aren't going well.

SUMMARY One of the key components of successful coaching is the ability to designand implement daily practice sessions. Everything that your team does in games is learned in practice. If you want to be a good coach, and produce winning teams, you have to be a good practice coach. Game coaching is also important, but 90 % of your teaching and coaching takes place in practice. Preparation for the game in practice is equally, if not more important as playing the game itself. Remember that success in games comes only when "preparation meets opportunity."

CHAPTER 5

GAME TACTICS AND STRATEGIES

Deciding what kind of tactics and strategies a team will use in a game mainly involves the manipulation of the offense and defense during different times of the game. In deciding what kind of offense your team will play, the coach needs to consider what the strengths of his team are, what kind of defense the other team will play in order to counter your strengths, and the game situation at the time (time of game, score, time of possession, etc.). The key to designing your offense is flexibility and movement. When the defense takes away part of your offense, you must be flexible enough to counteract what the defense does, by doing something else.

The other key to the offense is movement without the ball. Movement on offense causes the defense to react to that move, thus helping to take the defense out of its defensive alignment. It can also create confusion and take a defensive player out of his comfort zone; creating more opportunities for the offense. In the extra man offense, moving and shifting players can take a defensive player out of position and open up a teammate for a shot on goal.

A player can free himself to receive the ball against a strong press by driving and/or by releasing for the ball. Driving against a zone defense can clear out a defender who is dropping back on the center forward. Staying in one place and waiting for something to happen can stagnate an offense.

The key to designing a defense is to determine what defense the rules will allow your team to use in order to stop the other team from executing their offense. To be effective, teams need to learn more than one kind of defensive alignment, and also to have the ability to change from one defense to another at anytime during the game. Changing defenses has to be practiced over and over again, until the team can make the change smoothly and without hesitation.

SET THE PACE OF THE GAME

I feel that it is very important for my team to set the pace of the game. I want to take advantage of our speed and conditioning, to wear the other team down by playing a fast paced game. The fast game starts with a pressure defense that leads to bad passes, hurried shots and turnovers from the other team. This feeds our counterattack and the fast paced kind of game that we like to play. As mentioned previously, a fast team can adjust to a slow game; but a slow team will have problems adjusting to a fast game.

TACTICS

Many of the tactics in games have to do with clock management, be it the shot clock or the game clock. The correct tactical use of the clock during a game can help a team to win close games, and in critical situations at the end of a game. This can make the difference between victory and defeat. Managing the shot clock is an important part of the game for all teams, and can make a difference of a several goal swing in either direction.

The ability to manage the clock just doesn't happen, however. A coach has to prepare his players for these situations by going over them in practice until they know instinctively what to do, without the coach having to call time-outs to go over every situation. The introduction of the 30-second shot clock makes it even more important for players to know what to do when the shot clock is winding down. Teams should always use a shot clock in practice.

A coach should go over all the possible situations that can occur in the game, so that the players are prepared for anything that can happen. Not only must players know what to do at the end of the shot clock, on both offense and defense; but the players should know what to do at the end of the game when there is little time left on the clock, their team has a 1-2 goal lead, the game is tied, or their team is 1-2 goals behind. These situations can be critical to the success of the team, and can sometimes make the difference in a winning or a losing season; or whether the team makes it to the post season or not.

SHOT CLOCK SITUATIONS- DEFENSE

LEAVING EARLY

As a defensive player, you are expected to counterattack the other team when there is a turnover, shot on goal, or when the shot clock runs out. A smart defensive player can also create goal-scoring opportunities by leaving his defensive position before the shot clock expires, and as the team on offense is running out of time. As the shot clock is winding down, a defender who is guarding an offensive player who not in position to be a scoring threat, can take advantage of the situation and take off early on the counterattack, towards the other end of the pool.

THE PSYCHOLOGY OF LEAVING EARLY

The idea here is that the defender hopes to take advantage of the offensive player, with or without the ball, who has to stay on offense, is not in a good shooting position to take a high percentage shot, and will not be able to follow the defender down the pool. The offensive player that the defender leaves has to make a decision on whether to stay on offense, pass the ball, shoot the ball, dump the ball, or follow the defender down the pool.

If the defender does this correctly, the offensive player will not be in a good position to shoot, and he also will not be in a good position to follow down the pool. In other words, "He is caught between a rock and a hard place". Taking off early may not work every time that you try it; but once a player learns the correct time and situation to leave early, it can work several times a game, and give your team a few more scoring opportunities that you would not have had otherwise.

If you can score several goals a game with this strategy, it will be worth it. In addition, it will make the other team more hesitant on offense, for fear of the defender taking off down the pool every time.

WHO DO YOU LEAVE?

Part of the strategy of leaving early has to do with leaving a player who is not a direct threat to score. This can be accomplished if the player that the defender is guarding is holding the ball: or even a player without the ball, as long as he is not a position to score. An example of this would be a wing player, or someone far enough away from the goal that he is not a threat to score, or receive the ball and score. Timing is critical in this situation.

The defender has to be aware of the shot clock and how much time is left. There cannot be enough time remaining on the clock that will allow the player that is left alone to become a threat to score. Players have to try this in practice every day, so that they start getting a feel for when to leave, and who to leave.

Examples of who and when to leave from:

1. Foul the wing-player with a bad angle on the goal, with less than five seconds on the clock, and then immediately take off down the pool. Fouling takes away his opportunity to shoot the ball, because he is inside the five. He cannot chase you until he does something with the ball. The wing player either has to pass the ball or dump it in the corner.

2. With less than 5 seconds on the clock, take off on a wing player with the ball, without fouling him, so that the clock doesn't stop. The wing has a very bad angle shot and doesn't have enough time to move in for a better shot. Taking off on a right-hander playing on the left-handers wing position 05 is even better; because his chances of scoring from that wing are less then they are from the 01 wing.

3. At the end of the shot clock, foul the player with the ball at 8-10-yards away from the goal, and then take off down the pool. He has to take a long distance shot, or pass the ball to someone else. Once he gets the ball back, he will not have time to move in and take a closer shot. If you want to avoid stopping the clock, then take off without fouling.

4. At the end of the shot clock, take off on an offensive player who does not have the ball, and is far from the goal or on the wing, and not involved in the offense. Even if he receives the ball, he will not have time to move closer for a shot, or improve his angle on the wing. (See diagram 5-1 on the next page)

5. Defenders should always position themselves in front of the wings and counterattack the wing player late in the shot clock; when another player takes a shot, or every time the ball turns over. (See diagram 5-1 on the next page)

6. A defender can try and take off on a player with the ball who is inside the five-meter line; but this is a risky move unless there is very little time left on the clock, and your team is desperate for a goal. It is better to foul the player inside the 5-meter line so he cannot shoot, and then take off on him.

If the timing is right, he will not have enough time to pass the ball, and then get it back again for a shot near the front of the goal. Do not try this unless it is at the end of the game, and the team is desperate for a goal. All you can hope for in this situation is that the offense takes a risky shot, and your team gets a free man in the other direction.

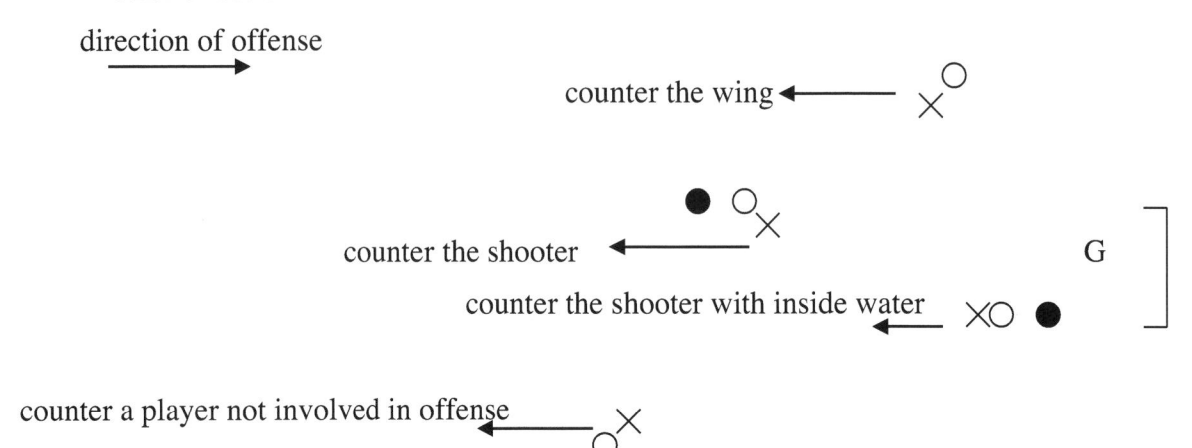

direction of offense →

counter the wing ← ×O

counter the shooter ← ●O×   G

counter the shooter with inside water ← ×O●

counter a player not involved in offense ← O×

Diagram 5-1: Counterattack and "leaving early' situations.

7. An outside gap defender in a gap defense like the m-zone, who is not attacking the ball, can leave early with little time left on the clock. (See diagram 5-2 below)

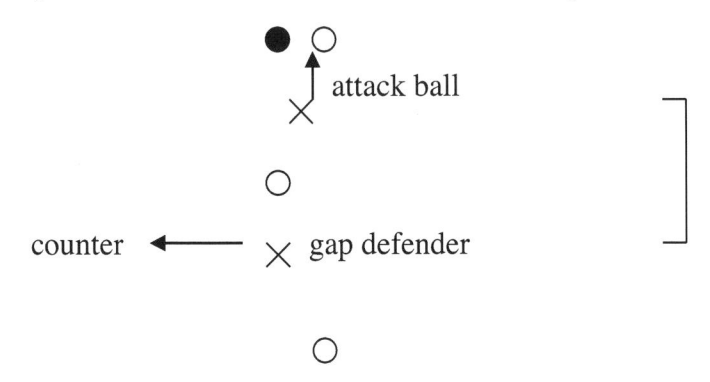

●O
× attack ball
O
counter ← × gap defender
O

Diagram 5-2: Gap counterattack from defender not attacking ball, with less than 5-7 seconds on shot clock.

"LEAVING EARLY" OFFENSE

One of the top high-school teams in Northern California, Sacred Heart Prep coached by Brian Kruetzkamp, has used the "leaving early" offense for the past two years with a lot of success. Just as the opposing team is starting to set up their front court offense (15 seconds or less left on the shot clock), a perimeter player on the defensive team simply takes off down the pool by himself, forcing the team on offense to make a decision on whether they should send someone to cover him. Note: It is easiest to try this maneuver from an "M" zone defensive alignment because it eliminates the possibility of the ball going into the 2-meter position.

If the offense tries to take a shot while they have a six-against-five man-advantage, and they miss the shot, the other team will have a free man all by himself at the other end of the pool. Sending an offensive player down to the other end to cover the player who "leaves early" can take anywhere from 7-8 more seconds off the clock. During that time, the offense has to wait to take the shot until the free player is covered. Once he is covered, the offense is left in a 5 on 5-situation, but with only 5-7 seconds left on the shot clock.

This is a very precarious position for the opposing team to be in, as it is very difficult for the offense to get off any kind of meaningful shot in this situation. They usually end up either forcing a bad shot, or dumping the ball in the corner; which is exactly what the "leaving early" offense is designed to do. It can easily be classified as a defense, as well as an offense; because it can effectively limit the opposing team's offense; as well as give the offense an early presence at the other end of the pool. Note: This is an excellent strategy for the end of the game when your team is losing and needs a quick goal.

CHERRY PICK OFFENSE

The cherry pick offense is similar to the "leaving early" offense; but instead of sending a player to the offensive end early, the last man down the pool (usually the 2-meter player), purposely hangs back, and does not come all the way down on defense. Even with one more player on offense, it is often very difficult for a team to score a goal. Any turnover or missed shot by the offense, results in an easy one on nobody at the other end of the pool by the cherry picker. This is also a good tactic to use at the end of a game when a team is losing by a few goals, and needs an easy score to tie or get closer to their opponent.

COUNTER THE SHOOTER

Always counter the player who shoots the ball, because he will have to turn around and chase you after he takes the shot. Always take off on any player who takes a bad angle shot from the wing, a player who forces an 8-10-yard desperation shot at the end of the 30-second shot clock, or a player who takes the shot from an inside water position and facing the goal.

The proper technique in this situation is to take off as the shot is being taken. The defender should take off on the shooter any time the shooter takes a low percentage shot (as described above), even if there is a lot of time left on the clock. The goalie should be able to make an easy block on these kinds of shots, and defender who takes off will be swimming free at the other end. (See Diagram 5-1 above)

SHOT CLOCK MANAGEMENT AND TACTICS ON OFFENSE

END OF THE SHOT CLOCK

A team on offense has to know what to do in the situation where there is a short time left on the shot clock. The offense must keep the ball in a scoring position, preferably in front of the goal. The ball should never be passed to a wing with less than 6-8 seconds left on the clock. The wing player can easily be countered; because he has a bad-angle shot on the goal that can easily be blocked by the goalie, and he doesn't have time to move in to improve his angle. The wing player can also easily by fouled and countered in this situation; stuck with the ball on the wing, and with no opportunity to shoot.

Teammates must always "cover up" for the player who is stuck with the ball. If the player with the ball is in good position to shoot, he should shoot high and hard; so that he might get a new 30-second shot clock if the goalie blocks it out of bounds. If he can't take a good high percentage shot, then he should dump the ball in the corner of the pool. He should never shoot a lob shot in this situation, unless the goalie is way out of the goal. The shooter is not necessarily trying to score in this situation; so he doesn't need to force a bad angle shot; or take a shot from way outside that will put him in jeopardy of getting countered.

A good shooter knows when to shoot, and more importantly, when not to shoot. He should never take the kind of low percentage shot that will allow a team to counterattack, unless his team is in a desperate need of a goal at the end of the game. The best possible shot to take as the clock is running out, is to try and draw a foul outside the 5-meter line, and then take the free shot after foul. Since everyone on the offense knows that a shot is coming, they can all cover back on defense as the shot is being taken.

Another good tactic at the end of the shot clock is to pass the ball into the 2-meter player. This is even more effective at the end of the shot clock, because several defenders may have already left early for the other end of the pool. Consequently, there won't be as many defenders to help back and double team the 2-meter player. He can usually get off a good shot in this situation; or draw an exclusion foul on the 2-meter defender.

COVER BACK AND HELP

Knowing when to start peeling back on defense when your team is on offense, is one of the most difficult situations to learn as a player. If your team is about to shoot the ball, or you are getting to the end of the shot clock, and you are not directly involved in the offense, than you should start releasing back to defense before the ball is turned over. Try to anticipate when your team is about to loose the ball and start thinking about helping back on defense. Usually the person shooting the ball is not in good position to come back on defense, and will need help from teammates.

Offensive players have some control over situations when they know a teammate is going to shoot the ball; so at least they can be in a position to help the shooter. Situations that you cannot control, such as offensive fouls, or bad passes that are intercepted by an opponent, can make it more difficult to help out a teammate because they are unexpected.

DUMPING THE BALL

As the shot clock winds down, and the player with the ball doesn't have a good shot opportunity, he has to "dump" the ball. He wants to place the ball in a position that will make the defender who has left him recover the ball; or put it somewhere in the corner of the pool, so that the goalie has a long way to swim to get to the ball.

A good strategy for a player with the ball, whose defender has left him, is to dump the ball along the side of the pool; so that the defender has to stop and retrieve the ball, thus losing the advantage he has gained by leaving early. If the player on the counterattack has to detour to the side of the pool, the player who dumped the ball will be able to chase and catch up to him. (See Diagram 5-3 on the next page).

direction of offense
→

dump ball into corner

offensive player without ball cover back
←—O✕

G

✕ dump ball to side of pool

counterattack detour

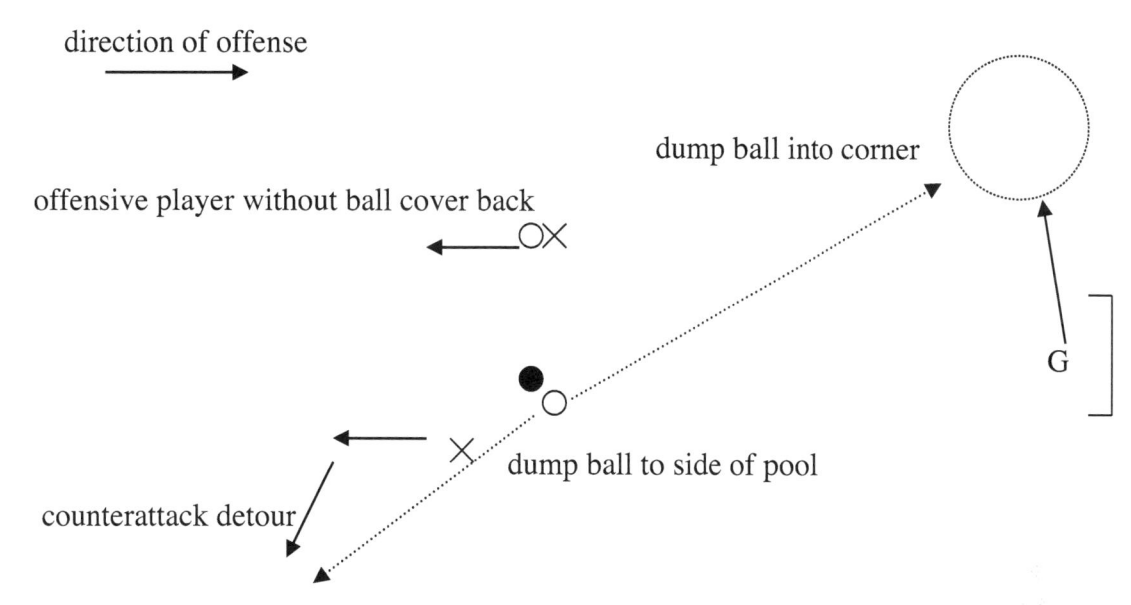

Diagram 5-3: End of shot-clock-dump the ball in the corner or to the side of the pool.

When it is obvious that the man with the ball has to shoot or dump the ball, his teammates who are not involved have to start "peeling" back; or releasing back to cover up on defense. In a situation where a player must shoot the ball at the end of the shot clock, every player but the center forward and the shooter should be swimming back on defense. As the opposing goalie recovers the dumped ball in the corner of the pool, the players covering back should have enough time to catch anyone who has released and gotten free.

The more defenders covering back, the harder it is to score for the counterattacking team. By covering back early, the team can force the counterattacking team into a higher risk 6 against 5, or 5 against 4 counterattack, rather than a low-risk one-on-nobody, 2 on 1, or 3 on 2 counterattack.

OFFENSIVE TACTICS TO PREVENT THE COUNTERATTACK

Once a good counterattack team gets a free man on the counterattack, there is not a lot that the defense can do to stop it. The best way to stop the counterattack, while your team is on offense, is to keep it from happening in the first place. To stop the counter before it happens, the team with the ball must become very conservative on offense as the shot clock winds down; and not put themselves in situations that feeds the other team's counterattack.

They must control the ball, without turning it over by a bad pass or offensive foul; and they must take only high percentage shots on the goal. Turnovers give the other team an excellent counterattack opportunity. Even a poorly taken, or low percentage shot, can be considered a turnover. I would rather have my team dump the ball than force a bad angle or weak outside shot that the other team can counter on.

A critical situation that requires offensive players to cover back is when the offense is on the counterattack, and has a free man (man advantage). Players have to be very alert for the possibility of a turnover while on the counterattack. It is during the counterattack that a team must protect and control the ball the most; because that is when they are the most susceptible to getting countered in the other direction. The counterattacking team cannot afford to throw the ball away on a bad pass, or take a low percentage shot that doesn't have a good chance of scoring.

Unless there is a good chance to score on the counter, then the team should just control the ball and set up their frontcourt offense. Any offensive player who is not in position in front of the goal to receive the ball, or is not the free man, has to be thinking about helping back to cover up, in case the offense loses the ball. This is a good time for players on the counterattack to be "thinking defense" when they are still on offense.

END OF GAME SITUATIONS- PLAYING FROM BEHIND

IF YOUR TEAM IS LOSING, PRESS AND STEAL

If a team is losing by several goals late in the game, they need to do everything that they can to get the ball back in their possession. They should play a pressure defense and steal and/ or foul the ball at every opportunity to stop the clock. I would rather have the players try to steal the ball in these situations, rather than foul every time. They have to take a chance and go for the steal. If the player doesn't get the steal, then he should commit the foul to stop the clock.

Players have to be careful and not commit an over-aggressive foul that results in an exclusion from the game. It is imperative during the "press and steal" defense that the ball be kept out of 2-meters. Because the defense will be spread around the pool, it will be difficult to help back (crash) on 2-meters. Playing in front of the 2-meter player, and both wings, should be part of the "press and steal" defense.

2-MINUTE DEFENSE

The "2-minute defense"(press and steal defense) has to be practiced ahead of time; so that the players know what to do in the situation where they find themselves losing by a goal or two late in the game. The coach should only have to command "press and steal", or "2-minute defense", and the players should know what to do without the coach having to call a time-out.

The question is when does a team start the press and steal defense? It depends on the score and how far behind the team is. The further behind they are, then the earlier they must start the press and steal defense. As the game nears the end, the team that is behind has to take more and more chances in order to get the ball back.

Depending on the how far behind your team is, the "2-minute press and steal" can be anywhere from 2-minutes from the end of the game, to even longer than that. My team once started the "press and steal" in the middle of the third quarter of an NCAA Championship final game, when we found ourselves trailing by six goals. By using this defense, we were able to come back and tie the game late in the 4th quarter; and almost won the game with a few seconds left in regulation.

YOU NEED A GOAL- DRAW AN EXCLUSION

It is a close one goal or tie game, and your team needs a goal. Under present day rules, it is probably best to get the ball into 2-meters and try to draw an exclusion foul, instead of running a play. The odds of drawing an exclusion and scoring a goal are a lot higher than scoring a goal from a set play.

In order to get the ball into 2-meters, the center has to get front position on the defender. With little time left on the clock, the offense cannot afford to have the 2-meter player fronted, and then have him take a lot of time fighting his way into front position. Your team can assure front position at 2-meters by running a screen to help your 2-meter player gain front position. After a time out, start your 2-meter player (06) at the 01 wing position, and then have 02 drive forward to block defender X6. The resulting "loop around" screen will help get O6 front position on defender X2, who switches on to him (See Diagram 5-4 below).

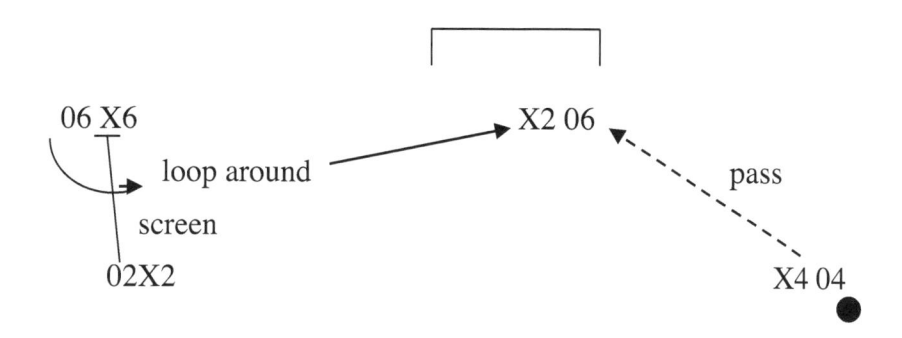

Diagram 5-4: Loop screen to get ball side position.

POSTING UP TO GET A GOAL OR EXCLUSION

This same technique can be used to "post-up" a second player on a second post position, while moving the hole-man over to the other post for a "double post" offensive set up. Start with your best driver at the 01 wing position and have 02 run a screen as described above. When he gets ball-side position on the post, the ball should immediately be passed to him.

Because the second post is considered as having the same status as a second 2-meter player, the chances of drawing an exclusion or scoring from this position are very high. It is certainly higher than attempting a lower percentage outside shot. If the defense does not commit an exclusion foul, then the post player has to attempt to take the shot. The odds are in favor of the offense in this situation. It is either going to be an exclusion, or a shot from right in front of the goalpost by the post player.

YOU NEED A GOAL- DRAW THE 5-METER DIRECT SHOT FOUL

If you don't have a lot of time to run a play or post up a player, simply put your best shooter at the 03 point position, just outside 5-meters. If he cannot get a shot off, he can draw a foul and take the direct shot on goal that he is entitled to under the rules. This may be the best shot that a team will get with little time left on the clock. From a position on the five, the defender either has to let him shoot or foul him. Either way, the chances of scoring are a lot higher than just taking a shot from outside.

PULLING YOUR GOALIE

Recent rule changes allow a team with a lead in a game, and in their last possession of the ball (less than 30 seconds left), to simply give their goalkeeper the ball, and let him hold it for the full time of the possession. The team without the ball, and losing by a goal, needs to gain possession of the ball in order to attempt to tie the game. The only recourse by the losing team in this situation is to attack the goalie that is sitting on the ball. Attacking the goalie will inevitably leave a field player open somewhere in the pool.

The losing team must cover all players in the pool (ladder down the pool), leaving the last player closest to the losing team's goal without a defender. This player has to be covered by pulling the goalkeeper out of the goal to guard him; thus leaving the goal open. The team that is behind is hoping for a mistake by the team that has the lead; either an errant pass and interception, or a shot on the open goal that misses it's mark. This strategy is a last recourse, and only a mistake by the other team will result in getting the ball back in the last 30 seconds of the game (See Diagram 5-5 below).

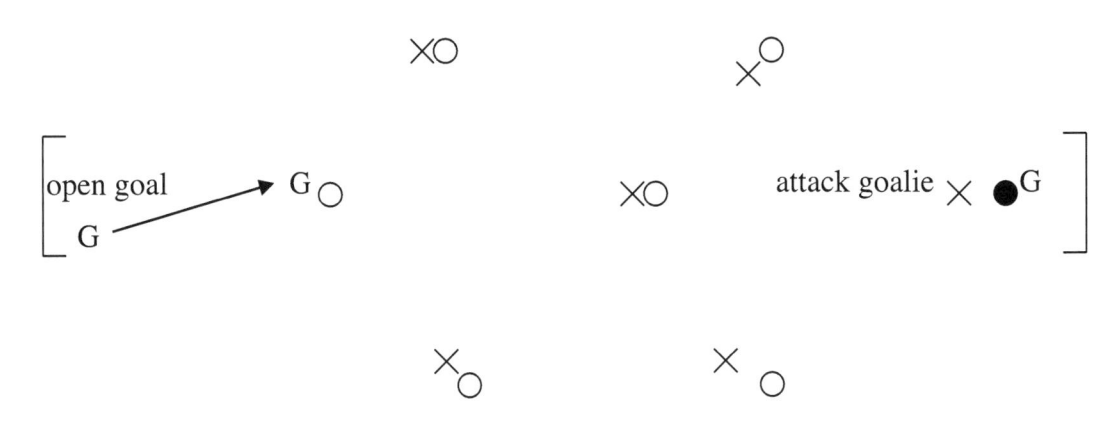

Diagram 5-5: Attack goalie at one end, ladder down the pool and cover everyone but the last player. Then pull your goalkeeper to cover him.

END OF GAME STUATION-YOUR TEAM HAS THE LEAD

TWO-MINUTE OFFENSE

When your team has a slight lead late in the game, they must do everything they can to protect that lead and keep the other team from scoring. Players need to rehearse this situation in practice, so that they know what to do keep their lead and win the game. The way that the team plays when they are protecting their lead is called a two-minute offensive drill; and includes all of the things that a team must do in this situation. The necessary tactics of the two-minute offense are as described below:

BALL CONTROL

Ball control is critical to the success of protecting the lead in the two-minute offensive drill. Ball control means using as much of the clock as you can, protecting the ball with good, safe passes and movement, taking high percentage shots, dumping the ball in the corner if you don't have a good shot, keeping the ball away from a position that will allow a counterattack from the other team (like a deep wing), and not creating turnovers that will help feed the other teams counterattack.

MOVEMENT- MOVE THE BALL AND HELP THE BALL

With little time left in the game, and a team with the lead in possession of the ball, the other team is in a desperate situation; and will try to do anything they can to get the ball back. They will become very aggressive and will be trying to steal the ball, or foul to stop the clock and force a pass. Many times, the referee in this situation will subconsciously help the team that is behind by letting them foul aggressively, or by allowing them to steal the ball. The team with the lead can prevent this from happening with movement.

Sitting in one position and waiting for the ball to come to you is a sure way to get the ball stolen. This is called "sitting on the lead". The player who is to receive the ball must "help the ball" by moving towards the ball. This keeps the defender from jumping in front of the stationary player for the steal. At the same time, the player with the ball should not force the pass to a player who is not open, is not moving towards him, or is not ready to receive the ball. He also must not sit with the ball, but must keep moving as much as possible.

Options for the passer, instead of forcing a bad pass, include keeping the ball and swimming with it, or simply throwing the ball back to the goalie that is not being guarded. At the end of the shot clock, the ball has to be passed all the way to the other end of the pool; forcing the team who is behind to bring the ball the full length of the pool in order to start their offense.

LEADING WITH LAST POSSESSION- STALL

The best way to protect a one or two-goal lead, with your team in possession of the ball, and with less than 30 seconds in the game, is to stall. This is done by spreading out around the pool, with your goalie in possession of the ball. The following principles must be followed when stalling: 1) two players must not be so close to each other that they can get "double teamed", 2) avoid corners of the pool where a player can get trapped, and 3) stay away from the opposing teams goal in order to avoid being guarded by the team who pulls their goalie.

If the goalie with the ball is attacked, he must pass the ball to a field player who is usually better prepared to protect the ball. Once a field player receives the ball, he must protect it at all costs. It is better for a player to keep the ball, rather than risk passing to a teammate.

After the player with the ball is fouled to stop the clock, he must put the ball into the water and swim away from the defender; then continue swimming until he is fouled again. Repeat this maneuver over and over again until time runs out. It is better to swim towards your own offensive end of the pool in case the ball is stolen. This forces the opposing team to take the ball the length of the pool in order to score. (See Diagram 5-6 on the next page)

Remember that your team is leading and does not need to score a goal. Avoid taking a shot on the goal, even if the opposing team leaves the goal open by pulling their goalie. A hurried shot on an open goal can easily be missed, giving the opposing team possession of the ball. Rather than shooting the ball, the best way to insure a goal against an open goal is to swim the ball into the goal or just simply to run the clock out.

                                                                    If fouled, swim the ball

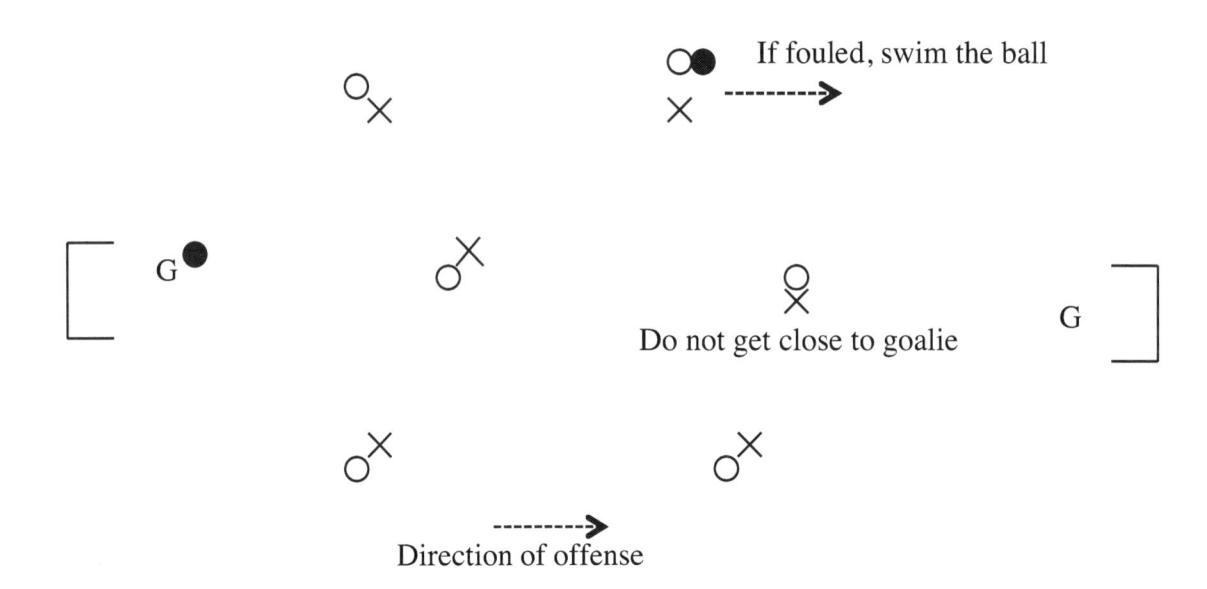

Diagram 5-6: One goal lead, in possession of the ball, and with less than 30 seconds left in the game. Stay spread out as shown. Goalie keeps ball until attacked, then makes safe pass. If player with the ball is fouled, it is better to swim the clock out rather than attempt another pass.

CHERRY PICKING

Whenever the losing team sends players down to the other end of the pool when your team is on offense, you must send players back to cover them. A team that is behind by a goal, with little time left, will have a player stay in the back-court, while the other team goes down on offense; or they will have a defensive player "leak out" early towards the other end of the pool. This is called "cherry picking" (Described above).

Everyone on the team has to be aware of this situation (especially if your opponent is losing late in the game), and keep someone back with the cherry picker. If nobody notices the "cherry picker", your goalie certainly should see this; and should call someone back immediately to cover up.

Always cover up the cherry picker before any shot attempt is made. Remember, you don't need a goal or a extra man! This situation has to be communicated to the person with the ball, so that he doesn't take a shot until the cherry picker is covered. If the opposing team sends more than one player to the other end, then they all must be covered.

PROTECTING THE LEAD- DON'T GIVE UP THE EASY COUNTER

When your team has the lead at the end of the game, you also have to be careful that you don't put yourself in position that will give the other team an easy counterattack. You should keep the ball on the outside positions of your frontcourt offense; and keep it away from the wings. This keeps your opponent from countering your wingman; who is usually not a threat to score from his weak position in the pool.

The objective in this situation is to control the ball for the full 30 second period, without giving it up too early on a turnover or shot. Movement and helping the ball is the key to not giving up the ball. If the team that is leading does attempt a shot, it should be at the end of the shot clock, and it should not be the kind of shot that creates a counterattack for the other team. An early shot taken before the expiration of the shot clock should only be taken if it has a "100 percent chance" of scoring.

Since the other team is probably trying to get the ball back by pressing, they may leave the 2-meter player uncovered from the outside. However, your team should keep the ball on the outside, and avoid the temptation to pass the ball into 2-meters (the ball is too easy to lose there) until the shot clock has less then 5-6 seconds left. The defense than has two choices as the ball is passed into two-meters. They might have to foul the 2-meter player, taking the exclusion to keep him from scoring from that position. The result will be a man-up situation and a new 30-second shot clock. The other choice for the defense is not to foul, and hope that the 2-meter player does not score, and the defense will get the ball back.

If the ball cannot be passed into 2-meters in the last 5-6 seconds of the possession, then a player with the ball outside 5-meters should try to draw a foul for a shot on goal. Whether the ball goes into 2-meters, or an outside shot is attempted, all other offensive players not involved in the shot must release back towards the other end of the pool in order to prevent the easy counterattack. If a good shot cannot be attempted, then the ball should be "dumped". (See above tactics).

While trying to control the ball, it is also important that offensive players avoid an offensive foul, by not being overly aggressive in trying to gain offensive position. Drives toward the goal are not recommended for fear of the offensive foul, or because of over-committing on offense. Both of these situations can lead to a counterattack by the defensive team.

SITTING ON THE LEAD

In a situation where your team has a several goal lead and still a few minutes left in the game, you have to be careful and not sit on your lead; or you will let the other team back into the game. It is human nature to let up when you have a lead, and the game is almost over. This can be disastrous to your team! You have to keep playing with the same intensity that got you the lead in the first place, and you must keep trying to score; although you do not need to force a bad shot, or be over-aggressive and commit an offensive foul.

A shot on goal is good, but not at the expense of giving the other team a goal at the other end. A bad-angle wing shot, for instance, is not recommended because it gives the other team an opportunity to counterattack. All of the tactics, as described above, still apply in this situation. In summary, try to score if you are able to take a high percentage shot; but be sure to protect the ball, keep moving to avoid the steal, do not give any easy counterattack opportunity, and cover up on defense. A team that sits, and tries to passively protect their lead, will usually lose their lead.

KNOWING WHEN "NOT" TO SHOOT

Knowing when NOT to shoot, is many times just as important as knowing when to shoot. Basically, if your team doesn't need a goal, and/or your shot will give your opponent a chance to score at the other end of the pool to tie the game or get the lead; don't take the shot. An obvious situation occurs when your team has a one-goal lead, in possession of the ball, and less than 30 seconds in the game, and a new shot clock. All you have to do is run out the clock.

Other situations are not so obvious; but if you think about them, there is a certain amount of logic involved. It all boils down to a situation where your team has a lead at the end of the game. You have to make sure that the shot that you take doesn't put your team in jeopardy of losing the lead, or the game. If it does, then don't take the shot. It would be good to gain an extra "insurance" goal at the end of the game; but only if the attempt doesn't cost your team the lead.

END OF QUARTER SITUATION

End of the quarter situations depend on how much time there is left on the shot clock. You often hear coaches directing their team to "get out of the quarter." This means that with about 30 seconds left on both the shot clock and the game clock, and your team in control of the ball, you want to protect the ball, get off the last shot of the quarter, and not give the other team an opportunity to counterattack and score.

If you don't get a good shot opportunity before that, and with 1-2 seconds left in the quarter, you can probably take a bad shot or lob and hope that it goes in; or try to draw a foul outside five-meters and get a shot off; as long as the other team doesn't have enough time to swim down to the other end and get off a last second. The safest thing to do is to simply sit on the ball, until the clock runs out, and then take a last second shot.

SUMMARY: ONE-MINUTE DRILL- OFFENSE

How a team handles the end of game situation depends a lot on whether you have a lead or not, how big or small your lead is, and how much time is left on the clock. If your team has a one goal lead, and you are on offense with less than a minute left in the game, then you should try and take as much time off the clock as possible, giving the other team as little time as possible to run their offense at the other end.

This is the time to run the "one minute drill" that has been practiced by the team. The one-minute drill consists of all of the aspects of controlling the ball and controlling the clock as described in "Protecting the lead" above. Once you have run the clock down with the one-minute drill, try to get off a good shot at the end of the 30-second shot clock; or dump the ball in the corner and cover up on defense.

There is no need to force a bad shot that will give your opponent a counterattack opportunity. If you get a shot opportunity that has a very good chance of scoring a goal, then take the shot and cover back on defense if it doesn't go in. The rest of your teammates should also be covering back on defense when it is obvious that you are going to shoot.

The least amount of risk is to stall by giving the ball to your goalie. Then he should make sure that he runs the full 30 seconds off the clock, and then throw the ball to the other end of the pool; leaving little time or opportunity for the other team to come down the pool and score.

ONE-MINUTE DRILL- DEFENSE
How you handle the last minute, when you are losing, depends on the number of goals you are losing by. Assuming the other team has the ball, and you are behind by two goals, then you have to get the ball back immediately by performing the "press and steal" drill, as described above. If you are losing by only one goal, then it is not so critical that you get the ball back immediately.

With a minute left in the game, simply let the other team use-up the 30-second time on the clock, without letting them score or draw an exclusion foul. They probably will be reluctant to take a shot; but they may attempt to draw a kick-out. The best way to avoid this is to press and keep the ball out of 2-meters by fronting.

Once the opposing team gives up the ball, your team will still have some time left to try and score. Hopefully your team has a time-out left in order to set up a special play (that has been practiced) for scoring a quick goal, draw an exclusion foul, or draw an outside 5-meter shot after foul. When the ball turns over, it is best to first try and score on the counterattack; and then call a time-out if the team doesn't get a free man.

Another tactic that the losing team can try in the last minute is to play an "M" zone defense. Not only will the "M" keep the ball out of 2-meters, but it also puts the outside "gap" defenders in a great position to counterattack, and perhaps score the tying goal. Because your opponent has the lead, they will be reluctant to force a pass into the 2-meter player when he is fronted; and they will also be reluctant to take the outside shot because of the threat of the "gap" counterattack. Leaving early from the "M" defense is another option that is discussed above.

SHOT CLOCK DRILL
An excellent drill to create an "end of the shot clock" situation for both the offense and defense is to set up a half-court 6 on 6 situation. Set the shot clock at anywhere from 5 to 25-seconds and then give the ball to the offense. The coach can create different situations by giving the ball to players at different positions in the pool; and also create different end of quarter/game scenarios by setting different scores for each team, setting different defenses, and setting different times on the shot clock. When the ball turns over, or the shot clock runs out, allow both teams to counterattack to a conclusion at the other end of the pool. Then repeat the drill again at the other end of the pool.

This is a great drill for teaching both the offense and the defense about what to do at the end of the 30-second shot clock. It also is a good way to teach the team on offense how to cover back on defense when their team is about to lose the ball; and a good way to teach the defensive team when and how to leave early on the counterattack.

OTHER GAME TACTICS

WINNING WITH LESS TALENT

There are certain things that a team can do to win, even if that team has less talent than the other team. The less talented team, with good coaching, can be taught the necessary parts of the game that will help them to overcome the more talented team. First it is necessary for the team to play good pressure defense. It doesn't take great talent to play defense, just good discipline that puts pressure on the offense everywhere in the pool.

A coach can also teach a team to react and counterattack every time the ball turns-over. Again, it doesn't take great talent to anticipate and react to turnovers. It doesn't even take great speed. With good positioning and reaction, a player can gain the advantage over his opponent. Once he has gained the advantage, all he has to do is maintain it to the other end of the pool. Players can be taught to swim fast for the relative short distances of 15-20 yards. At the very least, they can be taught to maintain their advantage by staying in front, and not allowing the player they have just beaten to get around them.

Most importantly, the players have to be taught to reduce turnovers by playing ball-control on offense. Ball control is taking only high percentage shots, using as much of the clock as possible, making safe passes, and not turning the ball over; and then covering up on defense once the team takes a shot or loses the ball. If a coach can teach his players to play this kind of disciplined game, play good pressure defense and counterattack, then they have a chance to beat any team that they play.

HOW TO PLAY A TEAM THAT IS FASTER THAN YOURS

The best way to play a fast team is to not give them opportunities to counterattack. Besides controlling the ball on offense, and not creating turnovers that lead to a counterattack, a slower team has to have players come back early to the defensive end of the pool. Individually, if the person that is guarding you is faster, then you have to anticipate the ball changing hands and react before he does in order to get a head start on him.

If he gets the jump on you, even if you start even up with him, then you will not be able to catch him because of his speed. Once you get ahead of a faster player, you have to maneuver and keep your body in front of his so he can't use his speed to get around you. If all of your teammates use the methods as described above, then your team has a better chance of stopping a fast team's counterattack.

Another way to prevent a lot of counterattacks by a faster team is to play only a four-man offense, while keeping two players back at half court. This should take away the easier one-on-on-nobody, 2 on 1, and 3 on 2 counterattacks; and force the fast team to try and score with the more difficult 4 on3, 5 on 4 and 6 on 5 counterattacks.

HOW TO BREAK A HARD PRESS AND PASSING LANE DEFENSE

The best way to break a hard press is with movement, especially from the player who is to receive the ball. The player who has the ball and is being pressed, must first try to draw a foul and gain a free pass. When the whistle blows, the player who is to receive the pass must then make a release move to get away from the pressing/fronting guard.

As the team is moving the ball down the pool, the pass receiver simply swims towards the ball to get away from his defender. Sitting in one spot will usually result in a steal by the defense. In the frontcourt, releasing may require waiting for the whistle that indicates a free pass for your teammate; and then moving towards the man with the ball (helping the ball).

Two players working together can also run a pick or screen in order to release one of them to get free to receive the ball. Screens are not only effective during the counterattack, but also against a press in the frontcourt. A team that sits against a hard press and passing lane defense, will usually get the ball stolen from them; and then get beaten on the subsequent counterattack. Players must be taught how to release for the ball with movement or by running screens.

The drills shown in Diagram 5-7 below are basic release drills in the frontcourt. Start the ball on one side of the pool and have the center forward set to the opposite side. With the defense in a hard press, the offense has to move the ball around to the other side by using movement releases or screen pick. In this diagram, O2 releases "ball side" for the pass from O1. Also shown is O4 running a screen to help 05 to release for a pass from 03.

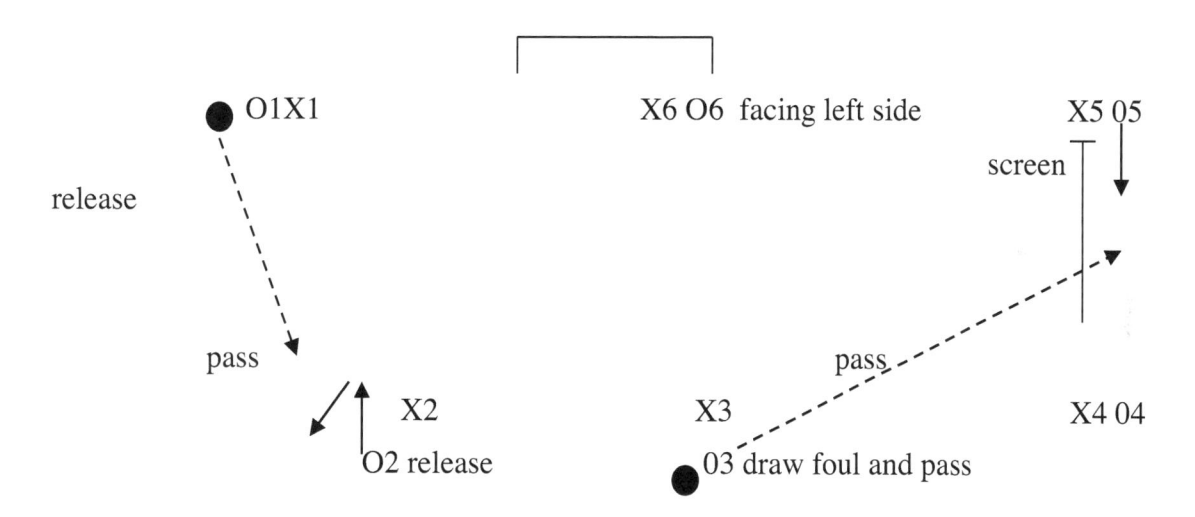

Diagram 5-7: Release moves to move ball around perimeter against a press.

BEATING THE PRESS WHILE MOVING THE BALL DOWN THE POOL
In order to beat a pressing defense when your team is trying to move the ball down the pool, it first requires that all six players counter past half court before the ball is passed from the goalie. All six players must remain a threat, so that it doesn't allow the defense to easily play front positions that takes away the pass from the goalie.

The first priority is to try to get the ball deep on the first pass, before the defense has time to press hard. Most defenses will not pay a lot of attention to a deep wing release because he is not a big threat. A couple of strokes toward the goalie should make the deep pass to the wing an easy pass to complete. If the wing is being fronted, than another player can run an "interchange" screen that will block the defender, and free the wing for receiving the pass from the goalie (See Diagram 5-8 below).

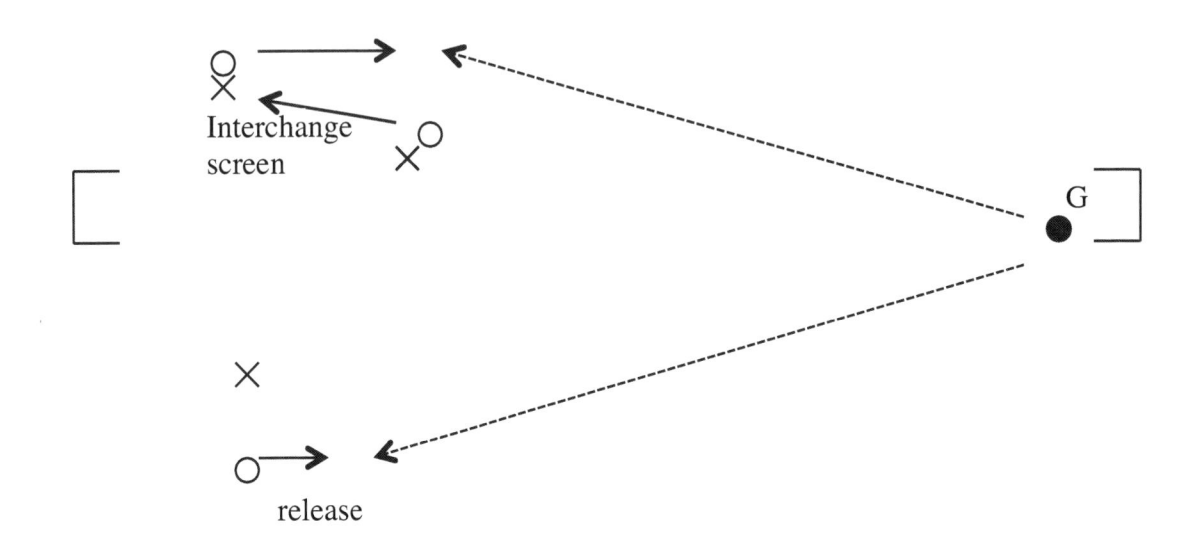

Diagram 5-8: Beating the press by passing the ball to a deep wing. Against a tight press, do an "interchange screen" to free the wing. Against a "soft" press on the other wing, simply release towards the ball by taking a stroke or two.

If the deep pass is not open, than the last three players down the pool can turn around and release towards the goalie to receive a pass. They can also run a screen to get one of them free. This should only be done if the players are past half court when they release back. Releasing before they reach half court not only makes it easier for the defense to press, but usually results in the first pass being made to the goalies side of half court. Once again, the more passes the attacking players have to make, the easier it is for the defense to press and front and steal the ball (See Diagram 5-9 on the next page).

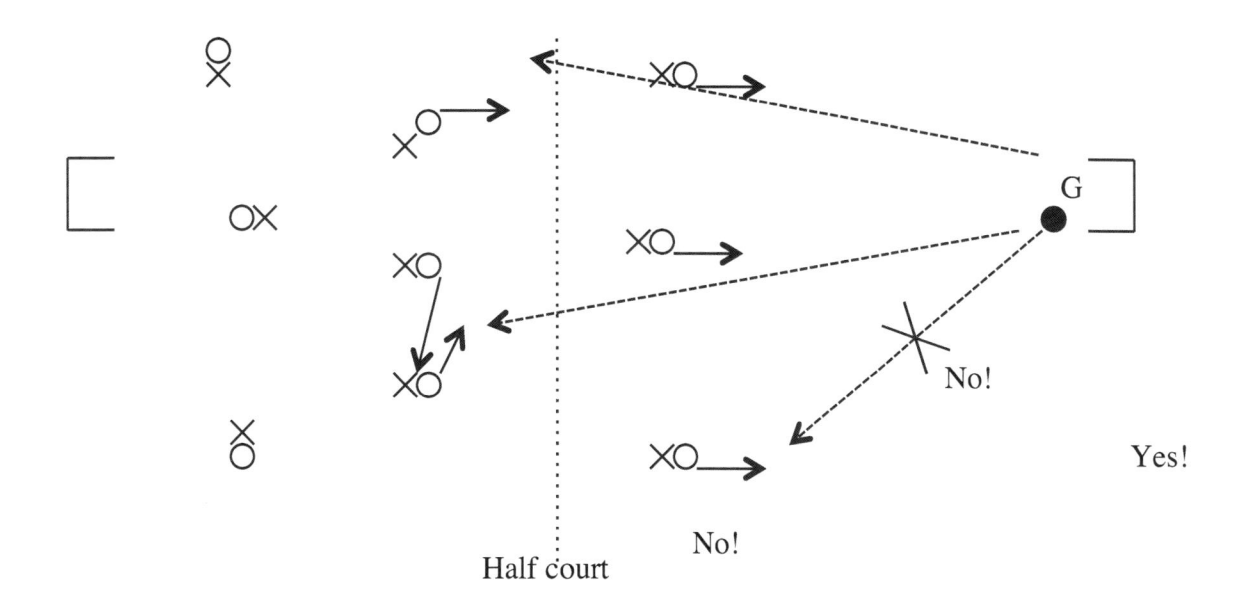

Diagram 5-9: If deep wings are not open for goalie pass, then (Yes!) the last three players can run a screen or release back for the pass. (No!) Last three players should not release on the goalies side of half court.

HOW TO BREAK A 2-METER FRONT

There are several ways to beat a team that plays in front of the 2-meter player. First, the 2-meter player who is being fronted can move out to the 4 or 5-yard line; and then turn and face the goal, leaving a space between him and the goalie. As he does so, the ball must go to a wing player; who in turn passes the ball inside to the 2-meter player.

Never try to pass the ball inside to a fronted hole-man from an outside position. That is a difficult pass to make, and by the time the hole-man and defender untangle, the goalie will intercept the ball. If the team on defense is fronting the wingman, if they foul and drop from the wingman, or if they bring the goalie out, this plan will not work.

The 2-meter player might be able to fight his way back into a side or front position by performing an outside spin move. The hole-forward should at the very least, turn to a side position, and have the team get the ball around to that side for the entry pass.

If the ball cannot be passed in from the wing, or the 2-meter player cannot gain front position, then only thing a team can do then is to bring in a new hole-man; or move the hole man to one post and bring in another hole man on the other post, for a double post offense. Both of these moves will work using a "loop pick" as shown in Diagram 5-4 above.

Other options for bringing in a "new" hole-man include an offense similar to what the Spanish National Team ran during the '84 Olympic, and what my team ran one year when we did not have a dominating 2-meter player. It requires the ball at 04 or 03 positions, and the player at the 2-meter position to swim out to the left-handed wing position. Then a player from either the 01 or 02 offensive positions drive "ball-side" into 2-meters, where they receive the pass from 04. (See Diagram 5-10 below)

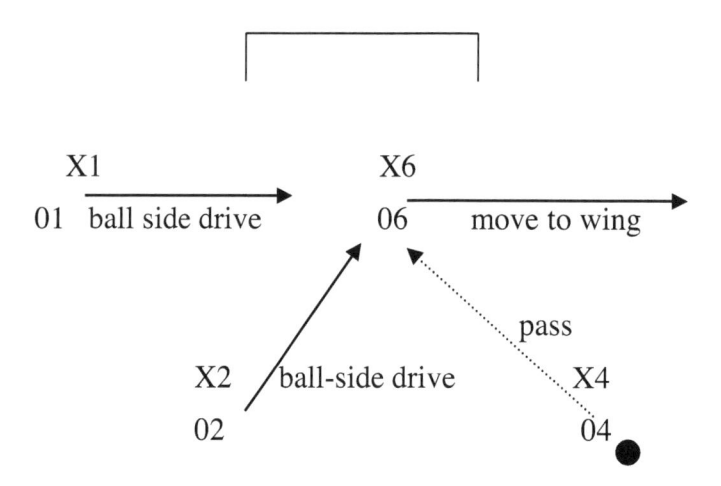

Diagram 5-10: Bringing in a new 2-meter player. Move 06 to a wing and then do a ball side drive from 01 or 02 to bring in another player; or have 02 sets a screen for 01 for a ball side drive. (See Diagram 5-4 above for a 2-1 screen).

Another option that will bring in a new 2-meter player against a press/front defense is a rotating center-forward type of offense, similar to the "wheel" offense shown in Diagram 5-11 below. This offense is a constant motion (rotation) by three players on one side of the offense, on the side opposite the ball. This rotation is initiated by the 2-meter player who first swims towards the wing.

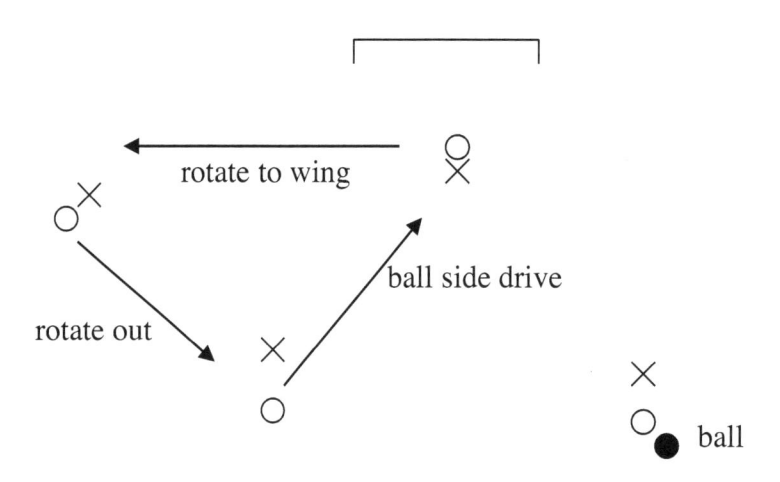

Diagram 5-11: Wheel offense

HOW TO BEAT A ZONE

One way to beat a zone is to clear out the defender playing directly in front of the hole-man. The best way to do this is to drive him through to a wing position. If the defender doesn't honor the player who is "driving through", then a pass to that open driver should result in a good shot on goal.

Once the point defender has been cleared, the team on offense will have two players at the 02 and 04 offensive positions, with no one between them. One or two passes between 02 and 04 to move the goalie, and the defenders, can result in an open shot by one of the two players, or an open pass into the hole-forward.

Another way to beat a zone is to drive the 01 wing player all the way across the goal and to the opposite wing. 02 can then take the ball and start moving toward the open space that has been created. The 2-meter player should face 02, so that X2 defender has to make a choice to drop back on 2-meters, or come out and take 02. Either 02 has a shot, or the ball can be passed into 2-meters for an exclusion or a shot.

It is important that the player who has "driven thru" to the wing area stay in that area along with the wing player. Neither player should come back to an outside position; or the offense will be back in the same position that they were before the "drive thru". The two players who end up on the wing must be careful to avoid being countered from those positions.

CREATE MISMATCHES- POSTING UP

Offensively a team should try to create mismatches, especially at 2-meters. Anytime that you have a smaller player guarding a bigger one, then the bigger player should take the smaller player into a double post set position. This is called "posting up". If the set position is occupied, then the 2-meter player can move out of the way by moving to the opposite post.

The primary 2-meter player can also create a mismatch situation before he moves into 2-meters. While he is in a perimeter position, he can run a screen with a teammate who is being guarded by a smaller player. When the defensive players switch positions to defend the screen, a mismatch will be created.

STOPPING THE DOMINATING PLAYER AT 2-METERS

When the 2-meter player is on defense, the offense should try to tire him out by driving him all the way down to the 2-yard line at the other end of the pool, or take him to 2-meters and try to get him to commit an exclusion foul. When the ball turns over, the 2-meter defender has to make him work to get back down the pool and to get back into his offensive position on his own two. If he has been taken to the wing, he will have to swim about 25 meters every time he returns to his position at the other end of the pool.

Once the 2-meter player gets down to the 2-meter area, the defender has several choices on defense. The defender can front the hole-man, press the ball on the outside, and hope that the offensive team cannot get the ball to him; or play behind and double down on him (crash) from an outside defensive position. If all else fails, it is better to commit an exclusion foul that will prevent the 2-meter man from scoring, than allow him to take a shot from a position close to the goal. A team has a better chance of stopping the other teams 6 on 5 than stopping a good hole-man from scoring out of the 2-meter position.

OFFENSIVE STRATEGY- DELAY THE 2-METER OFFENSE

Offensively, a team's first objective is to get the ball down the pool as deep as they can on the pass from the goalie, before the defense has too many players at that end of the pool. The main strategy of most teams is to get the ball into the 2-meter player, and either draw an exclusion foul, or get an outside shot. Before that happens, however, a team should delay moving the two-meter player into his position in front of the goal; and then drive or set a screen in order to drive a player into the open area in front of the goal.

It is at the end of the counterattack, when a defense is less organized, that they are most susceptible to being beaten by a drive towards the goal. A good drive or screen should open up inside water for a shot on goal, or even possibly for drawing a 5-meter penalty. If that does not open up, then the driver can clear out to a wing, while the 2-meter player drives into position; or the team can set a screen for him so that he gains a ball side position. Then the team can run their normal offense, depending on what kind of defense is being played against them.

DEFENSIVE STRATEGY- DELAY OR DENY THE BALL TO 2-METERS

The primary strategy of the defense is to keep the ball out of 2-meters; or delay the ball from getting into that position, with as little time left on the shot clock as possible. Keeping the ball out of 2-meters will result in the offensive team not being able to run their offense, and will put them into a position where there is little or no time left on the clock. Then they either have to take a hurried and predictable shot, or dump the ball into the corner.

This can be done at first with a pressing and passing lane defense that coincides with playing in front of both wings and the 2-meter player. Once the defense loses front position and comes back into a zone, they have to design the zone so that the outside defenders are in a position to crash back on the 2-meter player. The more a team can keep the ball out of 2-meters, or crash back and steal the ball from 2-meters, the less chance the offense has of drawing an exclusion and setting up their 6 on 5 man-up offense. This will severely limit their chances of scoring goals; which is really what the defense wants to do in the first place.

SPECIAL PLAYS

A team should have a few plays set up for special situations when they need to score a goal; or even when they don't need a score. The coach should have a play for the line-up at half court after a goal, a play for the half court offense after a time-out, a play when you need a goal at the end of the game, a corner throw play, and a play for a last minute 6 on 5 situation. A special play should be simple to execute, and should be rehearsed ahead of time so that the players know how to run it.

A simple play, that is not difficult to execute, sometimes can be the most effective play. If a team needs a goal, getting the ball into two-meters after setting up a double post, or having your best shooter draw a 5-meter foul for a free shot on goal falls into this category.

GAME TACTICS- WORKING WITH REFEREES

The relationship between coaches and referees is much better in today's water polo, because a coach can now at least speak to the referee. There is nothing more frustrating to a coach than not being to say anything to the referee about a call that he disagrees with. As a result, the coach would usually shout out his disagreement and embarrass the referee. The referee would then yell something back at the coach, and it usually ended up with both of them angry at each other.

The one thing that the coach doesn't want to do is to show up the official in front of everyone by questioning his call, or by yelling a derogatory remark from across the pool. To avoid these confrontations, the coach should get close to the referee at the first chance he gets, and speak to him in a calm manner about why he didn't like or why he questioned the call.

A good method to use when addressing the referee is to put your protest in the form of a question. IE. "I don't understand. What was that last call that you made against my 2-meter defender? I though it was a normal foul" The referee should let the coach say his piece, acknowledge that he heard the coach; or answer the coach's question. That should put an end to the situation. The coach will be happy that he got to say his piece, and the referee will be happy that he wasn't embarrassed.

If the coach continues his argument, then he should be warned, and then yellow-carded if necessary; unless the situation needs further clarification. Feel satisfaction in knowing that in today's water polo, coaches are at least able to talk about the call to the official. Officials can help to diffuse situations by giving the coach a verbal warning, instead of just automatically sticking out the yellow or red card. Officials must realize that it is embarrassing to the coach. If he persists after a warning, then he deserves the card.

QUESTIONABLE TACTICS IN TODAYS GAME

During the past ten years, I have coached and observed many water polo games, both at home and abroad. The game has changed a lot since I first became involved in the sport fifty-four years ago, mainly because of the many rules changes over the years. Many of the basic fundamentals of the game, by and large, have remained the same.

In my opinion, the changes in the game have led to an erosion of the fundamentals and the necessity of teaching these fundamentals. We used to teach defensive positioning and guarding a player with the ball; now we teach fouling. We used to teach driving towards the goal and shooting after receiving the ball. Now we teach holding the ball in one place for a period of time and then taking the shot.

Some of the tactics used by many of today's teams are questionable at best. I constantly scratch my head and question, "why did a player do that?" or "why is this team doing this?" In the following paragraphs are examples of questionable execution of basic fundamentals and tactics that I have observed in recent years.

THE DELIBERATE FOUL

The deliberate foul in water polo should only be used if trying to stop the clock when executing a "press and steal" defense, to prevent a goal inside of five meters, or to prevent a pass from a wing into a fronted hole-man. It is really perplexes me when I see players committing a deliberate foul for any other reason. This probably annoys me more than any other aspect of the way the game is played today.

I don't understand why players, who don't have to foul, purposely commit the foul anyway. Why are they fouling when they don't have to? Did they forget that there is a shot clock in the game, and every time they commit a foul, they stop the clock and give the offensive player a free pass? Not only are they giving the offensive team extra time to run their offense; but they are making it easier for the offense to move the ball into the scoring area, and consequently giving them more opportunities to score goals. What is even more perplexing to me is that a coach would let his players deliberately foul when they don't have to.

In a game that I observed recently, a team in possession of the ball was running out of time; and the player with the ball was in trouble; pinned against the lane line at the side of the pool. Instead of letting the clock run out, the defender deliberately fouled the player with the ball, stopping the clock. The awarded free pass went directly into 2-meters; resulting in an exclusion and goal by the team, who only a few moments before was in danger of running out the shot clock and losing the ball. The only explanation that I can come up with to explain the "deliberate foul" is, "if the referee is going to call a foul anyway when I press, then I am going to get my money's worth.

POSITION DEFENSE AT 2-METERS- PLAY ON THE SIDE

This leads me to another questionable move on defense that I see all of the time. I see a defender guarding the 2-meter player, playing directly behind him, and with one or both arms draped over the shoulder(s). When the ball arrives in front of the 2-meter player, and the defender is playing directly behind him, it can't help but be called an exclusion-foul against the defender.

If the defender plays around to the side of the 2-meter player, the same side that the ball is on; he has a chance of making the steal instead of committing the exclusion foul every time. In addition, playing on one side of the 2-meter player puts the outside defenders in position to crash back and steal the ball from the opposite side. It also is easier to maneuver behind the 2-meter player when the defender is low in the water and with his hands on the shoulder blades, instead of hanging on top of the shoulders.
 (See Pictures 5-A and 5-B on the next page).

Pictures 5-A: Playing behind the center, a certain exclusion foul.

Pictures 5-B: Playing on the left and right shoulders, ready to intercept pass.

NOT PUTTING BOTH HANDS UP
As the outside defender is about to steal the ball from the 2-meter player, the 2-meter defender has to immediately put both hands in the air; so that he is not called for the exclusion. How many times have you seen the "sure" steal taken away because the 2-meter defender fails to put his hands up? Actually "hands-up" is a misnomer. For the foul not to be called, both arms (including elbows) have to be out of the water and not resting on the players back, as shown in Picture 5-C on the next page.

Picture 5-C: Both hands (and elbows) up to avoid foul

GIVING UP THE 5-METER PENALTY SHOT

I have observed this situation over and over again, and I don't understand why it happens? A player receives the ball inside the 5-meter line and is facing the goal. The defender who is playing behind the player with the ball reaches over the shoulder and is called for a 5-meter penalty. Why is it necessary to commit the 5-meter penalty, when the defender has the shooter covered and in a very poor shooting position?

Think about it! The defender is following directly behind the shooter. The shooter can't pick the ball up because the defender can grab his arm or the ball. The shooter is forced to shoot the ball off of the water, with the goalie directly in front and towering above him. He is trapped into having to take the lowest percentage shot in water polo!

Why commit the deliberate foul and give up the "for sure" much higher percentage penalty shot? Let's see now? The defender deliberately fouls a player who has less than a 25% chance of scoring the "off-the-water" shot; and gives up a penalty shot, which has a 90% chance of scoring. Makes perfect sense to me! (See Picture 5-D below)

Picture 5-D: Giving up the 5-meter penalty to a shooter with a low percentage shot.

NOT TAKING THE SHOT AFTER BEING FOULED AT 5-METERS

At a recent tournament I watched about twelve water polo games between many of the best college teams in the country. In a total of 48 quarters of water polo, I saw only a total of six or seven shots attempted after a player was fouled at 5-meters. In some games I didn't see any attempts at all. Why not? A player is not going to get a better shot than a free shot on goal from five meters from the goal. The shooter only has to beat one arm up and the goalie.

I can understand not attempting the shot if you don't have good body position to take the shot; or if the opportunity occurs very early in the 30-second possession when you are still trying to work the ball into 2-meters. But, not attempting the shot at all! I don't understand the reason for this?

I recently saw a player fouled just outside 5-meters, directly in front of the goal, with three seconds left on the shot clock. He picked up the ball and dumped it in the corner, rather than attempt the free shot on goal. Why not attempt that shot? You might score a goal or get a new shot clock to retain possession of the ball. Shooting the ball is much better than dumping the ball into the corner, especially with only 3-seconds left on the shot clock.

I have several times observed another situation that is even more questionable. The player with the ball is fouled just outside 5-meters and doesn't even look at the goal; but instead looks at his teammate, asking his teammate to release and pass the ball back to him so he can get "live". He passes the ball to his teammate and receives the pass back. Only then does he turn towards the goal and look for his shot.

Why go to all the trouble to get "live", when the player with the ball had a better chance to score right after he was fouled outside 5 meters. Players should always take a shot when a good opportunity presents itself during the game. It shouldn't matter whether it is early or late in the shot clock, unless it is at the end of the game, and your team is protecting a lead. Then you might want to take a little time off the clock before you take the shot.

PASSING THE BALL BACK TO THE GOALIE

A player steals the ball near half court, is fouled, and then makes the free pass back to the goalkeeper, instead of looking down court for a player breaking down the pool. This is another situation that has to be corrected by a coach. The player who has stolen the ball can make a shorter and much more accurate and immediate pass to a breakaway player, than the goalkeeper who is situated way back in the goal.

I always had a rule for my teams that if the ball was stolen within 8 yards of our goal, the ball should go back to the goalie. The only exception to this rule occurs when there is breakaway by the team that has stolen the ball, and the pass to the breakaway player needs to be made immediately.

The time it takes to throw the ball back to the goalie may result in the breakaway player losing his advantage. At the very least, the player who has stolen the ball should first look to see if there is a breakaway, before he passes the ball back to the goalie. A player stealing the ball outside of 8-yards from our goal must never throw the ball back to the goalie; but has to immediately look down court to make a pass to advance the ball.

FIRST PASS ON COUNTERATTACK
On the turnover or shot on goal, six players streak down the pool on the counterattack. One player takes a few strokes and then stops and turns towards the goalie. The goalkeeper then passes him the ball. I don't know why the player would stop before half court (maybe he is tired and doesn't want to swim all the way down the pool), and I don't know why the goalie would make this short pass, when he just as easily could have passed the ball down to the other end of the pool. The other possibility is that the goalie is not a good passer in terms of accuracy (on long passes), and needs help from a teammate.

I want my team to get the ball as deep as possible on the first pass from the goalkeeper. The deep pass puts the ball into immediate scoring position, it gives the offense more time to score, it puts much more pressure on the defense, and it means there are fewer defensive players to contend with. Getting the ball deep on only one pass is much better than having to make several passes to get the ball into scoring position. The more a team has to pass a ball, the more chances for an errant pass and an interception by the defense.

The only time the ball should be passed to the goalies side of half court is when the last man going down the pool is the free man. He should be the only player to receive the ball in this situation; because a deep pass might be intercepted and the opposing team will have a free man in the opposite direction.

REACHING FOR THE BALL ON DEFENSE
I see this quite often when a perimeter defender is pressing, and guarding a right-handed player. The defender invariably reaches over the right shoulder for the ball, with the right hand, even before the player with the ball picks up the ball. The result is a foul!

The defender must be patient and wait until the player tries to pass the ball. He must position himself correctly on the left shoulder, and reaches for the ball (or elbow) with the left hand as the passer starts to turn to attempt a pass. Not only is there less of a chance of the foul being called (because he is not reaching over the shoulder or hitting the head); but the result can be a steal, blocked shot or an errant pass by the passer. Reaching with the right hand is a useless foul that is almost as bad as the deliberate foul as described above. All it does is stop the clock and give up a free pass, and usually does not result in a steal of any kind. (See Picture 5-E on the next page)

Pictures 5-E: Instead of reaching with the right hand and committing a foul, wait until the passer turns to make the pass and then reach with the left hand and a possible block or steal.

GIVING UP BALL SIDE OR INSIDE WATER- HIPS DOWN DEFENSE
I see this a lot in today's game (even at the college level), because defenders are not used to guarding players who drive to the goal. A simple, but effective after goal play is to toss the ball to the 05 left-handers wing, and then have the player at 03 drive "ball-side" to open water on the two yard line to receive the pass from the wing. The result is often times a goal, an exclusion foul, or even a 5-meter penalty foul.

This kind of drive would not be successful if the X3 defender would be playing on the ball side of the perimeter player, and with his hips on the surface of the water, instead of in a vertical position. Even if the defender is correctly playing "ball side" position, the common mistake of not having the hips near the surface of the water, allows the driver to drive right past the defender to open water in front of the goal.

Defensive players are not taught correct positioning in today's water polo; but instead rely on holding and grabbing to stop the driver. Taking away the "ball-side" drive is one of the first defensive skills that a coach should teach his players.

HOLDING THE BALL AND THEN SHOOTING
What ever happened to "shooting off the pass"? With a preponderance of frontcourt and extra-man zone defenses being played, the opportunities to take an outside shot are many. However, it is difficult enough to score against a zone, without decreasing your chances even more by holding the ball, and then shooting. I constantly see players catch the ball from a cross-pass and then fake several times, allowing the goalie and defenders to position themselves in front of the shooter; and then attempt the shot right into the defender's arm or a block by the goalie.

The chances of scoring against a zone are greatly increased if the player shoots immediately upon receiving the ball, before the defender and goalie can set themselves; rather than holding the ball and then shooting. The longer a player holds the ball, the less chance he has of scoring a goal, and the greater chance of someone blocking the shot.

DOES ANYONE PRESS ANYMORE?
We invented the press defense in this country. We probably got it from basketball. Now I see the Europeans pressing, and teams in the USA playing nothing but zone defenses. The country that invented the press has forgotten how to press! It is time for coaches in this country to wake up and get back to what the rest of the water polo world is doing.

Following is a direct quote from Bruno Cufino, Director of Water Polo Development.com, the major website for water polo in Italy:
"The choice of pressing is today common in the early stages of defense of all men's teams in the world, especially at a high level. The last major international competitions tell us that the teams who can keep, as long as they can, this kind of defense during the time of enemy attack, end up being the best teams in the world".

Don't get me wrong, a zone defense is fine at the appropriate time; and I understand why teams are playing a zone. They want to keep the ball away from the 2-meter player and avoid the subsequent exclusion foul. What gets to me is that many teams don't attempt a press at all. They just turn around and swim down the pool, stop in front of their own goal, turn around and put their arms up in a zone defense.

Come on coaches! You are allowing the attacking team to easily move the ball down the pool; and giving them all kinds of time to run their frontcourt offense. At least make it a little more difficult for the attacking team by initially pressing the ball on the counterattack. Then, after you press, you can turn around and go into a zone if you want to. It is not that hard to accomplish.

In conjunction with the press, try to avoid another of my pet peeves (as mentioned above); and that is fouling the player with the ball when you don't have to. When you are pressing, get your hands up and don't foul! You are just helping the ball get down the pool. When you foul, you are defeating the purpose of the press; namely, to delay the ball down the pool and to create turnovers.

WHAT DO YOU DO WHEN YOU ARE LOSING BY SEVERAL GOALS LATE IN THE GAME?
I rarely see teams even make an attempt to get the ball back in their possession, late in the game, when they are losing by one or two goals. Players don't seem to have a clue on what to do in this situation. Don't teams ever work on this in practice? I will give you a few hints. First you need to get the ball back in your possession, because you need to have the ball if you want to score. You cannot allow the team that is leading to retain possession of the ball and just run the clock out.

Secondly, you need to stop the clock? I have seen teams who are losing simply come back into their zone; or play a very soft press. All this does is to allow the clock to just keep running down; which is exactly what the team that is leading wants to accomplish. This is the one time in the game where you need to press hard, and deliberately try to steal the ball or commit the foul to stop the clock!

A player guarding the ball should go for the steal every time, by going for the ball. I don't mean once in a while; I mean EVERYTIME! Then if you don't make the steal, you have to foul, EVERYTIME! A team has two choices: 1) Try to steal and foul and get the ball back, or 2) do nothing but run your regular defense, and simply allow the other team to run the clock out and win the game.

CHAPTER 6

TRAINING AND CONDITIONING FOR WATER POLO

Water polo is a unique sport that has similarities in style, skill, and energy requirements to other team sports such as soccer, basketball, team handball, lacrosse and ice hockey. However, it is the only team sport that is played in the water; making it even more unique in the world of sport. Consequently, water polo has certain energy and physical requirements that are similar in some respects, but in many ways different than other sports.

Players must be trained according to the requirements of playing a high-energy game in the water. Water polo coaches must train their players based on knowledge of the principals of exercise physiology and fluid dynamics, while applying training techniques that are based on reliable scientific research. After the science, coaching experience is vital in making the minute technique adjustments needed during practice and games.

Most successful water polo coaches around the world are well versed in the tactics and skills required to play the game of water polo. However, many, including National Team and professional coaches, are lacking in the knowledge to properly train their athletes to achieve success. There are many misconceptions that coaches have about training water polo athletes. These are based on a misunderstanding of physiological principals and how to apply them to the requirements of the sport.

These misconceptions also come about in water polo because of the lack of knowledge of how muscular force is applied in a fluid medium (water) in order to achieve movement (propulsion). Because water is the medium in which our athletes compete in, we use swim conditioning in order to train our athletes. However, the improper use of swimming for training water polo players can be a detriment to the athlete.

Even though swimming is a necessary skill for water polo players, they must also learn the techniques, skills and tactics to play the game. For training to be effective, you must make the same demands on your body, and in the same way that they are made in the game. The closer the training routine is to the requirements of competition, the better the outcome.

The purpose of this chapter is to present a system of training water polo athletes based on the practical application of sound scientific principles, and the specific physical and energy requirements of the sport of water polo; one of the more physically demanding sports in the world.

The well-trained athlete is better able to handle the rigors of the game, and more importantly the rigors of long arduous practice sessions. The result is better execution of the fundamentals of the game during stressful periods, and a win for the well-conditioned team.

For the past 32 years, I have tried to combine my knowledge of exercise science and fluid mechanics, and my experiences of coaching water polo at the top level in this country in order to effectively train the athletes on my teams. In this chapter I will present the techniques that I have utilized, based on science and experience. The results have been successful well-conditioned teams that have out-swam and worn-down our opponents in the critical fourth quarter of many games.

PART ONE
Part one of the chapter explains what happens to a player's body from an exercise science perspective. Specifically, what happens to the cardiovascular and neuromuscular systems of the water polo player when he swims up and down the pool, performs the eggbeater, or performs a water polo skill.

PART TWO
Part two of the chapter deals with specific training methods used in water polo, based on an assessment of the energy requirements of the sport and the correct application of the principals of exercise physiology and fluid dynamics. Specific information on "how to train" for water polo is described, including information on water polo swim sets, conditioning drills, as well as information on conditioning the legs.

PART 1

THE SCIENCE OF EXERCISE

ENERGY FOR MUSCLE CONTRACTION
The human body will always require energy just to function, whether it is asleep or awake, resting or working. Our bodies get the energy they need from food, through metabolism; the chemical reactions in the body's cells that convert the fuel from food into the energy needed to do everything from moving, to thinking, to growing. When the body starts moving at a faster and faster pace, as it does during exercise, more energy is required by the muscles of the body to be able to contract at a faster rate, and produce faster and more efficient movement. It is the mechanical work of the muscles that is the pass key to the metabolic machinery that takes place within the muscle cells (fibers).

The energy requirements of the muscles depend on the stimulus of different kinds of activities, specifically the intensity and length of the activity itself. While all of us have muscles that are used for everyday function, the muscles of the athlete have to be trained to perform under the stressful conditions of a more intense athletic activity.

It is up to coaches to train athletes in the correct manner, so that they will achieve maximum performance in their particular sports activity. However, before physical training for athletes can be prescribed accurately, a basic understanding of how energy is produced in the human body is essential.

WHERE DO WE GET THE ENERGY TO FUEL OUR MUSCLES?

The human body is perfectly designed to move by a series of coordinated muscle contractions. When the brain tells the body to move, nerve signals trigger a powerful release of muscular energy through a special molecule called adenosine tri-phosphate (ATP). When the chemical bond that holds ATP together, snaps apart, energy is released and used by the muscles (fibers) to contract; and away you go. ATP must be present before a muscle can contract.

ATP is stored in small amounts in the muscle, but can only sustain activity for a few seconds. If activity is to continue, ATP must be produced in the muscle cells (fibers). The process that causes this to happen is simply converting chemical energy from food, into mechanical energy for muscle contraction. Three systems in the body create the ATP energy required for physical activity:

ATP-CP (ALACTACID) SYSTEM

ATP for the immediate use of the muscle cells at the start of any activity, is produced by the breakdown of another high-energy phosphate found in the muscles, creatine phosphate (CP). The ATP produced by this system is readily available; but there is only enough CP available to provide energy for approximately an 8-12 second athletic activity or other rapid muscle contraction. The activity of the ATP-CP energy system does not require the presence of oxygen, and is considered to be part of the anaerobic (without oxygen) energy system.

Since lactic acid is not produced by this system, it is also called the "alactacid" system. It is used primarily in speed and strength activities that are of short duration. If a person stops and rests after the short muscular effort, stocks of CP are remade in the muscles during the rest period (about 20-30 seconds); to be utilized again in order to repeat the activity.

GLYCOLYTIC (LACTACID) SYSTEM- ANAEROBIC GLYCOLYSIS

Other forms of fuel are also stored and made available in the muscles for more sustained bouts of exercise. These are stored carbohydrates (glycogen) and fat, which are degraded by different mechanisms to again produce the "chemical of contraction", ATP. During a sustained high-powered activity, when both stored ATP and CP and the delivery of oxygen are insufficient to meet the demands of the effort, the high energy carbohydrate compound glycogen can be broken down to glucose, and then ATP, and eventually lactic acid. This is called the "lactacid" or the "glycolytic" energy system.

This process also does not require oxygen and is sometimes called "anaerobic glycolysis". The glycogen used for this process is found in the muscles and in the liver; and is actually the storage form of the carbohydrates that your body digests as part of your diet. This system produces enough ATP, along with the stored ATP and CP, to sustain the exercise for a longer period of time; about 40-50 seconds or longer, depending on the level of training of the athlete.

The drawback to anaerobic gylcolysis is the production of lactic acid. Even though an athlete can swim or run at near maximum speed for this time period, the accumulation of lactic acid will eventually cause the muscles to fatigue, and muscular contraction to slow down. When the muscles reach a point where enough lactic acid has accumulated, the pain and heavy feeling of the fatigued muscles requires the athlete to stop or slow down.

AEROBIC SYSTEM (OXIDATION)
If exercise is not very intense, it can be prolonged even longer. The rate of energy release (ATP) in the muscles, can then be maintained by the process of oxidation. For oxidation to occur, oxygen must be transported from the air that we breath, from the lungs, and then to the muscles by the cardio-respiratory system (heart, lungs and blood vessels). Oxygen is then utilized by the muscles, along with carbohydrates and fats, for ATP production. The system that uses oxygen is called the "aerobic" energy system, and is used for events that last for long periods of time (greater than 2-3 minutes), like long distance running and swimming.

Although both fats and glycogen can be utilized by the aerobic system for more intensive and prolonged exercise, glycogen is preferred over fat; because it produces more ATP and produces it more efficiently than fat does. However, the problem with glycogen is that it is limited in supply, and can be depleted by prolonged exercise.

The heavy-legged and tired feeling referred to by marathon runners as "hitting the wall" is closely associated with severe muscle glycogen depletion. Glycogen can also be depleted by long practice sessions as well, and needs to be replaced by diet, before the next practice session or competition. (See "glycogen depletion" below)

WHAT IS THE PRIMARY SYSTEM USED FOR PLAYING WATER POLO?
The intensity of the exercise, and the bodies ability to deliver oxygen to the muscles, are important factors in which system is being utilized by the muscles. As long as the activity is slow paced and the cardio-respiratory system can deliver enough oxygen, the body utilizies the aerobic system for producing ATP. However, as the intensity and pace is increased, the body relies more on the anaerobic alactacid (CP/ATP) and glycolytic systems that are fueled by glucose (glycogen). The cardiovascular system simply cannot deliver oxygen fast enough to supply the demands of a high intensity exercise.

During exercise, all three systems come into play; but it is a selective system, where one of the three is utilized more than the other two, depending on the speed and intensity of the performance and the conditioning of the athlete. Generally, fast pace swims utilize more of the anaerobic systems, while slower paced swims utilize more of the aerobic system. The highly trained athlete can compete at a faster pace than the untrained athlete, without having to utilize the anaerobic lactic acid producing energy systems.

Water polo is a sport of high intensity sprints of short duration, and is considered primarily "anaerobic" in nature; utilizing predominately the ATP-CP and glycolytic/lactacid systems described above. It has been shown by sports scientists that the ATP-CP is the predominant sysytem of the two that are utilized in playing water polo.

WHAT HAPPENS TO THE LACTIC ACID PRODUCED BY GLYCOLYSIS?

Scientists used to believe that trained athletes could "tolerate" higher levels of lactic acid than untrained athletes. We now know that high levels of lactic acid doesn't mean the end of the road for athletes. Lactate formed during intense exercise can actually be converted back to glucose during the aerobic recovery period, and can be utilized by the working muscles to produce ATP; or if not utilized, can be converted and stored as glycogen.

This can occur during training, in the rest intervals of a work/rest interval system, and during periods of slow paced activity or while resting during an intense match or game. The trained athlete will not only produce less lactic acid for the same high intensity activity; but will utilize more in conversion back to ATP. No matter how well trained an athlete is, if he/she encounters meaningful muscular exertion that lasts more than 10-15 seconds, they will eventually accumulate enough lactate to cause fatiguing effects to the body.

THE IMPORTANCE OF GLYCOGEN FUEL STORES

Glucose (carbohydrate) is stored in the muscles and liver as glycogen. We refer to glycogen as the primary muscle fuel. It is specially structured to break down quickly to glucose, as required by the muscles to produce ATP. Carbohydrate in food is digested, absorbed into the blood, and transported to the muscles and liver where it is converted to glycogen and stored for later use.

The average 160-pound person will have about 40 calories (measure of energy) of glucose in the blood, 260 calories of glycogen in the liver, and 1400 calories of glycogen in the muscles. If an athlete wants to train and compete efficiently, he/she needs a full tank of glycogen every time they start to exercise. During high intensity exercise, glycogen is used at a very fast rate and may become depleted after 30 to 45 minutes, depending on the condition of the athlete and how much glycogen he starts the activity with.

The glycogen that is utilized during training has to be replaced every day, or performance will start to suffer. Graph 6A on the next page, shows a hypothetical situation for a water polo player, starting the training week on day one with a large amount of glycogen stored in his muscles and liver. After completing a strenuous 2 1/2 hour water polo workout, the player will use up a large portion of the glycogen that is stored in the body.

Eating a high carbohydrate dinner that night, and breakfast and lunch the next day, will restore some of the glycogen that was used up. However, the athlete will not completely restore the full amount, and will consequently start the next day's practice with less than he had the previous day. This cycle is repeated every day, until about the fourth day, when the glycogen is almost completely depleted.

After depletion, how well do you think the water polo player will perform in the practice or game the next day? If something is not done to increase the amount of stored glycogen that he starts the practice or game with, he will find himself competely fatigued early in the next practice or game. As shown in Graph 6A, it can happen to water polo players who train hard every day, and fail to restore the glycogen in the body.

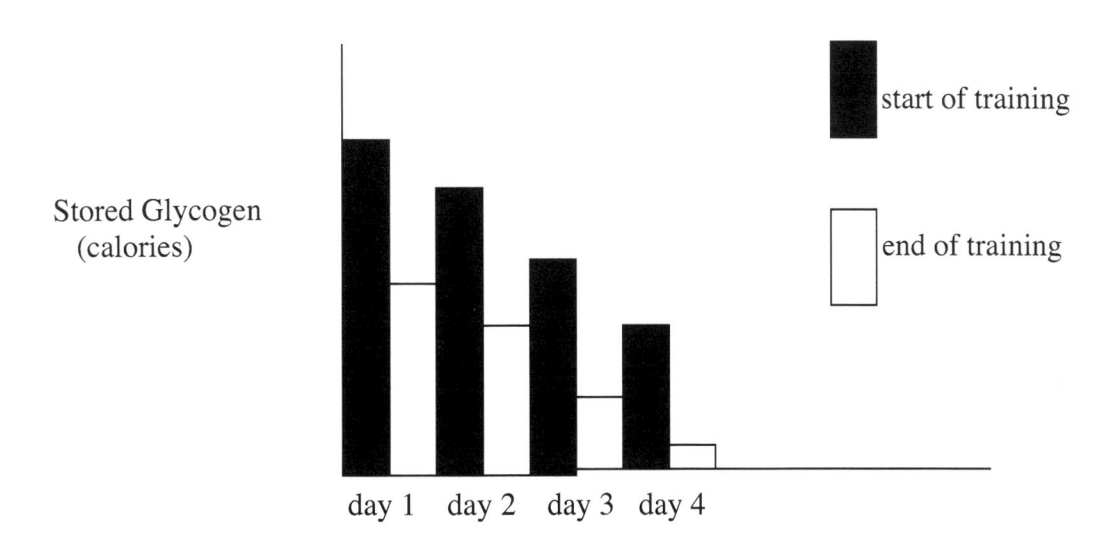

GRAPH 6A: Depletion of glycogen by a water polo player after four days of intense practice.

HOW DOES THE ATHLETE RESTORE THE GLYCOGEN LEVELS IN HIS BODY?
Both diet (carbohydrate intake) and rest are critical factors in performance; and both are required for maximum restoration of glycogen, and for maximum performance to occur. Water polo coaches should take note. If you want your team to perform well in an important game, then you must rest them a few days by cutting back on the length and intensity of your workouts, along with encouraging the players to add more carbohydrates to their diet.

HOW THE MUSCLES WORK
The main function of skeletal muscle is contraction, the result of which is movement. The endurance and speed of movement of an athlete depends largely on the muscle's ability to produce energy and power. In looking at a cross-section of a muscle, we see that muscles are composed of thousands of long fibers (cells). The number of fibers in different muscles ranges from 10,000 to as many as a million in some larger muscles. Not all muscle fibers are alike however. A single skeletal muscle contains fibers having different speeds of shortening and fatigability, and different levels of strength and endurance.

Microscopic examination of muscles has made it possible to identify two basic types of muscle fibers in human muscle. These are termed fast-twitch (red) and slow-twitch (white) fibers. The characteristics of these two types of fibers, and their distribution throughout the body are critical to the success of all athletic endeavors.

Despite their differences in structure and function, muscle fibers do have one thing in common; and that is, they are innervated by nerve fibers (motor nerves) from the central nervous system.

FIBER TYPES AND THEIR INFLUENCE ON MOVEMENT

It is the brain that perceives the need for movement, and then recruits muscle fibers to meet those needs. To activate the amount of muscle fibers required to generate a specific amount of force, the brain, through the central nervous system and motor nerves, recruits motor units in the muscles involved. The brain does not recruit fibers at random, but ascertains the precise amount of force your muscles require to move a precise resistance; and accordingly recruits the precise amount of fibers needed to do the job.

The motor units recruited, and when they are recruited, depend on the kind of force required to perform the movement, and the kinds of fibers that make up the motor unit. Slow-twitch fibers (ST) are generally regarded as endurance fibers, while fast-twitch fibers (FT) are regarded as speed fibers; and are characterized as producing greater force and are more anaerobic in nature.

Both kinds of fibers are found throughout the body, and in many people there is an equal proportion of ST and FT fibers distributed throughout the muscles of the body. The percentages of muscle fiber types that are found in the body go a long way in determining success or failure in certain kinds of athletic activities. The abilities of different fiber types to increase their performance can be improved with training (up to a point); but the proportions in the body muscles that you were born with always remain the same.

This is important in athletics, depending on the kind of event that an athlete participates in. Endurance athletes, such as marathon runners, have a greater portion of ST (red) endurance fibers in the leg muscles, as much as 80% in some runners. The exact opposite is true of sprinters (100-meter runners), who have a higher portion of FT (white) sprint fibers (as high as 80%) in their leg muscles.

Once again, we see the influence of heredity on athletic performance. Athletes tend to gravitate to activities that their body types will allow them to successfully compete in. Body size is a determining factor in many athleteic activities; but the percentage of fast twitch and slow twitch muscle fibers are also a major factor in success in many activities.

BASIC PRINCIPLES OF EXERCISE

OVERLOAD AND ADAPTATION PRINCIPLE

The goal of physical conditioning is to train the muscles in practice, so that there is an improvement in their performance capabilities in a game. In water polo, while both types of muscle fibers can be utilized, it is important for the anaerobic fast-twitch fibers that will be used in competition be trained correctly. In order for the fast-twitch fibers to improve in their ability to contribute to the high speed actions of the water polo player, they have to be stressed during practice, with a high enough load that the muscles perceive as a stimulus. Fast twitch fibers that are anaerobic in nature, are very unlikely to be stimulated to produce a training response in work that is consistently at, or below, anaerobic threshold (long and slow-speed aerobic swimming).

In other words, the stress has to be strong enough so that there is a weakening, or tearing down, of the contractile mechanism of the muscles. Acting as a biological agent, the body makes an "adaptive" response to the stimulus of tearing down or weakening, by building up the mechanism for contraction; resulting in a more efficient and stronger response to the demands of the muscles.

In the case of a sport like water polo, that relies a lot on fast-twitch fibers for short intense movement, the stimulus of the workload has to be great enough to require the body to recruit and fatigue them. This requires a stimulus of high intensity, like sprinting, in order to "overload" and stress the FT fibers. Only when they are stressed with a heavy load, will the body respond and increase the capabilities of the fibers to contract. The body simply will not "adapt" and build-up and improve the mechanisms of muscle contraction; unless the stressor (load) is high enough to overload the fast-twitch mechanism beyond the normal requirements of that particular system.

THE PRINCIPLE OF PROGRESSION

The principle of progression implies that there is an optimal level of overload that should be achieved, and an optimal time frame for this overload to occur. Overload should not be increased too slowly, or improvement is unlikely. Overload that is increased too rapidly can result in injury or muscle damage. An athlete should not (and cannot) train hard all the time. Doing so will lead to over-training; and a great deal of physical and psychological damage will result.

The Principle of Progression also makes us realize the need for proper rest and recovery. Continual stress on the body, and constant overload, will result in exhaustion and injury. This occurs in water polo at the beginning of a season, in the so called "hell week" training, when coaches just pile on the intensity and duration of training, in hopes of getting the athletes in shape quickly for the start of the competition. The coach should gradually increase the intensity and length of training at the beginning of the season, instead of piling it on with high intensity workouts for hour upon hour each day.

THE PRINCIPLE OF SPECIFICITY OF TRAINING

The Principle of "Specificity" is the cornerstone of all of the principles of training the body for physical exercise; and is the one most widely accepted by sports scientists, coaches and trainers throughout the world. The Principle of Specificity states that, "the maximum benefits of a training stimulus can only be obtained when it replicates the movements and energy systems involved in the activities of a sport". The Principle of Specificity applies to all areas of sports training to include both "physical" conditioning as well as "skill" conditioning.

Both the physical parts of a sports activity, and the skills associated with participating in the activity, require some kind of muscle action that involves motor-units controlled by the central nervous system. The basic premise of the "specificity principle" is that all of these muscle actions, whether they require one or many motor units, occur in a way that is specific to the action. In order for the muscular action to be performed correctly, and in an efficient way, the neuromuscular action has to be repeated again and again, and in the same "specific" way.

SPECIFICITY OF PHYSICAL CONDITIONING

Physical conditioning is a type of training performed with the goal of improving overall physical strength and metabolic condition (energy systems). In order to improve the physical conditioning of a body in a particular sport, the workload imposed must exactly duplicate the muscular movement patterns of the sport, and the exact energy systems utilized in the sport.

The greater the similarity of stimulation that is experienced at practice, is to competitive settings, the greater will be the transfer of benefits derived from training and practice. This is the fundamental principle that is supported by the "Principle of Training Specificity", and cannot be ignored when exercising serious athletes. A lot of research by sports scientists has shown that both the specific energy systems (anaerobic, aerobic), and the groups of muscles used in a sport (fast twitch, slow twitch), have to be trained exactly as they are used during competition in order for the athlete to perform better.

TRAINING THE ENERGY SYSTEMS

Whether it is primarily the alactacid and lactic acid anaerobic systems, or the oxygen related aerobic systems, that are utilized by the body to produce ATP for muscular contraction, the predominant system used in a sport has to be trained by overloading and stressing that particular system in practice. In order to gain training benefits to a particular system, the same intensity has to be utilized in practice as it is in competition.

Training at a rate of intensity that is required for one system, will not necessarily transfer to another system. The lower rate of intensity required to improve the aerobic system (slower pace) will not transfer to the faster paced anaerobic systems. Because the alactacid and lactic acid systems require much more intensity than the aerobic system, improvement of these systems must occur by practicing at higher intensities.

It has been found in numerous studies, that the effects of a slower paced practice intensity will not transfer to the higher paced requirements of a fast paced system; because it does not stimulate the stress required for adaptation to take place. However, training at a higher intensity will stimulate all three systems to a certain degree, because the faster pace stresses all three systems.

SWIMMING FAST

Swimming fast, although it is dependent on inhereted muscle characteristics like fiber type and muscle structure, is a learned skill that can be developed by coaches of sprint swimmers and water polo players. Everyone can learn to swim fast through training the muscles and energy systems involved. However, if two athletes perform the same speed training and use the same techniques, the athlete that starts with a body that has the required muscle characteristics of a sprinter (FT fibers), will eventually swim faster than the athlete who does not have these characteristics. The same goes for an athlete who has inhereted the endurance characteristics of a marathon runner. Despite doing the same training, he will be able to run a marathon faster than a runner who does not have these inherited characteristics (ie. high percentage of slow twitch fibers).

Since the muscles learn to function in particular ways to particular situations, training at a particular rate or intensity will produce specific adaptations to that intensity. In other words, repetition of the skill of sprinting over and over again, using proper technique and speed, will stimulate the adaptive processes of the body to swim faster.The neuromuscular patterns of performance are specific to each speed of swimming.

When a desired performance level requires a high velocity, then one should train at that velocity (or greater) to become skilled at that specific movement pattern. If one wishes to swim 100 yards in 50 seconds, then some training must be repeated at a velocity of at least 6 feet per second or faster (equivalent to 50 seconds per 100 yards). To perform at a slower speed would result in training for a slower than desired performance.

INTERVAL SWIMMING
The best way to achieve faster speeds for swimming and water polo is to practice at race pace, or in the case of water polo, practice at game (counterattack) pace. These types of swims are called "high-intensity" swims. These fast/high intensity swims have to be repeated over and over again; or the "skill" of swimming fast (neuromuscular patterns) will not be developed fully. This can best be achieved by using the "interval" system of training. That is, repeat work intervals followed by repeat rest intervals.

The beauty of the interval system is that each repeat swim can be swum at a faster pace, than if the swim was one long continuous swim. For instance 10 x 100 meters with a rest interval after each repeat hundred, can be swum at a much faster pace than a continuous thousand-meter swim. If a swimmer tries to swim 1000 meters at the same fast pace as the 100-meter intervals, he would have to quit or slow down before the end because of the accumulation of lactic acid. In order for the interval system to work for water polo, then each interval swim has to be of sufficient length and intensity that will allow the swimmer to swim at, or faster than, game (counterattack) pace. Details of water polo specific swim sets will be discussed in Part 2 of his chapter.

HIGH-INTENSITY SWIMS AND FATIGUE
Unfortunately, speed work, as it is presently practiced, is so stressful that few athletes develop any great skill for sprinting. When a swimmer does an all-out swim that lasts longer than 10-15 seconds; lactic acid starts to accumulate. Thus, a longer rest period is required, so that some of the lactic acid can be dissipated, and the fast high-intensity swim can be repeated. Swims of this sort require 2-3 times more rest than the time required for the swim. For instance, an all-out swim requiring 30 seconds to complete, would require 90-seconds of rest, if the work to rest ratio was 1 to 3.

Even with a long rest period, after completing a number of these kinds of swims, lactic acid will accumulate; and the players will find that are exhausted from the effort. It takes time to recover from these kinds of swims, and the carry over can go into the next day. Because of the fatigue effect, athletes end up not performing sufficient trials (repeats) to develop strong consistent sprint-movement patterns.

Water polo coaches are confronted with a perplexing problem: How can more sprint training be undertaken, if it is so stressful? If a coach increases sprint training, then participating players will succumb more quickly to excessive stress. One solution is to have the players perform these kinds of swims at the end of practice, so that they will have a day to recover. Another solution is to perform "ultra-short" swim sets.

ULTRA-SHORT SWIM SETS
Research findings from psychology and physiology suggest another alternative that allows both sprint skill and appropriate physical adaptation to be developed simultaneously, without the fatigue associated with long (> 15 seconds) high intensity swims. The players can perform swim sets that do not cause the accumulation of lactic acid, by repeating short swims that take less than 15 seconds to complete; and rely mostly on the alactacid ATP-CP system that does not produce lactic acid. These kinds of swim sets are called "ultra-short" swim sets, and will be covered in detail in the second part of the chapter.

PROPULSION AND THRUST
In the sport of water polo, an athlete must propel himself through the water in a horizontal position (swimming) and thrust himself out of the water vertically by performing the eggbeater or breaststroke leg kick. The objective of swimming is to propel oneself forward through the water (propulsion) by pulling the hands backward, while the objective of the eggbeater kick is to provide upward movement (thrust) of the body by pushing the feet down on the water.

POWER (P= F X V)
The key factor that explains both of these movements in the water is power. It has long ago been determined that power is important in all sports in order for athletes to perform at their maximum capacity. Many people mistakenly confuse power with strength. They state that if you have strength, than you also have power. In truth, strength is only one component of power. Speed is the other component.

When you multiply strength (force) times speed (velocity), then you have power (Power = force x velocity). Power is necessary to provide forward or upward movement in water polo. The more force that you can apply, or the more speed that you can apply the force with, the more power you will have. If you want to run faster and jump higher on land, then you need power. If you want to swim faster or get higher in the water, then you also need power.

We can apply this formula to movement on land and in the water, except for one important difference. In the water, propulsion cannot be generated by pushing-off from a fixed point, like the runner who pushes off the solid ground. Instead, propulsion is the result of pushing-off from the water, that gives when you push on it. This aspect alone may go a long ways in determining the need for force to generate power in the water.

An example of how power is generated on land and in the water is shown in the Diagram 6-1a and 6-1b below. In Diagram 1a, a swimmer uses his hand to push against a solid object that is anchored to the bottom of a shallow pool. In Diagram 1b, the swimmer pushes against the water.

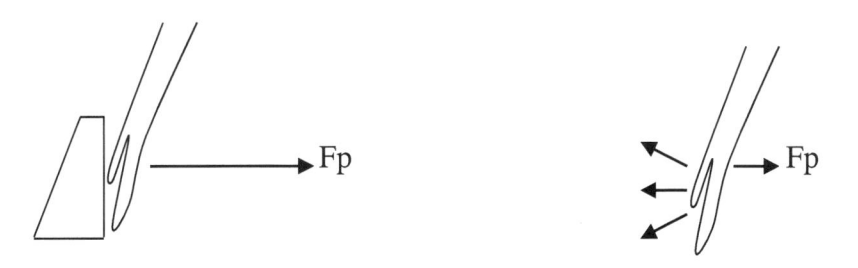

a) Pushing against a solid object   b) Pushing against water

Diagram 6-1: Generating power against a stationary object and against the water

In 6-1a above, the force generated by pushing the hand against the solid object will produce an opposite reaction (Fp, as indicated by the LENGTH of the arrow) to move the body forward at a certain speed. In this case, most of the mechanical force that comes from pushing on the wall is transferred to the forward propulsion of the body. The harder the arm pushes on the solid object (more force/strength), the more power is generated to push the body forward at a greater speed, and thus a greater distance.

In 6-1b, the same swimmer pushes back on the water instead of a solid object. The mechanical force the swimmer delivers with his hand and arm helps to generate the power to propel the swimmer forward (Fp, as indicated by the SMALLER arrow) but at slower speed than the runner, and thus for a shorter distance.

Why is there less power created when pushing against the water than on a solid object? Because a larger portion of the force is dissipated into the water by being converted into the kinetic energy of moving water, rather than contributing to the forward speed of the swimmer. In other words, the mechanical force generated by the muscles is mostly wasted on pushing the water backwards, whereas almost all of the force generated by pushing against the solid object goes into pushing the body forward. Consequently, the forward speed of the body generated by pushing against the solid object is much greater than the speed generated by applying the same force to the water.

OTHER VARIABLES TO PROPULSION- OVERCOMING RESISTANCE
Besides the differences in applying force on land and in the water, there are also differences in the resistance encountered on land and water, that will act to slow the athlete down. To run fast or jump higher, the athlete on land has to mainly overcome gravity (the weight of his body). On the other hand, to swim fast, or get higher in the water, the water polo player needs to be able to generate enough force to overcome the drag forces of the water acting on the body.

Because of the buoyant force of the water pushing up on the body, the swimmer does not have to worry a lot about overcoming gravity, only on overcoming drag resistance. The weight of a swimmer in the water is negligible. The weight that a runner must overcome to move forward, requires much more force than the force required to overcome the drag resistance of the water. An obvious conclusion and overall generalization is that it takes more strength to run than it does to swim.

ANALYSIS OF THE FORCE REQIRED TO SWIM OR EGGBEATER

PROPULSION OVERCOMES DRAG
When swimming through the water, the body experiences a braking force that is called drag. In order to create forward propulsion, the power created by moving the hands and legs through the water, have to overcome the negative forces of drag on the body.
This total drag force has three components when swimming at the surface; friction, pressure drag, and wave drag. These forces are dependent on the swimming speed and on the shape and size of the body.

Frictional drag is caused by the movement of water past the skin of the body, and is more of a concern to the competitive swimmer than the water polo player. The effects on water polo of friction drag are minimal; mainly because of the shorter distances swum during a game (20-25 meters). Wave drag also plays a small part of the drag on a water polo player.

Pressure or form drag, however, is more of a concern to the water polo player, and arises as a result of pushing the body through the water. The frontal area (surface area of the head, shoulders, arms and legs) of the body that pushes through the water, causes a pressure differential between the front and the rear of the swimmer, resulting in "pressure drag". The competitive swimmer can reduce frontal area by streamlining, or elongating the body with each stroke. The swimmer that presents less body surface area (frontal area) to the water as the body moves through it, will create less drag, and thus allow the swimmer to go faster.

A water polo player has to overcome even more resistance from frontal area then a swimmer does, because of the angle of the body in the water. Swimming with the head out of the water when playing water polo, causes the hips and the legs to drop below the surface of the water; creating more need for power to overcome the increased frontal resistance. (See Diagram 6-2 on the next page).

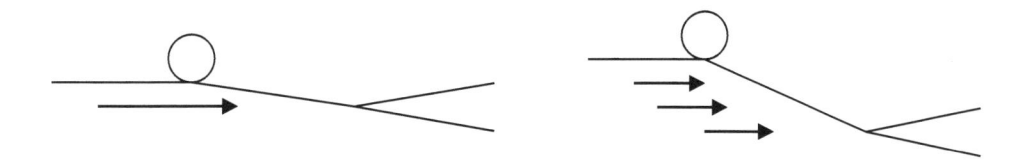

Diagram 6-2: Normal swimmer –hips up   Diagram 6-3: Water polo player. Head high, hips low- increased frontal resistance.

Increasing the speed of the arms, and increasing the tempo of the kick, helps bring the legs and hips higher in the water; and thus creates less frontal resistance. One of the factors in streamlining is the mass of the body. A bigger mass presents more frontal area (the area of the front of the body that pushes through the water) and thus creates more drag to slow down the swimmer. Girls, with less body mass then boys, for example have on average 20% less drag than boys when compared swimming at the same speed.

Eventually a point will be reached where the mass achieved from bigger muscles is a negative influence on speed; mainly because of more frontal area. The biggest water polo players in terms of mass (2-meter players) are also the ones that have the most difficulty moving through the water. Long, tall and lean is preferred over big and massive when it comes to moving fast in a water polo match, as well as a swim meet.

SO HOW DOES THE WATER POLO PLAYER INCREASE POWER TO SWIM FASTER, OR GET HIGHER IN THE WATER?

One way to increase power is to increase the force component (F) of F x V = P. This is done by increasing both the drag and lift on the arms and legs while swimming, or using the eggbeater. By positioning the hand or foot so that more surface area is presented to the water, more force is created. Positioning the hand and the foot is mostly a matter of correct technique and bone, joint, and muscle structure.

While using proper technique can help increase the force that is applied to the water, a lot of the force generated by the hand and the foot goes into pushing water backward or downward. Consequently, these methods of increasing force are not that efficient in creating propulsion. So what is the answer to swimming faster or getting higher in the water?

Remember that Power = force x velocity. So, if we can't produce more power in the water by increasing the force component (F) of power, then we have to increase the velocity component (V). In other words move the arms and the legs faster through the water. Not only does the increased velocity help to increase the drag on the arms and legs, but it also increases the lift on the arms and legs, similar to the lift produced by an airplane wing. This is why water polo players must move there arms faster to gain speed and move their legs faster (eggbeater) to gain more height in the water. This ability to move the arms and legs fast for a short period of time can be trained.

TRAINING TO INCREASE ARM AND LEG SPEED

In considering all of the factors mentioned above, it would seem that increased arm speed would be more effective than increased force in helping a swimmer to swim faster. In essence, the swimmer and water polo player are using arm speed, instead of arm strength, to increase swimming speed. So how is a player able to move the arms and legs through the water rapidly, and then repeat this fast movement over and over again during a game or practice?

The best way to increase speed is to perform the activity (sprinting and eggbeater) in practice, at a high enough intensity that will stimulate the muscles to contract faster. In other words, the arms and legs have to be specifically (there's that word again) trained to move faster through the water!

What we are really training here are the energy systems responsible for supplying energy (ATP) to the contracting muscles, namely the anaerobic creatine-phosphate (CP) and the anaerobic lactic acid (LA) systems. While performing these activities in practice, the intensity must high enough to overload these energy systems; so that they will adapt and improve. This adaptation CANNOT be accomplished by slow swimming, or performing easy eggbeater. Only sprint swimming and fast and explosive kicking can do this.

The effect of this kind of specific training (sprint swimming and explosive kicking) is due to the motor-learning of the skill associated with the activity (rapidly moving the arms and legs). The most specific way to train the neuromuscular system involved in the activity is to perform the activity itself at a high intensity. The most specific way to train for water polo is to perform the sport itself, namely playing water polo. By performing the sport activity in practice and games, the exact amount of strength and speed necessary for power production will be developed.

HEAD-UP SWIMMING IN WATER POLO

Specificity not only occurs with the energy system involved; but also with the technique and form utilized in the stroke. Remember, this a "learned behavior" that is characterized by the neuromuscular patterns of recruiting motor units. Most, if not all, of the high-intensity swimming performed in water polo practice should be performed with the head out of the water, in order to exactly duplicate the water polo stroke.

The water polo player cannot just wildly move the arms through the water at a fast pace, however, and expect good results. Correct technique must be followed in terms of high elbows, hands wide of the shoulders, pulling through only to the rib cage before recovering (short stroke), and fast turnover of the arms. Streamlining can be achieved by correct body position in the water; with a hips high position created by a strong flutter kick.

In SUMMARY, we can conclude that it doesn't take a lot of force for a water polo player to overcome the resistance of the water, especially when compared to a runner or jumper on land. Getting as much applied force as possible (efficiency) by positioning of the hands and feet, is more important than just sheer force aquired from muscle strength.

Because of the low hip position in the water, and the negligible effects of streamlining, a water polo player must use more energy than a swimmer going the same distance and speed. Both the swimmer and the water polo player can increase speed by increasing the velocity of their arms and feet; more so than by increasing strength. Streamlining and correct technique are also factors in swimming faster; but are more of a consequence to the swimmer than the water polo player.

Training for speed is relatively straight-forward: the activity itself should form the basis of the form of movement, the technique should be as correct and economical as possible, and the training action should be as intense as possible, so that overload and adaptation takes affect. Both swimmers and water polo players can benefit from high intensity and high speed training that will overload the muscle's energy systems, and consequently improve the speed of the swimmer and the lift of the body higher out of the water.

PART 2
TRAINING FOR WATER POLO

ANALYSIS OF THE REQUIREMENTS OF PLAYING WATER POLO
In order to determine the requirements for training a water polo player, the movements of a player during a game have to be analyzed to see what a player actually does in a game. Only by determining what the player's actual movements are during a game, and the relative intensity of those movements, will we be able to know what energy systems need to be trained, and what skills need to be trained.

Observations of the frequency and duration of the different activities occuring in a game, and of the physiological responses to participating in a water polo match, are initial sources of information for designing training programs specific to the game, and specific to the different playing positions.

Water polo has been promoted as one of the toughest sports in the world. While it takes a lot of athletic ability to play the sport, some of the aspects of the game have been greatly exaggerated, especially the physiological requirements of playing the game (i.e. "It requires great stamina to play water polo, with players swimming at all out sprint speed for distances of up to two miles").

European sports scientists, who are interested in the metabolic demands of the sport of water polo, have done video analysis of players in international water polo games. The results, in terms of distance swum, intensity, and amount of time spent in vertical and horizontal positions, may surprise you! It is a demanding sport; but perhaps not as demanding as one would like to think.

Be aware that most of the film analysis is done on players who are competing in 8-minute quarter games and in a 30-meter long water polo course. We will assume that every player plays every minute of the game without substitution, although in an actual game this very rarely happens.

Rest intervals that occur during quarter breaks and time-outs also allow recovery during a game; but are not taken into account when analyzing the energy demands of the game. The distances swum also have to be adjusted down when we are speaking of young players or females playing in 25-yard or 25-meter pools. Most of the movements analyzed will be of field players who play the driver/perimeter positions. Other positions that require more specific training are the 2-meter offensive and defensive positions and the goalkeeper positions. Both will be discussed in Book 2 of the "Water Polo Series".

HOW FAR DOES A WATER POLO PLAYER ACTUALLY SWIM IN A GAME?
A water polo game lasts, on average, somewhere between one hour, to one hour and 10 minutes in length (perhaps the shortest game time of any team-sport); depending on the number of stoppages during the game, level of play by different ages and sexes, the number of time-outs called by coaches, and whether the game goes into overtime or not. For purposes of this discussion and for ease in calculating times of certain activities, we will choose an average number of 60 minutes for a game, which is a number that covers all levels of water polo.

Film analysis of a complete game show that the total linear distance traveled by an active player, who plays most of the game in a 30-meter course and 8-minute quarters, ranges from a distance of 1300 meters and up to a maximum of 1600 meters (Approximatelty one mile). Distances swum in a smaller pool (25 meters) and with shorter quarters are somewhere around 1200 meters average distance. For our purposes we will choose 1500 meters as the distance that a top player would swim during a high level game. Many players will swim less than that.

Calculations from time and motion analyses indicate that field players spend only 45% to 55% of actual game time in a horizontal body position. The remainder of the time is spent performing activities in predominantly vertical body positions, with and without contact with an opponent, and at low, moderate, and high intensity. Reflecting the increase of zone, and extra-man offense and defense, in modern water polo, we will choose 50% as the amount of time spent swimming in a horizontal position, and 50% spent in a vertical position.

Subtracting two time-outs (2-minutes each), two 2-minute quarter breaks and a five-minute half time break during the 60 minute game, a total of 20-25 minutes of actual playing time is spent moving in a horizontal position, and about the same amount of time (20-25 minutes) is spent in a vertical position.

HOW FAR AND HOW FAST?
When a coach is trying to decide how to train a player who swims about a mile during a game, the total distance swum is not as important as how it is broken down in terms of distance, and how intense each portion is. A player does not swim 1500 meters without stopping; but swims a variety of shorter distances of 2-25 meters in length. A player also does not swim the full 1500 meters at all-out speed. So, in determining the energy demands of playing a game, we have to look at the intensity and duration of each swim that makes up the total 1500 meter distance.

Most of the high intensity swimming in a game occurs during the counterattack and defending the counterattack. Assuming about 8 possessions for each team during each quarter played, a player who plays the whole game must swim up and down the pool a total of 16 times per quarter (offense and defense), or about 64 times per game. Assuming that a player swims from the 4-6 meter line at one end of the pool to the 4-6-meter line at the other end during a counterattack, that is approximately 18-22 meters per swim maximum (about 20 meters per swim on average in a 30 meter pool), for a total of about 1100-1200 meters of high intensity counterattack swimming.

This is for a player who is never substituted for. Since this rarely happens in a game, the most any one player would play would be about 80 percent of the game, or a total of approximately 800-1000 meters of high intensity counterattack. For purposes of this discussion we will use the higher figure of 1000 meters.

The rest of the distance swum (approximately 500 meters) is to gain position over an opponent, or defend an attacking maneuver. These kinds of swims are lower in intensity and of shorter distance (2-5 meters); and are not considered intense enough that they have to be trained for. Most of the training for these types of movements can be performed with short, start and stop, and change of direction drills.

SUMMARY OF MOVEMENTS IN WATER POLO
Following is a summary of the kind of swimming that occurs in a high level water polo game for a starter who plays about 80% of the game:
1. 40 to 50 high intensity counterattack swims of 18-20 meters of length, that take about 12-14 seconds to complete.
2. Each high intensity swim is usually followed by 10-15 second "rest" period of lower intensity swimming, holding or gaining position, or in a vertical position in the water.
3. In addition, every player has rest periods when he is "on the bench" and rest periods between quarters and time-outs.
4. The maximum longest period of intense time during each quarter that a player has to endure before taking a long break would be about 12 X 20 meters with a 15 second break between each swim. This would be like doing a swim set of 12 X 20 meters @ a 30 second interval. This is equivalent to a one to one (1:1) work to rest interval; 15 seconds of high intensity work, followed by 15 seconds of rest.
5. There will be times during a game where a player might have to endure two or three counterattacks in a row, with little rest in-between each one; but these occur infrequently, perhaps twice each quarter at the most. This would be the equivalent of swimming 8-10 x 40-60 meter repeats, dispersed throughout the game.

ENERGY REQUIREMENTS FOR A WATER POLO GAME
Most of the energy to contract the muscles, in order to perform each of the 40 x 20-meter counterattack swims (10-14 seconds duration) as described above, can be derived from the breakdown of the ATP molecule in the muscle cells that is produced by the breakdown of creatine-phosphate (CP).

A short rest period of about the same time interval, will quickly restore CP levels; allowing the athlete to repeat these short and intense activities over and over again. If enough rest is allowed, the water polo athlete can rely almost entirely on the ATP-CP energy system to perform these swims and complete a water polo game. So in order to train the exact energy system used in a game, the training should duplicate the intensity and duration of the swim, as well as the rest periods in the game. This can be accomplished in practice by performing 20 meter intervals every 30 seconds, approximately a one to one work to rest ratio; the same as in a game.

A final game analysis of the movements during a water polo game, brings us to the conclusion that "the creatine-phosphate (CP) energy producing system is ultimately the predominant energy system utilized during a water polo game".

As mentioned above, there will also be several times during a game where rest periods are very short; or a player has to put together two or three swims without any rest at all (as in back to back counterattacks). Although these kinds of swims do not occur often in a game, they still have to be trained for. Even though the CP system will still contribute energy for these kinds of swims, the use of creatine phoshate has its limits. Consequently, another energy system must take over the chore of producing ATP for muscle contraction.

These kinds of swims that require sprinting for distances of 25-50 meters, and take more than 15 seconds to complete, will use the glycolytic (lactic acid) energy system that utilizes stored carbohydrates (glycogen) and blood sugar to produce ATP. It has been estimated that the glycolytic system produces up to 20 percent of the energy for muscle contraction during a water polo game. While this system produces more than ample ATP for muscle contraction, it also produces lactic acid that can cause fatigue to occur in the muscles. For the most part, players in a game should have sufficient time to recover from the lactic acid accumulation during quarter and time out periods and other times of relative inactivity.

There may be a few times during a game when a player will accumulate higher levels of lactic acid. This can occur from several consecutive sprints without an opportunity for sufficient rest. Without immediate rest, it could impede performance during subsequent play. Since these occasions of insufficient recovery time can occur during the course of a game, although infrequently, the cumulative effects of the production of lactic acid have to be trained for, by occasionally swimming sets of 25 to 50 meter sprints in practice.

In planning for training of the two systems, both of which are classified as anaerobic (without oxygen) in nature, a coach can figure that about 80% of the intense swimming (about 600-800 meters) will require use of the ATP-CP system, and 20% (about 200-400 meters) will require the use of the glycolytic-lactic acid system.

HOW INTENSE IS THE GAME, REALLY?

In reality, the intense swimming as described above is only a smaller portion of the time of the entire game; at most about 30-35% of the total time (about 20 minutes of a one hour game). In analyzing what a water polo player actually does during a game, we can dispel the notion that while water polo is a high intensity game, only about a third of the time, or less, of the 60 minute game is actually spent in high intensity swimming activities. The rest of the time is spent performing short distance, less intense maneuvering swims, performing in vertical offensive and defensive positions; or doing nothing at all during periods of inactivity.

Since most players do not play the whole game without being substituted for, we can safely say that the above estimates of high intensity swims is about the maximum that could occur at the collegiate and international levels of men's water polo played in a 30 meter course. The above estimates should be downgraded by another 20% for women, and boys and girls, who play in 25 meter (yard) courses.

So what we are really talking about here, in terms of actually training athletes to play a water polo game, is training the water polo athlete to perform about 40 short intense swims of 15-20 meters in length, and about 10-15 intense swims of 25-50 meters in length; all in about one hours time. The question that begs to be answered is, since a distance of more than 50 meters at a time is rarely covered during a game (if at all), and the total distance of intense swimming covers only about 1000 meters, why are some water polo coaches training their players by swimming total distances of 4000-10,000 meters per day in practice, and requiring them to perform repeat practice swims of 100, 200, 400 and 500 meters at a time? That kind of training just doesn't make sense.

HOW THEN SHOULD WATER POLO COACHES APPROACH TRAINING?

After analyzing the specific physical requirements of playing a water polo game, coaches have to apply the principles of training and scientific research (as described in Part 1 of this chapter) to the physical requirements, and then learn how to correctly train their athletes to meet these requirements. There are several ways that a coach can go about training his athletes.

One way is to just load hours and hours of all kinds of physical training and swimming on the players, and hope that something works. This method is a wasteful use of the short and precious pool time that we have to train our athletes; and is by far the least efficient method of training a team. Not only that, it is absolutely unnecessary! As a water polo coach, you cannot allow yourself to fall into this trap of "more is better".

The key to efficient training of your athletes is to do just the right amount of the correct training that will get your players in the best shape to play the game. Any more than that is a waste of time that should be spent playing water polo. The best way to train the players with swimming, is to duplicate the total distance swum in a game, the intensity and the duration of each swim, and the rest period that occurs in the game.

Ideally, in order to duplicate the kind of swimming done in a game, the daily swim workout should be only about 800-1500 (max) meters in total distance, consisting of 10, 20, 25 and 50 meter intense swims to cover that distance, while allowing a one to one work to rest interval. No more than that is necessary! After that, the rest of the training session can be used to condition the players to play the game, by actually playing the game (drills, counterattack, scrimmage, etc).

At the very least, the training and conditioning should be water polo related. Don't worry coaches, your players will be more than ready to play a water polo game with this kind of training; especially if you spend the rest of the practice performing high intensity water polo related activties instead of swimming. The bottom line here is that water polo is a sport that requires that the athletes be trained to perform the specific activities of the sport, exactly as they are performed in competition. Train your athletes to play water polo, not to be competitive swimmers and competitive weight lifters! More on strength training later.

ADDITIONAL WATER POLO SPECIFIC TRAINING
In addition to straight swim sets, swim sets that incorporate water polo skills and simulate game conditions (head-up swimming, change of direction swims, stop and go swims that require acceleration, etc.) should also be performed on a regular basis. The most effective and specific type of water polo swim training can be performed during full-court counterattack drills and scrimmages.

Because 45-50% of the game is spent in a vertical position in the water, legs must be conditioned every day; including specific leg conditioning drills that utilize the way that the legs are used in a game (shooting, shot blocking, horizontal to vertical, 6 on 5 passing and 6 on 5 defense, etc). (See "Training the Legs" below).

There are positional differences in the skills and abilities required of field players that also have to be trained. Two-meter offensive and defensive players spend more time in contact with opponents, spend longer in a vertical body position, have more frequent transitions between horizontal and vertical body positions and perform a different variety of actions at different frequencies than other field players. These positional differences have to be trained for. The same thing holds for training the specific position of goalkeeper. (Covered in Part 2 of the Water Polo Series)

INTERVAL TRAINING
As mentioned above, the most efficient method of training water polo players, aside from actually playing the game, is to use the interval training system. An advantage of "interval swimming" is that a coach can exactly control the distance, frequency, and intensity that each athlete swims, by changing the work and rest intervals. The kind of swimming that occurs in a game or practice is the most specific swimming in water polo. However, because of the variety of the distances swum and the intensity of each swim in a game, these kinds of game swims can be more haphazard and different for every player.

Interval training is more consistent, and insures that every player gets the same training. Interval swimming is also great for water polo conditioning because it stimulates game conditions; which is bursts of speed followed by slower paced or no swim rest intervals. By alternating rest intervals with work intervals, and changing the time of the rest intervals, a coach can duplicate any kind of conditions that occur in a water polo game.

BASIC PRINCIPALS OF INTERVAL SWIMMING

In water polo, we are most interested in the principle of interval swimming that says "the shorter the distance swum, and the longer the rest interval between each swim interval, the faster the player can swim". Water polo players need to swim at "game pace", or greater, in order for the body to be stressed enough that it will adapt and swim faster.

The best way to achieve this is to swim shorter intervals; and at the same time allow sufficient rest so that that swimmer can maintain the same fast speed for each interval. Even longer swim intervals can be swum at game pace, if enough rest is given between swims. Applying what we learned from film analysis and specificity of training, the distances a player swims in practice, should be similar to the distances swum in a game. So, repeating game distances of 5, 10, 15, 20, 25, 30, 40 and 50 meters is the best way to train water polo players.

Depending on the amount of rest between each swim repeat, players should be swimming these distances at counterattack game pace or faster. In general, the LONGER THE DISTANCE SWUM AT HIGH INTENSITY, THE MORE REST IS REQUIRED TO ASSURE GAME PACE SPEED.

HOW MUCH REST IS REQUIRED?

Training at shorter distances between 5 and 25 meters that rely on the ATP-CP energy system that does not produce lactic acid, only requires enough rest between swims to restore creatine-phosphate (CP) in the muscles in order to repeat the next swim. Usually a 1:1 work to rest interval will accomplish this. Distances of 30-100 meters that rely on the lactic acid producing glycolytic system, requires greater rest intervals in order to allow the dissipation of some of the lactic acid. Work to rest intervals of 1 to 2 for 30-50 meter swims are sufficient, while work to rest intervals of 1 to 3 or even 1 to 4 are common for distances of 75 and 100 meters.

A swimming set of 200 meter swims can be attempted once every 3-4 weeks, as long as sufficient rest is given between 200's to insure game pace speed (5 minutes rest). Swims of this sort take a lot out of player. Consequently not more than 600-800 meters of total distance of these kinds of swims should be performed at a time.

It is a coaches decision to have the team perform sets of 200 meter swims; but at the same time the coach must realize that at no time during a competitive water polo game does a player swim a distance of 200 meters with stopping. The best way to swim 200 meters is to break up the total distance into 25 and 50 meters hard swims interspersed with slower swims of 25 and 50 meters; thus simulating game conditions of hard swims followed by slower less intense swims.

SLOW SWIMMING BETWEEN REPEATS

Total dissipation of lactic acid requires several hours of rest to accomplish. Slow swimming during each rest period, rather than just floating in the water, does result in more lactic acid being utilized by the muscles, and converted back to ATP. Consequently, low aerobic type swimming is highly recommended during rest periods that are between longer intense swims of greater than 50 meters.

Some coaches make the mistake of thinking that because a player is swimming a short distance, that it is OK to make the rest interval very short. An example of this would be swimming a set of 10 X 50 yards, with only a 5 second rest between repeats. The result of this type of set is that the shorter rest intervals do not allow the athlete to recover, and so he must slow down to a pace that is much slower than game-counterattack pace.

What usually occurs is that little or no anaerobic training effect takes place (this is required for playing water polo); but instead the effect is more aerobic in nature. A better set of 50 yard repeats would allow 30-60 seconds of rest between 50's; so that the swimmer can go at game pace, and not have to slow down because of insufficient recovery time.

It is highly recommended by sports scientists, that any swims that build-up lactic acid should be done at the end of practice, especially if the coach hopes that the players have to perform or learn any water polo related game skills during the rest of the practice session. It is well known that the fatigue from the accumulation of lactic acid can affect sports skill performance and learning. Performing lactic acid swim sets at the end of practice allows the athlete almost a full day to recover, or at least until the next practice session.

ULTRA SHORT SWIM SETS

In the past, both swimming and water polo coaches have resorted to "race specific" or "game specific" sprint training in order to train swimmers to swim faster. This type of interval training is defined as "speed work" and consists of repeating all-out 25, 50, 75, 100 and 200-meter swims with long rest intervals interspersed between the work intervals. Because of the high quality of the swims over these distances, the lactic acid produced, and the fatigue that accompanies it; coaches have used these kinds of intervals sparingly during training sessions.

Coaches are faced with a dilemma, in that our athletes need to perform "game specific quality" swims in practice in order to swim those speeds during games; but the fatiguing affects of repeating these kinds of swims in practice detract from learning and performance during the rest of the practice, and in subsequent practices. What can we do to train our athletes to avoid the debilitating effects of all-out sprint training as we have done in the past?

The answer lies in what sports scientists, who specialize in "speed" training, have known for many years; but have not been readily adopted by coaches. They have found that during speed intervals, if the work duration is short enough, even though intensity is very high, and if recovery periods are short; energy sustains mechanically efficient "fast" work, while no buildup of lactate occurs.

Glycogen levels, as well, are not depleted and remain high throughout the short intervals; whereas with longer intervals, glycogen levels depreciate significantly. This type of training where work intervals were only 10-15 seconds long, became known as "ultra-short" training. This training facilitates better sprint performances than those fostered by typical, and mostly inappropriate sprint training that has been utilized by coaches in the past. "Ultra-short" training is very appropriate for water polo, a sport that utilizes more of the ATP/CP system than the lactic-acid glycolytic system; and improves both systems without the debilitating effects of lactic acid build-up.

RECOMMENDATIONS
Ultra-short swim set recommendations for water polo coaches:
1. All sets should be performed with one to one work to rest ratios.
2. The work interval should be somewhere between 5 and 15 seconds.
3. The sprints should start from a horizontal position in the water and performed with the head out of the water.
4. Sets of this sort can be performed daily during the competitive season, including the day prior to a game, without the debilitating effects of lactate accumulation and glycogen depletion.
5. Typical sets include 20 to 40 reps of distances of 10, 15, 20, 25 and 30 meters, utilizing a 1/1 work to rest interval. 50-meter repeats are not considered "ultra-short" because they take longer than 15 seconds to perform. They can also be utilized, however, once or twice a week to simulate the game situation that requires a player to counterattack in both directions with little or no stoppage of the action.
6. No additional swim training is required during a practice as long as the coach also utilizes water polo related conditioning drills, counterattack training, and game related scrimmages.
7. An all-out 100% effort is required of all swims.

SWIM TRAINING FOR WATER POLO

DISTANCE SWUM
Maximum daily swim conditioning for water polo teams should not exceed a total of 500 meters for age group players, 1000 meters for high school players, and 1500 meters for college and national level players. At the end of a typical week, and just prior to a game, the total distance should not be more than 400-500 meters of nothing more than 25 meter repeats. The majority of the swim intervals included in the total maximum distance should be water polo specific distances of 10 to 50 meters in length.

EFFECTIVE TRAINING? KEEP THEM MOVING!
Swim conditioning, as part of a water polo practice, should not require a lot of time to perform. The goal of the water polo coach is to get as much specific conditioning from swimming as possible, in the shortest period of time. This allows the coach to utilize the rest of the practice session to perform water polo specific conditioning that also teaches the skills, tactics and strategy to play the game.

In other words, the coach has to make efficient use of the short pool time that he is given.

A key to running a successful practice is to make it one of constant conditioning, by keeping the players moving at all times. This can be accomplished by combining swimming and skills into drills that will train the players to the maximum level possible. Every part of the practice must include movement of some sort.

Water polo is the only team sport where the athletes are asked to condition at the beginning of a practice session; before they train in their actual sport. In other words, they are conditioning for conditionings sake. This is like asking the basketball or soccer player to go to the track and run laps for a half hour before they do basketball or soccer practice.

Most of the effective conditioning performed in these other sports is "sports specific" training. Water polo can learn from other sports by keeping swim conditioning to a minimum, and concentrating more on sports specific conditioning during the rest of practice. Swimming can only be effective if it closely resembles the intensity, distance and technique that is similar to what is done in a water polo game.

WATER POLO SPECIFIC TRAINING

Head up sprints are the best water polo related swims that a player can do, and should be done every day in practice. The coach should insist that players keep there heads out of the water, so that in a game they will keep their heads up in order to see what is going on around them. A high percentage of the swims sets of 50 meter repeats should be done with the head up to simulate water polo type swimming. All sprint swims of less than 30 meters should be done head up, and all should be started without pushing off the wall to start the swim.

A good water polo swim set is to go all out from the 2-meter line to the opposite two meter line, 20 times, with the head up and not using a wall. When doing 20 sprints of 25 meters, the coach can divide the team into two groups. Set the first group off, and when they reach the other side of the pool, start the second group; thus insuring a one to one work to rest interval. A strong scissor kick should be used to start every swim. In order to simulate water polo starts, the coach can have the players start out by facing the wall, opposite the direction in which they will be swimming. On the whistle, they must turn around first, and then do a scissor or breaststroke kick to get a fast start.

TYPICAL ANAEROBIC SWIM SETS FOR TRAINING WATER POLO PLAYERS

Swim sets that primarily train the ATP/CP anaerobic energy system, the primary system utilized during a water polo game, include repeat swims of 10, 15, 20, 25 and 30-meters at one to one work to rest intervals (e.g. 10 sec swim/10 sec rest); covering a total distance of about 600 to 800 meters (the distance covered in a game).

A majority of the total distance swum should be with the head out of the water. Since sets of this kind rarely accumulate any lactic acid, they can be done anytime during the week leading up to a game, including the day before a game. The only thing that should be changed, the day before a game, is to reduce the total distance to about 400-500 meters.

Examples of these kinds of sets:

20 X 30 meters

25 X 25 meters

40 X 25 meters (20 at the beginning of practice, 20 at the end of practice)

4 sets of 10 X 25 meters with a slow 100 meter swim between sets.

30 X 25 meters

20 X 15 meters followed by 20 X 10 meters

40 X 10 meters

Or any combination of these swims that add up to 800-1000 (max) meters of total distance.

Swim sets that train the other anaerobic system used in water polo, the glycolytic (lactic acid) energy system should include repeat swims of 40, 50, 75 and 100-meter swims at a 1 to 2 or 1 to 3 work to rest interval (e.g. 30 sec swim/60 sec rest or 30 sec swim/90 sec rest) totaling a maximum distance of 400-500 meters (the distance of this kind of swim that is covered in a game).

Part, or all of the rest periods in these types of swims can be swum at a slow aerobic pace that will help the body convert any lactic acid build-up back into ATP. An example of this would be a 30 second swim (about 50 meters), followed by a 25-meter slow swim, followed by a 30 second floating rest period. Repeat 10-12 times. Another example is to swim an all out 100 meters, followed by an easy 50 meter swim, followed by a full minute rest period. Repeat 5-6 times at most.

High intensity lactic acid producing swims that are similar to this should be performed early in the week; or at the end of a workout, so that the players have time to recover. Twice a week is the maximum number of times that players should be asked to perform these kind of longer high intensity swims, and never the day before a game. Examples of these type of swims include:

10 X 50 meters (one to one work to rest intervals, every other one head-up)

10 X 50 meters (one to two work to rest interval, follow each swim with an easy 25 meters, every other one head up)

8 X 75 meters (one to two work to rest interval, follow each swim with an easy 25 meter swim)

5 X 100 meters (one to three work to rest interval, follow each hard swim with an easy 50 meter swim)

3 X 200 meters (4 minute rest period consisting of 100-200 yards of easy swimming folowed by a floating rest)

3-5 X 200 meters combination swims- Any combination of 25 and 50 meter sprints and 25 and 50 meter slow swims. I.e. 50 sprint, 25 easy, 25 sprint, 25 easy, 50 sprint, 25 easy.

CHANGE OF DIRECTION SWIMS

Changing direction at high speed in the middle of the pool is a common occurrence in a water polo game. Simulate this condition by doing a "6-whistle drill". Divide the team into two groups. Start the first group with a whistle until they have gone anywhere from 2-8 strokes.

On every whistle after the first one, they must change direction as quickly as they can; and then swim in the opposite direction as fast as they can. After six whistles and six changes in directions are complete, the coach can start the second group. Vary the distance swum between whistles and repeat about five times for each group.

In order to get the players to look up at the referee when the whistle blows, the coach can point in a different direction every time he blows the whistle. After some whistles the players will continue in the same direction that they were going; and after other whistles they will change direction, depending on which way the coach is pointing.

WATER POLO IM'S

100-yard water polo individual medleys should be swum once every two weeks, so that the same swim muscles used in water polo will be utilized and trained. A water polo IM consists of one length of butterfly head up with a breaststroke kick, one length of backstroke with the upper back and head high out of the water and with a breaststroke kick, one length of breaststroke with the chest coming completely out of the water on each stroke, and one length of head-up freestyle.

DON'T FORGET THE SCISSOR AND BREASTSTROKE KICKS

The scissor kick, as well as the breaststroke kick, are both used all of the time in water polo, but seldom practiced. Quick starts, change of direction, going from horizontal to a vertical position, defending a driver, shooting the ball, intercepting a pass, etc. all require the use of the scissor and breaststroke kicks. A good scissor (breaststroke) kick is essential in water polo for getting a quick start from a vertical position in the water.

Always start sprints by NOT using the wall for a push-off. Having the hips and legs near the surface greatly helps a player initiate the momentum necessary for a fast swim. Start with the hips up, while performing an eggbeater kick. On the "ready" command, start a more rapid eggbeater. On the whistle, explode by using a quick sidestroke/breaststroke kick and an arm pull. Another method is to start by first facing the wall, and then turning around to start the swim.

SWIMMING FAST IN PRACTICE

If the coach wants the players to swim fast, he should closely monitor all swim set times for each player. Use a pace clock or a stop watch, and time all swims. The coach must demand that the players swim fast. A player who loafs swim sets is doing himself and the team a disservice. I tell my players that we will swim less yardage than our opponents; but almost everything that we swim will be fast. Our daily workouts will also be shorter than our opponents; but everything that we do will be performed with intensity, including drills. I would rather make the swim sets shorter, and have the players go all out, then make the sets too long, and have the players swim at a slower pace. In 32 years as a college swim coach, I cannot remember ever swimming more than 2000 yards in a practice, ever! The results speak for themselves.

FITNESS IS HARD TO GAIN, BUT EASY TO LOSE

A coach should provide a year around training program for water polo players, to insure that they stay in water polo shape during the off-season. Consistency in training is one the most important factors in conditioning for any sport. There is an old saying that "Fitness is hard to gain, but easy to lose."

I want my players to get in shape and stay in shape. The worst thing they can do is to get into the vicious cycle of getting in shape, and then getting out of shape, and then getting back in shape again. Most successful water polo programs have some kind of year around training for the players that is closely monitored by the coach. Players left on their own during the off-season usually do very little in the way of conditioning. They will practice shooting until "the cows come home." but swimming on their own time; forget about it!

SWIM TEAM DURING THE OFF-SEASON?

If a coach can provide year around training for water polo players, swimming on the swim team during the off-season is not necessary for water polo players. Some of the top water polo players in the world have never been on a swim team, including many Olympians. Besides that, the training that a water polo player receives on the swim team is not necessarily beneficial for water polo. The water polo coach who spends the time training his athletes in the off-season, will get much better results than relying on a swim coach to train his players incorrectly for water polo.

EFFICIENCY OF TRAINING BY COMBINING

Conditioning by itself does not win water polo games. Players must also learn how to play the game. Most of us have a limited amount of time each day in order to condition the athlete, and to teach him how to play the game at the same time. As coaches, we have to learn how to become more efficient in our training, so that we can do both conditioning and learning the game at the same time. We can easily do this by combining water polo skills and swim conditioning together in a way that is specific to the sport of water polo.

As an example, shooting drills can involve some sort of swimming before the players take a shot. This simulates game conditions and teaches the players how to shoot when they are tired. Instead of having the goalie or a coach on the deck retrieve a ball after a shot, have the player react and quickly swim to retrieve his own ball. Every drill should involve some sort of swim conditioning, even if it is for a short 2-5 meter distance. Remember to "KEEP THEM MOVING" during practice, if you want a well-conditioned team.

WATER POLO SKILL SWIM DRILLS

Following are some specific skills that can be done during sprint swims of 20 yards to 30-meters:

>Head up "look-swims"- Look-swim means that the player should look back on every other stroke. This is useful on the counterattack when looking back for the ball.

>Start all swims without using the wall, so players must use a scissor kick to start. Start facing the wall and then turn to swim.

>Stop and start swims on the whistle, with and without the ball; or, throw the ball ahead about six feet, and then sprint to the ball. Repeat all the way across the pool.

>Change of direction swims, with and without the ball- Six whistles, change of direction on each whistle. Short and intense.

>Going from vertical to horizontal and from horizontal to vertical. Alternate swim bursts with vertical leg jumps. With the ball, go up into a shooting position and eggbeater forward. Without the ball, go up into a blocking position or do several jumps. Jumps can be straight up or lateral; one to the right and one to the left.

>Bursts of speed- Face each other, one player blasts around the other. Turn and catch the player who has just gone around you and pass him. One player starts first; the trailing player must catch him and get around him and into a defensive position. Or simply start one player first, and have the second player try to catch and/or pass the first player.

>Working in pairs, passing the ball while swimming- This drill teaches the players how to pass while on the move. Have the players pass with either hand, and pass to their teammate both wet and dry, to inside and outside arms, and in front of the face.

>Change of direction angle swims- Fast start with a scissor kick, swimming straight ahead. On the first whistle, change direction and swim at a 45-degree angle to the right; next whistle, change direction and swim at 45-degree angle to the left; next whistle, swim straight ahead. Repeat. Make a deliberate 45-degree turn. (With and without the ball).

SWIMMING FOR POWER
1. Use power racks, or stretch cords, tied around the waist and attached to the side of the pool, to create resistance as you swim.

2. Explosive start and stop swims. It takes more power to start an explosive swim from a stopped position in the water.

3. Acceleration swims- Swim 100 meters, starting at a slow pace. Accelerate and swim fast for 6 strokes when the player hears a whistle.

4. Sprints of any kind with the head-up.

DRILLS THAT STIMULATE THE ATP-CREATINE PHOSPHATE (CP) SYSTEM

1. 2-man chase and shoot drill- Swim from the four to the four, one player with the ball, and the other player trailing. Vary the distance the trailer is behind the shooter, vary the angle from the goal, and vary the shot. The coach can start the players in a shoulder to shoulder position, close together or wide apart; or the defender can start directly behind, or way behind the shooter. The closer the defender, the more the shooter has to shoot off the water. If the trailing defender is way behind the shooter, he can pick up the ball, move across the goal, and shoot. If the trailer is close behind as they both swim down the pool, the shooter must continually angle in front of the trailer in order to keep the defender from getting around him.

2. Basic counterattack drills- Start with any number of pairs, 2 on 2, 3 on 3, 4 on 4, 5 on 5, 6 on 6 offense and defense. Have one player hold back a few strokes in order to create a man extra on the counterattack.

3. 6 on 6 create an extra man drill- Starting with a half court six on six situation, the coach can create any kind of counterattack situation that he wants to, by calling out the hat number of one of the offensive players. When the coach calls out the hat number, everyone goes on the counterattack, except the player whose number was called. He goes underwater for several seconds and then chases down the pool.

4. One-way counterattack drill- Both teams play half court at one end of the pool, until a shot is taken or there is a turnover. Both teams counterattack on "anything", a turnover or shot and whether a goal is scored or not. This is a reaction drill as well. The same team counters ten times in a row after stopping and changing directions at each end of the pool. Then the other team does ten counters.

DRILLS THAT STIMULATE THE GLYCOLYTIC (LACTIC ACID) SYSTEM
1. One-on-one counterattack shooting drill (double hernia)- This drill start out in one corner of the pool, with one player starting out at the hips of the other player. They take off together down the pool with one player staying at the hips of the other. The third player in line passes to the player in the front position. The player chasing is harassing the shooter for the length of the pool. Then when the shooter takes the off-the-water shot at the other end of the pool, both players imediately react back in the other direction down the center of the pool. The chaser becomes the shooter and the shooter becomes the chaser.

At the other end of the pool, the type of shot taken depends on the distance between the two players and the speed of the two players; but in most cases the shooter should have time to pick up the ball and shoot. After the first two players are half way down the pool, the next two players in line will start the drill. There has to be enough spacing between pairs so that they don't stack up behind each other; but the drill must be continuous and on going.

In the first part of the drill, the coach must make sure that the chaser plays good defense and not allow an easy shot. Three goalies are required for this drill. Two goalies are in the goal blocking shots and the third goalie (or a field player) retrieves the first shot and passes to the player swimming down the pool in the other direction. Rotate goalies as necessary. This is one of my favorite drills, because it gets players in shape, simulates game conditions, and teaches players how to shoot when they are tired. (See Diagram 6-3 on the next page).

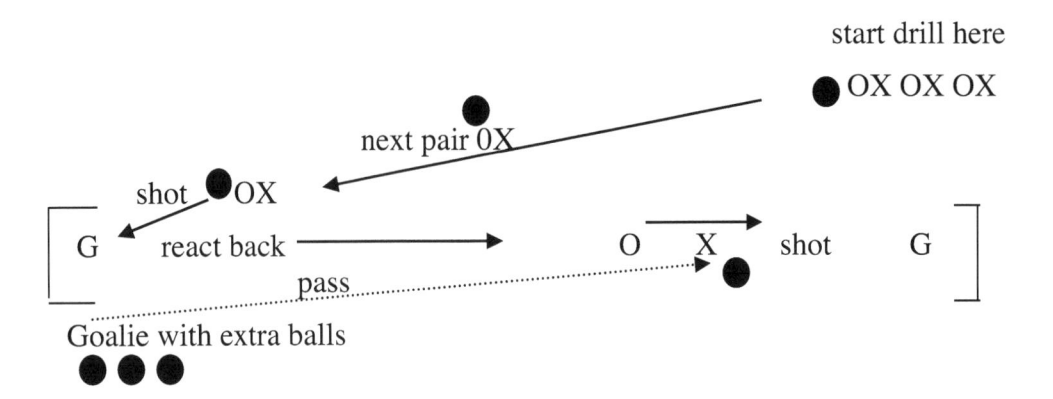

```
                                                        start drill here
                                    ●                   ● OX OX OX
                          next pair OX
              shot ● OX
          ┌────◄─────────────────────────────────────────────────────┐
          │  G     react back ────────►            O   X  ───► shot  G │
          └──────────────pass┄┄┄┄┄┄┄┄┄┄┄┄┄┄┄┄┄┄┄┄┄┄┄┄►●────────────────┘
            Goalie with extra balls
                ● ● ●
```

Diagram 6-3: Double hernia drill

2. 2 on 2, 3 on 3, 4 on 4 full court two-way counters- Create man up on first counter by calling out a player's hat number; or have one player start in a trailing position. Counter back in the other direction on the shot. There should be a free man in both directions. The coach has to make sure that all players chase and play defense on the first counterattack, as well as on the second counterattack in the other direction.

3. 6 on 6 two-way counters-Start by playing half-court offense at one end, then start by reacting to the shot; or start by calling out an offensive player's hat number and have him go under water. After the shot is taken at the other end. both teams counter back . This drill also is a great conditioner, and it teaches the players how to cover back when they have a free man in one direction. Players should react to the shot at both ends of the pool; whether or not it goes into the goal, is rebounded, or goes out of bounds.

4. Three-way counterattacks (Six on six)- Start with a six on six front court offense at one end of the pool. React to the shot in all three directions. No stopping for tipped shots, goals or rebounds. Stop after three counterattacks and discuss what went right or wrong. Then do the drill over again. This is a very tiring drill; but it creates all kinds of different counterattack situations. In order to insure that there is an extra man on the first counterattack, start by having an offensive player go under water.

5. Three-way counterattacks (four on four)- Same as above, but with two teams of four players. After the first two teams of four players complete the drill, insert two fresh teams of four players each. At the end of each three-way counter, re-insert the first groups of two 4-man teams.

SCRIMMAGE

The best way to train the energy systems used during a water polo game is to scrimmage during practice. The coach should not interrupt play for critique, except during natural breaks in the scrimmage, like after a goal is scored. To increase the workload during the scrimmage, the teams have to counterattack after a goal is scored; instead of resting by lining up in the center of the pool to re-start the scrimmage.

TRAINING THE LEGS

A strong eggbeater kick is probably the single most important physical attribute that a player can possess for success in water polo. Almost every aspect of the game requires leg strength to perform at your best. Shooting, driving, defensive positioning, man up, man down, shot blocking, hole position, hole defense, and the goalie position are just some of the areas that require a good eggbeater kick in order to be successful.

EGGBEATER TECHNIQUE

The skill consists of alternating circular movements of the legs, that produce an upward force by the water in order to keep the player afloat in a vertical position. The legs move in alternate circular directions during the kick. The right leg moves clockwise and the left leg moves counter-clockwise. The path of the feet traces an elongated oval during the kick. When one leg is in the recovery phase, the other leg is in the power phase.

All the joints of the lower limb are active during the eggbeater kick: the hips, knees, ankles and the joints of the foot. In diagram 6-4 below, the right leg is pushing down on the water in the power (propulsion) phase of extension and abduction (towards the center), while the left leg is in recovery phase of flexion and adduction (away from the center). The alternating motion of the legs produces a consistent upward lift, so that the body will always remain in a high position in the water.

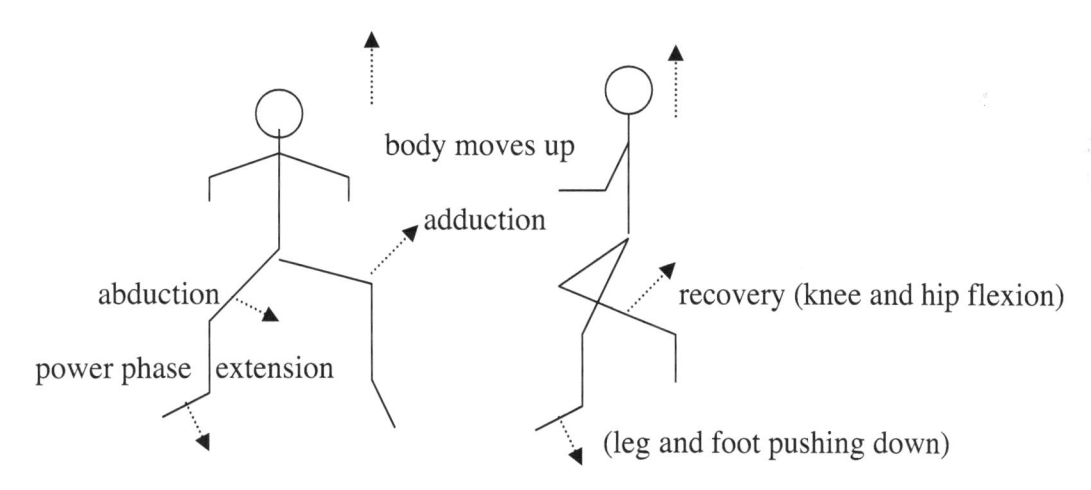

Diagram 6-4: Alternating eggbeater kick. Right leg is in the power (propulsion) phase. Left leg is in the recovery phase.

UPWARD THRUST

The force necessary to thrust the body upward occurs in two ways. One is due to the hydrodynamic lift forces of the foot as it pushes down on the water, and the other comes from the drag forces that are created by the rapid downward and inward movements of the foot and leg during the stroke. As the lower legs and feet are driven downward and inward towards the midline, the water passes faster over the top of the foot and leg, which acts like an airfoil of an airplane wing.

If the flow of fluid is faster over the top of the foot due to the movement and shape of the airfoil (foot), then a low-pressure area is created. The slower water moving under the foot creates high pressure. The difference of pressure (gradient) will help the body to be suspended or lifted in the water; and is similar to the lift that is created on the wings of an airplane.

While the lift provided by the foot as it pushes down on the water, is compared to the lift on an airplane wing; another force is created by the inward and downward movement of the leg. This force, which also contributes to upward thrust, comes from the drag resistance created by moving the legs through the water; much like the drag resistance produced in swimming, by moving the arm and hand through the water.

CONTRIBUTION OF BUOYANCY TO LIFT
Because the buoyant force of the water that is pushing up on the body largely negates the force of gravity pulling down on the body, it doesn't take that much force to lift a body up and out of the water. Because of the almost weightless condition of a body floating in the water, the athlete performing the eggbeater kick does not have to produce the same amount of upward force as would be required to support the body jumping off the solid ground. The only force needed is to supplement the upward buoyant force already being supplied by the water.

POWER IN THE LEGS
Similar to the hand pulling through the water while swimming, it takes power to produce the movement of the body upward. Power comes from both the force of the legs thrusting down and the velocity of the legs moving through the water. (Force x Velocity = Power). The force created by drag and lift can only do so much to lift the body out of the water; for the same reason that the force of the arms do not contribute a lot to moving the swimmer forward. Some of the force produced is dissipated into pushing water down; so does not contibute as much to the power that is needed to lift the body up.

The force (F) that is created by pushing down with the feet, has to be efficient in order to be effective and lift the athlete higher out of the water. In other words, it is important to get as much effective force as possible by correctly positioning the feet and legs during the downward thrust. This is similar to positioning the hand and arm during the swim stroke. This underscores the importance of proper technique in the eggbeater in order to get the maximum force possible.

The other way to create more power to thrust the body upward is to increase the velocity component (V) of power. This is accomplished by increasing the speed of the feet and the legs as they move through the water. It has been reported that the height maintained in the eggbeater kick is strongly related to foot speed. Water polo players who want to rise further out of the water by using the eggbeater kick, must increase the speed that their legs and feet move through the water. A rapid knee extension allows the athlete to maintain higher foot speed, and apply greater forces to the water.

This rapid movement of the lower leg and foot causes water to flow at a higher speed over the top of the foot, creating more propulsion from lift. The fast leg movement also increases the drag resistance forces that in addition to the lift forces, help to keep the player suspended. While a player can be trained to increase foot and leg speed, it is the joint structures of the legs, and the technique of correctly positioning the feet and legs, that also contributes a lot to upward lift.

SKILL AND TECHNIQUE
Skill in the eggbeater is likely related to the range of motion occurring in the legs, and the speed of movement of the lower leg and foot in the power phase. The key to the skilled eggbeater is the angle of the foot and lower leg that allows a larger surface area of the bottom of the foot to push through the water. The foot must be flexed and the ankle rotated out to start the stroke to provide this large surface area.

The increased surface area of the foot not only aids the lift forces that are created by the foil created by the foot; but also increases the frontal area (bottom of the foot) to create more force from drag resistance. The most difficult part of the kick is the ability to rotate the leg outwards, and at the same time flex the knee, hip and ankle in order to position the foot for the maximum surface area pushing on the water.

RANGE OF MOTION
The range of motion of the hip and knee will also determine the speed of the foot; as a greater range of motion over the same time will produce a faster foot speed. Power is produced throughout the full range of motion. The bigger the range of motion, the more power will be produced for a longer period of time. This requires that the starting point of the knee must be as high as possible and near the surface of the water.

Diagram 6-5 on the next page, shows the left knee in a high position at the start of the downward thrust, parallel to the surface of the water, and forming a 90 degree angle with the body. The dashed line shows the same leg at full extension at the finish of the downward thrust of the eggbeater. The difference between the starting (fully flexed) position and the finish (fully extended) position of the leg is the "range of motion" of the leg hip joint (as indicated by arrow). A player can get the maximum range of motion (and thus produce more power) by starting the knee at the highest point possible (bring it up near the surface), and then fully extending the knee at the finish of the power phase of the kick.

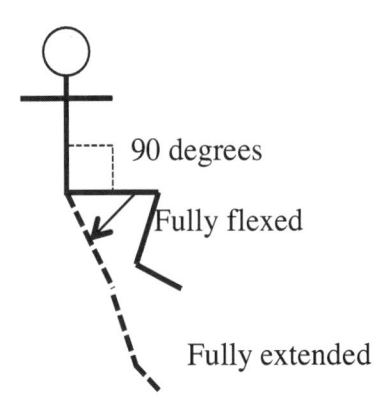

Diagram 6-5: Full range of motion from fully flexed (solid line) to fully extended (dashed line) as indicated by arrow.

It is been shown, that warming up the muscles and joints that will be used in water polo, is the best way to increase the range of motion around each joint. A good warm up will insure that the knee, hip and ankles are able to go through the full range of motion necessary for putting the leg and foot in the best position for creating maximum power and thrust. Note: Static stretching before a player perfroms the eggbeater in the water will do nothing to increase the range of motion of the kick.

An excellent range of motion, as well as conditioning drill, is one that I learned fron Genai Kerr, former UC Irvine and Olympic team goalie. After a good warm up, get into a vertical position in the water, with the hands at the surface of the water, both at a 30-40 degree angle out to the side of the body. Do a set of twenty eggbeater kicks by bringing the knees up to touch the hands on each kick of the legs. Do several sets of this drill to help increase your range of motion.

THE ROLE OF HEREDITY IN THE EGGBEATER KICK
Genetics is an important factor involved in the ability to correctly move the legs through the water and in the correct foot position. The ability to generate force as well as leg speed, has a lot to do with the bone and joint structure and skeletal muscle configuration that allows the leg and foot to be rotated and flexed to a position that produces maximum speed, as well a maximum foot surface area.

While some athletes have joint, bone and muscle structures that allow them to more easily get into the correct form to perform the kick, this ability is not inherent in all people. An example of this can be seen in competitive swimming, where certain athletes have the ability to swim the breaststroke and perform the "frog" kick, while others don't have that ability; but are better at other strokes like the crawl stroke, and kicks that require an up and down motion, like the flutter kick.

Since the breaststroke kick and the eggbeater kick use similar mechanics, both require a similar joint and muscle structure to perform them correctly. The bottom line is that if you want to be a good breaststroker, or have the leg structure to perform the eggbeater, choose your parents carefully.

THE ROLE OF TRAINING
The legs can be trained to move faster and with more power, by training the systems that supply the energy for the contracting muscles (muscle fibers) to move the legs rapidly through the water. This can be accomplished by overloading the eggbeater leg muscles in practice, with repetitive and explosive movements similar to the ones that are used in a game. Everyone can be taught the proper technique for performing the eggbeater kick, as well as be trained to perform the kick over and over again with maximum power.

That being said, the person who has not inherited the structural characteristics that allow the best application of force, will probably not achieve the same level as the athlete who has inherited the necessary leg structure; even if they perfrom the exact same training. Similar to swimming fast, performing the eggbeater kick has more to do with inherited muscle and joint structure, using proper form and technique, speed of leg and foot movement and range of motion; then it does with the actual strength of the muscles.

As mentioned above, it doesn't take a lot of leg force to power the body out of the water, especially with the contribution of buoyance to the upward movement of the body. It takes just the right amount of force, properly applied for maximum efficiency; along with fast leg movements that can be trained in the water. Lidting heavy weights to gain stronger muscles does nothing to improve the eggbeater kick. This is because having stonger muscles does not equate to more force in the water and to a stronger eggbeater.

Most of that force is just wasted, because it is not properly applied because of the position of the feet and legs; in addition to a lot being wasted on moving water. Moving water down when you push on it does nothing to add to the power necessary to create a propulsive force to lift the body. The value of resistance training exercises, like squats, is very questionable for improving the eggbeater kick.

PROPER FORM
The water polo player must utilize proper form during the eggbeater in order to insure maximum lift of the body. This includes having the leg and foot in the proper starting position, all the way through the power phase, to the recovery phase, and back to the starting position.

STARTING POSITION
To start the kick, the hips start in a position close to 80-90 degrees of flexion (bring top of leg up almost parallel to the water surface) with the top of the leg rotated out to the side at 30-40 degrees from the center of the body. The knee is flexed close to 15 degrees (bring heel up under buttocks) and laterally rotated at the start of the kick.

The toes of the foot should be brought up by flexing the ankle, while the lower leg is rotated outward so that the toes are pointing out and away from the center of the body. Placing the leg and foot in this position insures the largest surface area for the foil created by the foot, as well as the maximum range of motion of the leg. (See diagram 6-6 below).

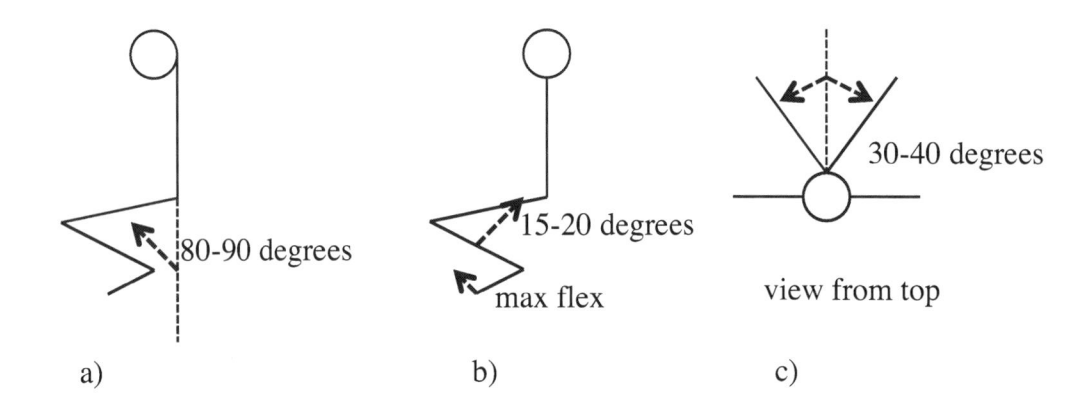

Diagram 6-6: Starting position of leg. a) top of leg flexed 80-90 degrees from vertical. b) knee flexed 15-20 degrees, maximum flexion of foot. c) both legs out to the side at about 30-40 degrees.

PROPULSION (POWER PHASE)
The major force-producing portion of the stroke occurs when the foot is brought down, forward and inward while the knee and hip are extending down. Propulsion is gained by the inwards and downward movements of the lower legs and feet that are moving alternately. Maximum propulsion occurs when the legs are rapidly and fully extended as shown in Diagram 6-4 above).

One of the keys to the skilled eggbeater is the angle of the foot and lower leg during the power phase of the stroke. To improve the airfoil shape, the foot is brought down (like pushing down on a car gas pedal) while the bottom of foot is turned inward. The shape of the foot must be carefully controlled by the swimmer, to ensure that the airfoil shape is maintained during the power portion of the stroke.

Common errors in the eggbeater kick are:
- Not enough flexion of the hip during recovery. The knee should be brought up as close to the surface as possible (80-90 degrees from vertical).
-Not enough extension of the hip so the power phase is limited. (Fully extend leg down)--
-Not enough hip medial rotation to cock the foot and lower leg to create an airfoil. (Lower leg and foot must rotate out to side)
- Keeping the hips too flexed throughout the stroke, rather than forcefully extending during the power stroke. (Extend top of leg fully)
- Not enough of a circular motion of the lower legs. Legs should be in constant motion.
- Moving legs too slow (Legs must move quick and fast)

- Too much up and down motion, which does not produce as much lift as movement forward and back and sideways (left and right).
- Too much bouncing or lack of stability, where player does not maintain a steady height and vertical posture. (Slight sitting position in the water, with the legs in front of the body and the trunk in a vertical position. One leg pushing while other is recovering-smooth and constant motion).
- Legs not positioned at correct angle out to the side. A starting position out to the side at about 30-40 degrees is preferred.

CONDITIONING THE LEGS

FOR BEST RESULTS, WORK YOUR LEGS IN THE WATER

You can improve your legs with training, up to a point. Be specific and do most of your leg training in the water. Water polo drills that involve the legs, like the shooting position, blocking position, hips up defense position, guarding 2-meters-changing sides, etc. are ways that a player can use the legs the same way that they are used in a game. Walking with both hands out of the water, hands on top of the head, or hands on a ball that is situated on top of the head, are other ways to condition the legs while walking.

Coaches should make sure that the player's elbows remain out of the water when walking. Changing body position while walking; so that the player goes forward, backwards, and sideways, insures that the legs are fully conditioned. Start out in forward position and rotate a quarter turn to the right on each whistle. On the next lap have then rotate to the left a quarter turn at a time. Walking distances should be kept short (less than 20 yards at a time) so that the players can execute the eggbeater at maximum intensity.

SHOOTING AND BLOCKING LEG CONDITIONING

Using the legs and moving forward in a vertical position, with the hand in a shooting or blocking position, closely resembles the way that the legs will be used in the game. If shooting with the right hand, the left shoulder should be pointed forward slightly, the left hand in the water and using a sculling motion, and the right hand in the air and held above the right shoulder and the head. (See Picture insert 6-A on the right)

The body position for blocking is more "square" to the shooter, with one hand straight up and slightly in front of the shoulder, and the other hand in the water, sculling for support. These skills must be practiced in both the shooting and blocking positions, and also performed while walking 5-10 yards at a time. (See Picture insert 6-B on the right)

Picture 6-B: Shot blocking position

HORIZONTAL TO VERTICAL

Alternating the shooting and blocking positions with swimming and changes of direction, is a great way to work the legs similar to a game situation. This also gets the player used to going from a horizontal to vertical position, a necessary water polo skill. Examples include sprinting 6 strokes with the ball, quickly pick it up and get into a shooting position, eggbeater forward 2-3 yards, put the ball back in the water and repeat until 100 yards is covered.

Or start in horizontal position, without the ball and facing the wall, rotate over the hips in the opposite direction, take two strokes and get up into a vertical blocking position, walk forward 2 yards; again reverse direction and swim back to original horizontal position; repeat ten times. Add a forward lunge at the end of the 2 yard blocking position to simulate knocking down the player with the ball.

RESISTANCE DRILLS FOR THE LEGS

Adding resistance during training in the water will overload the legs, and also help to improve them. Adding resistance while performing the eggbeater kick in the water, is the most effective way to strengthen the legs; because it exactly duplicates the motion of the legs, and in the same way that they are used when playing water polo.

Quote from Terry Schroeder (Four time USA Olympic hole-man and USA Men's Olympic Team head coach. "I always gained the most benefit in strength training for my legs with resistance type exercises in the pool".

There are a number of ways to train the legs by putting additional resistance on the body. This overloads the muscles and makes them work harder to perform the eggbeater kick. You don't need to risk injury by loading up the legs with very heavy weights; just enough to make the legs work harder than they are used to.

PUSH DOWN FOR RESISTANCE

Having one partner push down on the other partner's shoulders, while doing eggbeater repeats, is a great way to increase resistance on the legs. Players can alternate between having the hands in or out of the water. The time that the player is being pushed down can vary from 5 to 15 seconds. Less time means more pressure from the player doing the pushing, while more time means less pressure.

Pictures 6-C: Push down on shoulders to create resistance for the legs.

An example of this sort of exercise would be 10 reps of 5 seconds each, 8 reps of 10 seconds each, and 5 reps of 15 seconds each. The coach should also vary the rest period between each repeat, usually 5 or 10 seconds. Alternate the player who is pushing and the player doing the eggbeater, after each set.

PAIR RESISTANCE-COMBATIVE TRAINING
Have two players face each other, with their hands placed on each other's shoulders. On the whistle have both players do an eggbeater kick, trying to push the other player backwards. This is great resistance training for the eggbeater kick; especially if both players are evenly matched.

There are a multitude of drills that can be done one on one with a partner, including back to back, alternate spinning moves, front to back moves, etc. Drills for the 2-meter player and defender can also be done with a partner, and is a great way to train the legs to play those two positions. Fronting and holding position, no rules positioning drills, spin drills, step out drills and turning your man are all examples of these kinds of 2-meter specific drills. (See Pictures 6-D below)

Pictures 6-D: Partner combative drills for the legs

HEAVY BALLS
Using weighted balls in the water is a great way to add resistance to the legs. These drills can be done with one player holding the ball above his head, or with two players passing a weighted ball between them, using both hands at the same time. Both players can be in the water; or one player in the water and one player on the deck. The further apart the players are from each other, the harder they have to work their legs to push the ball to each other. While in the water, the distance between players can vary anywhere from 3-10 feet, depending on the weight of the ball.

Balls weighing from 6-12 pounds can be used for this drill. Add variety by changing from different weight balls and varying the distance between players. In order to overload the legs only, do not allow the players to put their hands in the water at any time during these drills. (See Pictures 6-E on the next page).

Pictures 6-E: Hold ball over head or pass between players with two hands

EXPLOSIVE JUMPS

Explosive jumps are an important part of the game and should be practiced every few days. On the whistle, players jump up as high as they can. You can have the players do this while walking, while in a stationary position, or even while swimming. Half of the jumps can be done by pushing off with the hands, and half without using the hands.

An excellent drill is to have the players sprint four strokes freestyle; then jump up and to the high left, followed immediately with a jump up and to the high right, repeat for 100 yards. Jump drills can include jumping straight up, high right and high left, and low right and low left. The coach can use his hands to indicate what kind of jump he wants; and the players must mimic his movement. (See pictures 6-F below)

Picturea 6-F: Jump high left and right, overhead, and low left and right.

OVER THE GOAL

A drill that can be done using the goal as a reference, is to have a player start at the left post, facing the goal, with his hands held at shoulder level. He then uses his legs to jump up and reach for the top bar (or higher) with his hands, moves 2-feet to the right, jumps again, repeating 6 times across the goal without the hands ever touching the water. Then he starts on the right post and repeat 6 jumps while moving to the left post. This can be repeated by pushing off with both the hands and legs. (See pictures 6-G on the next page)

Pictures 6-G: 6 times over the goal as player moves across from post to post. Start with and without the hands.

LEAP FROG

This is an excellent leg training drill for all players, especially for the hole-forward and defender positions. This drill can be done in pairs or with three players. The players line up facing in the same direction, with one player behind the other. The player in the back position puts his hands on the shoulders of the player in front of him and "leap frogs" over his head and shoulders.

They alternate leaping over each other until they have gone a set distance of 75-100 yards. The player that is being leaped over, must keep his head above the water, by using both his legs and hands for support. In the three-player drill, the players line up in a row and the last player must leap over each of two consecutive players before he stops. (See Pictures 6-H below)

Pictures 6-H: Start of the leapfrog.   Leaping over the top

LEG GAME DRILLS- HORIZONTAL/VERTICAL/HORIZONTAL DEFENSE

Going from a vertical position to a horizontal position, and visa-versa, are skills that are used in the game all of the time, especially when performing a zone defense. Drills as described above in blocking/shooting legwork should be done several days a week. The players should practice these skills until they become comfortable changing quickly from one position to another.

This skill is especially important when playing frontcourt zone defense and 5 on 6 zone defense. A good drill to practice this defensive skill requires three players to execute. Position one player between two other players spaced about 8-9 feet apart. The player in the middle starts on the shoulder of one player, in a horizontal position, and with his feet pointed towards the other player.

He starts by pushing off or sculling back and away from the first player, then pivots over his hips and up into a vertical blocking position, eggbeaters forward until he reaches the other player, and lunges forward with his hand towards the shoulder of arm of the other player. Once he touches the second player, he immediately turns around and swims quickly back to the first player. Repeat ten times and then switch the player in the middle. (See Diagram 6-6 below)

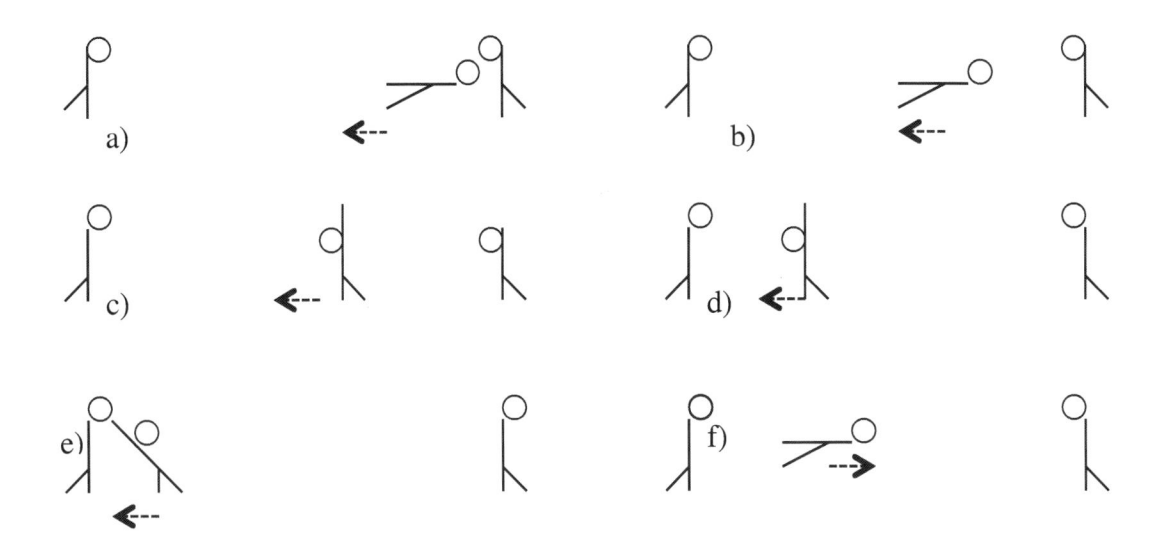

Diagram 6-6: Horizontal/vertical/horizontal drill. a) Push off post player, or b) scull backwards, c) pivot over hips to vertical-arm up, d) eggbeater forward in blocking position, e) lunge at shoulder or arm, f) turn around and swim back.

USING THE LEGS TO DEFEND- HIP-UP HORIZONTAL POSITIONING DRILL
Two players, a driver and defender facing each other, with the defender playing on the right (ball side) shoulder of the driver, with his right hand extended and looking back at the ball over his left shoulder. A third player, with the ball, is located on the right side of the driver. The driver has a choice of driving, releasing back, or popping-up to receive the ball for a shot. The defender has to react to what the driver does, using his legs and keeping his hips up at all times; always staying in ball side position. After the driver makes his move, the player with the ball attempts to pass the ball to him. The defender tries to intercept the ball. (See Diagram 6-7 on the next page).

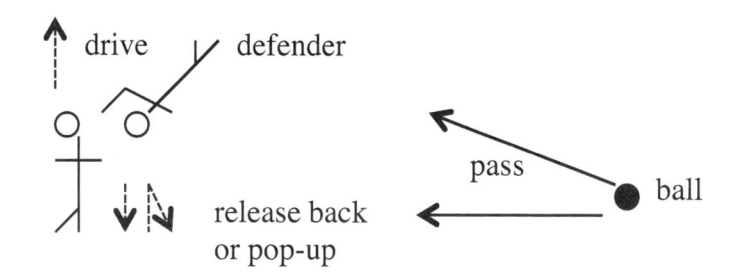

Diagram 6-7: Using legs to position against driver. Driver can drive, release back for a wet pass, or pop-up for a dry pass. Defender must react to take away whatever driver does.

USING STRETCH CORDS IN THE WATER

The player can perform the eggbeater with resistance provided by stretch cords or surgical tubing. One end of the cord is tied to a pool railing or ladder, while the other end is attached around the player's waist. The player starts in a vertical position close to the wall, and then gradually eggbeaters away from the wall.

The further the player moves away from the side of the pool, the more resistance is created. When a player gets to a point where he can go no further, then he must hold that position for 10-15 seconds; before stopping and letting the cord pull him back to the wall. (See Pictures 6-I below)

Pictures 6-I: Stretch cord tied around the waist. Eggbeater away from the wall.

TIPS FOR IMPROVING THE EGGBEATER KICK

The key to improving the eggbeater kick, is to practice doing it in the water every day. The coach should choose a variety of exercises such as described above and have the athlete perform these in practice every day.

Make sure that the athlete warms up the legs, first by doing some easy breaststroke kick and eggbeater kicking on a kickboard or ball; and then some easy vertical walking in all four direction until the legs are warmed up. Passing the ball is a good warm-up for the legs, as well as for the arms. Do a couple of easy jumps; at first using the hands; and then without the hands. Walk about 100-150 yards for a warm-up, before attempting any kind of resistance training, such as pushing down on the shoulders, heavy balls, or stretch cords.

HOW MUCH LEG TRAINING IS REQUIRED?

Specific leg conditioning drills (aside from game drills and scrimmaging) should be done in practice for about 15 minutes per day. Leg conditioning is often a case where "more is not necessarily better. A coach can over-do leg conditioning to the point where injuries occur, or where a "point of diminishing returns" is reached. Conditioning the legs by walking with the hands out and doing jumps and heavy balls is great for field-players; but don't overdo it by using excessive weight, or by spending too much time (more tan 20 minutes) doing specific training for the legs.

The result of too much legwork, especially with heavy weights, can be knee, hip and groin injuries. Besides the leg specific drills mentioned above, remember that players use their legs a lot during a 2-2 ½ hour practice; every time they are in a vertical position in the water, when taking a shot, during 6 on 5 offense and defense, during zone shot blocking, playing 2-meter and goalie positions and when scrimmaging.

Over-training can also occur when training goalkeepers. Some coaches over-train their goalies by overloading them with heavy weights and heavy conditioning, day after day. The result is tired legs. Get the goalies legs warmed up, do some conditioning (about 15-20 minutes), and then put him in the goal to block shots. Two hours or more a day of blocking shots is the major part of the conditioning that a goalie will need. It is essential to rest the goalkeeper by giving him some time away from conditioning on the day or so before a game.

ARE WE OVERTRAINING OUR ATHLETES?

In analyzing the energy requirements to play a water polo game, applying the principals of exercise physiology, and looking at the results of scientific studies performed on training athletes, we realize that we as coaches may be doing more than is required when training our players. Is the long distance swimming, 3-4 hour practices, six hours of training a day etc., really necessary in order to train our players? Are we overtraining our athletes by doing much more than is required? Are we causing unwanted mental and physical fatigue and injuries that are the result of overtraining?

Ideally, we should spend just enough time that is necessary for conditioning our players; so that the rest of the time can be spent learning water polo related skills. Research has repeatedly shown that the rate of physiological adaptation occurs primarily in response to the intensity of effort, rather than the total amount of effort. A point is reached for swimmers and water polo players, in terms of mileage, that allows for maximum improvement in performance. Anything beyond that point is wasted effort, and does not contribute to performance gains.

"It is not the QUANTITY of the mileage that is swum, it is the QUALITY of the mileage that will improve performance that is important, once that point is reached".

Fatigue occurs in the muscles, not the cardiovascular system, and the way to make the muscles more impervious to fatigue is not to slog through a lot of slow swimming. There is a maximum distance that can be covered to produce beneficial effects on performance. Further improvements can then only come from changing intensity, not adding more distance. Once the warm up is complete, the only slow swimming that should be performed is for recovery from an all out lactic acid producing session.

The difficult part for the coach is to determine how much mileage is needed to effectively train a water polo player. Once it is determined what that point is, there is no need to increase the distance any further. Therefore, the principle concept for swimming and water polo training is "effective yardage". Just the right amount of distance, and no more, than will get the job done.

It should not be necessary to swim more than 1500 yards a day in practice (even less for playing in a 25 yard (mtr) pool), if all of that swimming is effective swimming. In other words, it is similar to the distances and intensities performed in a game. The rest of the practice session should be used to perform water polo related skills and drills that require water polo specific swimming, i.e. heads up, change direction, counterattack, etc.

WARMING-UP

A player should warm-up by performing the movements that he/she is going to utilize in a game or practice, slowly at first, and then with more intensity as they go along. It has been shown that warming up also can reduce injuries related to the muscles, tendons, ligaments, and other connective tissues.

The right warm up should do three things: Loosen muscles and tendons to increase the range of motion of various joints, literally warm-up the body by increasing body temperature, and prepare the body for the intensity of the practice or a game. When you are at rest, there's less blood flow to muscles and tendons, and they stiffen. Warming up will increase blood flow to the muscles, fluid to the joints, and increase heat so that the muscles and tendons feel loser.

A warm-up must begin with easy aerobic activity, usually light to medium speed swimming of about 400 yards. Gradually increase the speed and change strokes as you go along, utilizing as many muscles as possible. The swim warm-up should also include some breaststroke, which will help get the legs ready to perform the eggbeater kick. The next 100 yards can be broken down into 25-yard "build" swims that start out slowly at the beginning of each length, and then ending with a short burst of speed at the end. These actions by them self should warm up the swimming muscles and help to increase range of motion.

Next the legs should be warmed up with easy eggbeater, and the arms with easy passing. The legs and arms can be warmed-up the same time by gradually increasing the distance between two passers, passing the ball while using the eggbeater kick. After warming up the legs and arms the players should take some shots on the goal, gradually increasing the intensity of the shot.

And then finally, about 5-10 minutes before the game is to begin, the team should do about four sprints at full speed. A few short sprints before a game starts will prepare a player for the intensity requirements at the start of the game. If the sprints are short enough (20 meters) and involve only the ATP/CP energy system, no lactic acid will be produced. These kinds of short sprints will only require a player a few minutes to restore the creatine-phosphate in the muscles, and recover completely before the start of the game.

The warm-up effect doesn't last that long (10-15 minutes), so it may be necessary for players to perform a second shorter warm-up to effectively get the body moving again. If the team has to get out of the pool for introductions after they have warmed up, especially on a cold day, they should all get in the pool after the introductions and swim across the pool and back a few times with a few quick arm strokes at the end; so they will be ready to go once the game starts.

The same holds true for a substitute who has been sitting on the bench for a while. When a sub gets into the game, he should swim from the corner of the pool to the centerline, again with a few quick strokes to get the blood circulating and to get him ready to go hard when the game starts. A half-time swim warm-up can be effective for players who sat on the bench for the first half. Players who played a lot in the first half can also do about 5 minutes of slow swimming at half time to help dissipate any lactic acid that has accumulated.

SUMMARY
Now that you as a coach knows and understands the principles of training and the requirements of performing the game of water polo, you should analyze the training and practice sessions that your team has performed in the past; using the above information as a guideline. Then you must ask yourself, is there anything that I can do more efficiently, and more effectively, to correctly train my athletes for playing the game of water polo?

CHAPTER 7
RESISTANCE TRAINING FOR WATER POLO

Dry-land strength training is part of the conditioning program of many water polo teams around the world, with the idea being that the stronger you are, the better your performance in the water. A big question that we have to ask as coaches, trainers and players, is strength training necessary to become a better player, or is it just something that has been perpetuated by strength trainers and coaches as necessary for all sports?

It sounds logical. Get stronger and improve your performance! Is it really that simple? Do the same principals of strength apply in the water as it they do on land? Is the dry-land strength training that many teams do really needed for better performance in the pool?

Gaining strength and power simply for the sake of being stronger, or more powerful, is of relatively little importance to athletes unless it also improves their athletic performance. Resistance training for field-event (shot-put, discus, etc) athletes, weight lifters and football players makes intuitive sense; because strength is an important factor in success in those events. The need for resistance training by the gymnast, distance runner, swimmer, baseball player, high jumper, water polo player, or ballet dancer is less obvious.

Every sport has a basic strength requirement that must be met to achieve optimal performance. Training beyond those requirements may be unnecessary and costly in terms of time. Athletes cannot afford to waste time on activities that won't result in better athletic performance. If we just want water polo players to become bigger in body mass or achieve bigger, stronger muscles, we can accomplish that by having them perform traditional dry-land weight training exercises.

Water polo, however, has unique strength requirements that are different from the mainstream dry-land sport. Most of the differences have to do with the water medium that the water polo athlete performs in. Because of water's lack of a solid mass that provides an athlete a base of support for application of force, and the effect of buoyancy on the body that takes away the force needed to overcome gravity; the need for strength may be much different for the water polo player, and the competitive swimmer, than for a land-based athlete.

Performing a sport activity in the water changes everything! Why? Because when a swimmer or water polo player pulls their hand, or pushes their foot against the water, the water gives way. So the biggest question we can ask is, if the water gives way when you push on it, how does a swimmer gain propulsion; and more importantly, how much strength (force) does it require to push your hand or foot through the water?

POSSIBLE STRENGTH REQUIREMENTS OF WATER POLO

Let's first start by looking at the sport of water polo, and what parts of the game might possibly need added strength for improvement in performance. I can think of four areas where strength might be of benefit to the water polo player: swimming speed, leg strength (eggbeater) to get higher out of the water, shooting the ball harder, and the grappling and holding that goes on underwater between two players. Since swimming relies on pulling the hand and arm through the water to create propulsion, we will look at the swimming part of water polo separately.

The other three areas that could possibly require strength for success are the eggbeater kick, shooting a ball, and wrestling in the water. All are related by one common factor; and that is the ability of the legs to perform the eggbeater kick. Even though the skills of swimming and eggbeater involve different parts of the body (the arms and legs), they are similar, in that the fluid mechanical principles of lift and drag apply to both the arm pull and the downward kick. Consequently they will be examined together when analyzing the thrust and propulsion that is created when the hands and feet move through the water.

PROPULSION AND THRUST

The objective of swimming is to propel oneself forward through the water (propulsion) by pulling the hands backward, while the objective of the eggbeater kick is to provide upward movement (thrust) of the body by pushing the feet down on the water. The key factor that explains movement in sports is POWER. It has long ago been determined that power is important in all sports in order for athletes to perform at their maximum capacity.

Many people mistakenly confuse power with strength. They state that if you have strength, than you also have power. In truth, strength is only one component of power. Speed is the other component. When you multiply strength (force) times speed (velocity), then you have power (Power = force x velocity). Power is necessary to provide movement in all sports. If you want to move faster or jump higher, then you need more power. The more force that you can apply, or the more speed that you can apply the force with, the more power you will have.

WHERE DOES STRENGTH (FORCE) FIT IN TO SWIMMING SPEED?

From the discussion on propulsion in Chapter 6 "Training and Conditioning for Water Polo", and the examples of a hand pushing against the water as compared to a hand pushing on a solid object, we concluded that it doesn't take a lot of force for a water polo player to overcome the resistance of the water, especially when compared to a runner or jumper on land. Most of the force just goes into the water and does not contribute much in propelling the body forward or upward. Even pushing back with more force on the water does not help to propel the body forward faster. Even though some force (strength) is required to propel the body forward, the question is just how much is required?

The conclusions of the discussions in Chapter 6 on generating power as it relates to swimming, and the relative contributions of speed and strength, have been based mostly on applying scientific principals of fluid mechanics. Researchers and sports scientists around the world have been trying to answer this question of just how much strength is required to swim.

Up until now, it has been difficult to collaborate the science with actual research; because of the difficulty of measuring force production in the water. In order to measure force produced by a swimmer, a fixed and immovable reference point is needed to get an accurate measurement. In other words, a solid reference point is needed so that the force generated by the arm can be measured. In a medium such as water, that is not fixed (it doesn't stay in one place), it has been almost impossible to measure how much force is actually applied by the hand as it pushes on the water.

Dutch exercise scientist H.M. Toussaint, who has probably done more studies on swim propulsion and drag than anyone in the world, has come up with a way to measure force while swimming, by having the swimmer push against a series of paddles, from which accurate force measurements can take place (this is called the M.A.D. system). Toussaint was actually able to measure the amount of force generated by the arm and hand that contribute to propelling a swimmer forward. In his latest research using the M.A.D system resulted in a 2007 published paper titled "Strength, Power, and Technique of Swimming Performance", Toussaint drew the conclusion that:

"Swimming is not a sport that requires much strength to swim fast".

This collaborates the idea that it doesn't take a lot of force to overcome the drag of the water, and that a lot of the mechanical force that is produced goes into pushing the water backwards, and not into propelling the swimmer forward.Toussaint concluded that the only strength that is necessary for swimming is the strength required to move the arm through the water.

This strength can be acquired by simply performing the event in question. In other words, a swimmer can acquire the strength necessary for swimming his/her event by swimming. A water polo player can acquire the strength to play water polo by playing water polo. Anything more than that is wasted energy that just goes into pushing water, and does not go into propelling the body forward.

STRENGTH CONTRIBUTION TO SPEED?
So if a swimmer can get the strength that he/she needs just by swim training, can't the swimmer also get faster by getting stronger? Why do swimmers lift weights if it doesn't make them stronger and faster? Over the years, swim coaches have used the positive correlation between power (strength x velocity) of swimmers, and their swim performances, to accomplish power improvement through strength training. This is mistakenly done by thinking that getting stronger can increase the (f) factor (force/strength) in the power formula of force x velocity.

In the discussion in Chapter 6 on "propulsion and thrust", we have theoretically shown, by using principles of fluid dynamics, that any extra strength (force) in the arms is simply dissipated into the water and does not contribute to more forward propulsion (speed). This is fine "in theory"; but can it actually be shown that increased strength acquired from dry-land strength training does not contribute to making a swimmer faster? I'm glad you asked.

This age old question has perplexed coaches and scientests for years. Several renowned researchers in sports science decided to answer this question once and for all. They first surmised that if there are any effects of strength training on swimming, it would have more of an effect on sprinters than endurance swimmers; because strength is thought to be more important than endurance to sprint swimmers.

This research on sprinters is also of interest to water polo coaches and players; because an important aspect of playing water polo is sprint swimming, and sprint swimming speed. Since both water polo players and sprinters utilize similar strokes, and swim approximately the same velocities and distances, studies done on sprinters should also apply to water polo players.

Over the past few years, many respected Exercise Physiologists who have specialized in doing research on all aspects of competitive swimming, have taken on the challenge of determining the influence of strength on the perfromance of swimmers. One of the objectives of the research was to learn how to train swimmers to help improve their performance; and to answer the question of whether strength gained from dry-land exercises is transferred to performance in the water, let alone necessary for swimming faster.

In many studies performed by sports scientists (Costil D. et al 1983 Swim Technique; Crowe S.E. et al, 1999, Med & Sci in Sport & Exercise; Tanaka H.U. et al, 1993 Med & Science in Sport & Ex; Sukolovas G, 2000, Olympic Trials Project, and Toussaint H. et al. 2001, European Journ. Of Sports Med.) sprint swimmers trained for a period of time approximating a competitive season, while using traditional swim training methods.

One group of the swimmers also performed traditional dry-land resistance exercises, in addition to their normal swim training. At the end of the training, all swimmers were tested for improvement of their sprint swimming times. It was found that despite the increases in muscle strength acquired by swim specific dry-land resistance training, these strength gains were not transferred to increased sprint speed in competitive swimmers.

In a classic study to determine whether adding resistance training to pool training might improve sprint-swim performance, Tanaka, et al. studied 24 experienced swimmers during their 14 week competitive season. The swimmers all trained by utilizing the same sprint-training program in the water; but half of the swimmers performed additional swim specific dry-land strength exercises.

The most important finding of this study was that resistance training did NOT improve sprint swim performance (time for a 25 meter swim) of the "swim/strength" group over the "swim only" group; despite the fact that those swimmers who combined resistance and swim training increased their strength in the resistance training exercises by 25-35%. In other words, they got stronger in the strength exercises; but it did not transfer to increased speed in the water.

The renowned Exercise Physiologist David Costill from Ball State, Indiana, also concluded that while dry-land resistance training is common practice in the swim world, evidence from many controlled studies supported the view that there does not appear to be any further benefit to swim performance from dry-land training performed in addition to water-based workouts.

WHY DOESN'T ACQUIRED STRENGTH TRANSFER TO SWIMMING?

As concluded in the above discussions, a factor that may explain why strength increases on dry land do not transfer to increased performance in the water, is the matter of the force generated by the muscles to push the hands through the water, is largely dissipated into the water; and does not go into propelling the body forward.

Another factor that may explain the failure of increased strength not increasing performance, is the results found in hundreds of studies, in almost all sports, including swimming, that strength training is specific to the activity involved (running, swimming, soccer, basketball, gymnastics and even football). An athlete has to strengthen the muscles in the same way that they are used in the specific sport activity. Because it takes place in the water, and because of the mechanics involved in the swim stroke, swimming is one the most difficult sports to exactly duplicate the movements involved with dry-land exercise. Dry-land strength training is simply not specific enough to duplicate the swim stroke or the eggbeater kick in sprint swimming and water polo.

Complex movement patterns are also involved, where the hand and arms change position during the power phase of the stroke or the kick. These movement patterns are difficult to imitate on dry land. This all suggests that during dry-land training, the strain on the various muscle groups strongly differs from that while swimming in water; so it is not obvious that dry-land strength training contributes to improved swim performances.

CAN WE INCREASE STRENGTH IN THE WATER?
Some physiologists and coaches have speculated, that based on observation and the application of the principals of the science of exercise physiology, that high intensity speed work, along with some in-the-water resistance training with swim benches, power racks, stretch cords and paddles, can increase the specific strength necessary to swim at maximum speed in the relatively short sprints that are part of sprint swimming and the game of water polo. To test their theories and observations, studies were performed of all of the resistance-training techniques mentioned above.

The conclusions, after years of study, found that only high intensity speed work in the water, and tethered-swimming, in which the swimmer actually swam in the water while attached to a resistance cord, achieved any significant improvements in speed. Swim bench training was not found to be effective because it did not exactly duplicate the swim stroke in the water (no shoulder roll or stabilizing kick), and hand paddles caused injuries to the shoulders while changing the actual swim stroke.

In conclusion then, the strength necessary for swimming fast does not have to come dry-land strength training; but can come from performing short, fast and intense practice swims and by adding resistance in the water by using stretch cords. Only by training the energy systems responsible for sprint swimming, can the water polo player achieve the increase in arm speed necessary for optimum performance in a game; and that will allow the player to repeat the arm and leg movements at a fast speed. A player has to have muscle strength to swim fast; but technique, streamlining, and faster movement of the arms and legs become more important than strength in increasing swim speed in competitive sprinters and water polo players.

CAN WE IMPROVE THE EGGBEATER WITH STRENGTH TRAINING?
The physical factors mentioned above for sprint swimming, also holds true for performing the eggbeater kick in the water. Technique, joint structure, and speed of the foot and leg are important factors in the eggbeater kick, along with correctly applied muscle strength. Similar to sprint swimming, strength training to improve the eggbeater kick can best be applied in the water by utilizing weighted balls, teammate assisted push downs, and explosive jumps; or simply performing the eggbeater kick in practice in a similar situation to that used in a game.

Heredity plays a big role in performing the eggbeater; because the structure of the knee and ankle joints that one inherits from his/her parents, is what allows the water polo player to properly position the feet and legs for maximum power. Similar to pulling the arms through the water, applying more force to the kick will not achieve desired results; because most of that force goes into pushing the water down.

The same principles that apply to swimming, also apply to performing the eggbeater kick. The kick has to be practiced with enough intensity to overload the systems that supply energy to the leg muscles. Training by performing the kick at fast speeds (i.e. explosive jumps) is necessary. Proper technique in positioning the bottom of the feet is also an important factor in performing a good eggbeater kick. Consequently, leg speed and technique, rather than strength, become the most important factors in performing the eggbeater.

THE VALUE OF SQUATS
I cannot see the value of water polo players performing squat training for the legs. If you look at most water polo players and swimmers, even those who are good breaststrokers, or have a good eggbeater kick, you will see that their legs and lower body are slim, and not bulky. There is a reason for this.

First of all, there isn't any need for heavily muscled legs in order to perform the flutter and breaststroke kicks while swimming, or the eggbeater while playing water polo; and secondly, the extra bulk in the buttocks and legs creates more resistance that the water polo player has to overcome in order move through the water.

More importantly, the strength gained from doing squats does not apply to the breaststroke and eggbeater kicks; for the same reasons as mentioned above. The complex movements of the legs cannot be duplicated in the weight room, and any additional strength (force) gained from squat training is dissipated into moving water. The strength gained in performing dry-land squats is not transferred into increased height in the water when performing the eggbeater kick.

Even in dry-land sports like volleyball, where the athlete pushes off the solid ground, numerous studies have shown that increased leg strength from squat training does not result in increases in the vertical jump of volleyball players. A conclusion that we can draw from these studies is "if squat training does not increase vertical jump on dry land, how can we expect it to increase height in the water from performing the eggbeater kick?" In other words, increased strength in the legs acquired from squats does not help performance on land, or in the water. So, why bother?

WILL STRONGER ARM AND SHOULDER MUSCLES HELP IN SHOOTING THE BALL HARDER?

In a classic study on water polo players (Bloomfield, B.A. et al, Australian Journal of Science and Sport) studied the influence of strength training on overhead throwing velocity of elite water polo players. Following strength training, no change in throwing velocity was observed in either the normal training group, or the strength-training group. The implications of this study, along with many on other activities, shows strength training on unrelated activities does not improve speed actions of an activity. Strength training had no carry over to the skill tested; because it was not specific enough to improve the neuromuscular reaction to the stress imposed on the muscles.

Also of interest to water polo was a study done on the "relevance of specific training (resistance training) for baseball pitching", published in the textbook of Exercise Physiology by Mcardle, W.D. et al (2004). Since the action of throwing a baseball is similar to the action of throwing a water polo ball, the conclusions of the study can apply directly to water polo. The conclusions were "to improve a specific physical performance through resistance training, one must train the muscle(s) in movements that mimic the throwing motion, with specific consideration for force, velocity, arm angle and power requirements".

"The direct application of this recommendation, is that hard-throwing is the only stimulus for improving muscular function in baseball pitching. Training on resistance machines, or doing different forms of throwing as training and practice items, will be irrelevant activities for improving pitching. Irrelevant training (such as weight training) should not be expected to produce pitching improvements".

Both in baseball and water polo, it is the application of power by the legs that is more important in throwing the ball, than upper body strength. The same leg action that is needed to get high in the water, is also necessary for shooting the ball faster. In throwing a ball while in a vertical position in the water, the power of the downward thrust of the legs (especially the front leg) is transformed to the upper body to help initiate the forward rotation of the upper torso.

While arm and shoulder strength are factors in throwing or shooting the ball with greater velocity; they are not as important as you may think. How a player applies that strength is even more important. Proper throwing technique (skill) is important, probably one of the "most important factors", in insuring that maximum force is translated from the legs to the arms. Shooting the ball starts from the tips of the toes and finishes from the tips of the fingers, putting all of the factors together in the correct sequence, and using the proper form.

Sometime take a look at the upper bodies of some of the top major league pitchers that can throw the ball 90 mph. Many of them do not have great upper body strength. Back-to-back Cy Young award winner and World Series MPV Tim Lincecum of the San Francisco Giants has a slim body, with hardly any shoulder and arm muscle definition. Yet he consistently throws a 95 mph fastball.

Major league pitching coaches will tell you that proper form and technique, shoulder and elbow structure, and using the legs to push off the ground, are the most important factors in throwing a baseball, similar to a water polo player shooting a ball at a goal. Some of the ability to throw a ball may even have to do with factors in joint, bone and muscle structure that may have been inherited from ones parents. Do not discount heredity as a very important part in success in throwing a ball.

In water polo, I have observed some of the best shooters in the game over the past 40 years. The players with the most powerful legs (eggbeater kick) and the best shooting technique were usually the best shooters on the team; not the players with the most well-defined upper bodies, or those who could squat 400 pounds. Just as in baseball and football, the players with the best technique, leg strength, arm velocity, and ability to apply force to generate power, are more successful in throwing the ball.

ISN'T STRENGTH A FACTOR IN THE PUSHING, PULLING AND HOLDING AT 2-METERS?
Another area where strength may be required in water polo is the constant wrestling for position (pushing, pulling and holding) that goes on between players at the 2-meter position. Many of these players are physically big and strong; but they would not be successful at their position without a strong eggbeater kick. It is the kick that gives them the platform for leverage; so that they can apply the upper body strength to gain and hold position in the water.

Do not confuse strength with size and mass. 2-meter players with large mass are necessary, because it makes it more difficult to get around them. However, if two players that are the same size are grappling with each other in the water, the one with the best legs and technique will win the battle. Think of 2-meter players as football linemen who are maneuvering against each other. The big massive 350 lb offensive lineman can just stand there and get in the way (by using his mass) of the on-rushing smaller defensive lineman. However, if the defensive player has the ability to apply more power by using leg strength and speed, he will win the battle between them; and eventually get to the quarterback.

Besides the importance of the legs, using correct technique to gain leverage is important for both the football lineman and the 2-meter player in water polo. Football line coaches spend hours a day working on using the proper technique, in order to utilize the strength of these massive players when they are manuevering for position. The same holds true in water polo. What goes on underwater has a lot to do with the success or failure of the 2-meter player.

Once again, do not confuse strength with leverage. Recently, U-tube showed the action between two ten-year old wrestlers. One young wrestler was throwing the other kid all over the mat. The TV commintator stated "look how strong that kid is, he is throwing the other kid all over the place." I watched the video and noted that the kid who was winning was exactly the same size, and just as skinny as the other kid; but he understood how to use leverage to throw his opponent. Strength had nothing to do with his advantage. He was simply using proper technique to gain leverage. Much like the football lineman and the 2-meter water polo player!

Because water polo is a game that involves other skills and tactics, players can perform better by learning how to play the game better, getting faster in the water, and using their quickness and smarts to gain good position. As mentioned above, effective sports specific dry-land strength training might help overcome other deficiencies; but because of the nature of the game that is played in a fluid medium instead of on dry land, strength training can only help improve your game up to a point. Additional strength gains beyond that point may not help improve a player's performance, because of the limiting factor of applying force in the water, and duplicating the swim stroke on dry-land.

THE NEED FOR STRENGTHENING THE STABILIZER MUSCLES OF THE SHOULDER

THE SHOULDER JOINT
The shoulder joint is a truly remarkable creation. It's quite a complex formation of bones, muscles and tendons, and provides a great range of motion for the arm. The only downside to this extensive range of motion is a lack of stability, which can make the shoulder joint vulnerable to injury. Injury to the shoulder is the most common water polo related injury.

This is no surprise considering that the shoulder joint is the most used joint of the body when playing the sport of water polo. Hundreds of hours of swimming, and overhead passing and shooting, are bound to stress the shoulder to the point where an injury occurs.

WHAT COMPRISES THE SHOULDER JOINT?
The shoulder is made up of three bones, and the tendons of four small muscles, each of which originates on the shoulder blade, or scapula, and inserts on the arm bone, or humerus. These four individual muscles, and more specifically their tendons, surround the shoulder joint to form a thick "cuff" over this joint. This is called the "rotator cuff." It is the tendons of these muscles, which connect to the bones, that help to move the arm. When an injury occurs to the rotator cuff, it is usually an injury to the tendons of the rotator cuff muscles.

The shoulder is made up of two main joints, the gleno-humeral joint, which is the "ball and socket" joint, and the acromioclavicular joint, which is the smaller joint above the gleno-humeral joint. The shoulder has an extremely large range of motion (more than any other joint in the body), primarily due to the lack of bony congruency; and the very shallow cavity of the glenoid, which holds the ball at the end of the large bone of the arm, the humerus.

Because of the shallow socket of the shoulder joint (gleno-humeral joint), it is difficult for the ball of the humerus bone of the arm to stay in place when the arm is rotated, especially when the arm is in an overhead position. The rotator cuff muscles are small, but their function is very important. Specifically, they act to keep the shoulder joint stable during movements of the arm by, in layman's terms, keeping the "ball in the socket". They also help in elevating and rotating the arm.

The large muscle that surrounds the outside of the shoulder, and forms the pad of the shoulder, is called the deltoid. The rotator cuff tendons and both the shoulder joints lie beneath the deltoid. The deltoid's main function is to lift the arm out to the side, or in front of the body. It also can help to stabilize the shoulder joint; especially when the arm lifts overhead against heavy resistance.

WHAT CAUSES INJURIES TO THE SHOULDERS OF WATER POLO PLAYERS?
Athletes with a long history of participation in sports involving repetitive overhead motions or throwing, such as water polo, swimming, volleyball or baseball, are more prone to suffering injuries to the shoulder. Water polo players are prone to shoulder injuries from both direct trauma and overuse.

Many water polo players start as competitive swimmers, and have accumulated a lot of mileage in the pool before they even pick up a ball. Overuse is caused by the repetitive rotation of the shoulder joint, especially when performing the crawl or butterfly swimming strokes. The repetitive stretching of the shoulder capsule and ligaments, that occurs over time, causes the shoulder to become loose or unstable.

The "tightness" of the ligaments, tendons and the muscle cuff around the shoulder is important for the joint to maintain its integrity. Adding together the effects of thousands of repetitive shoulder rotations every week while swimming, and hundreds of overhead throws, water polo players (especially those who have a swimming background) will stretch the tendons and ligaments of the shoulder over time; which leads to more instability of the shoulder joint.

STRENGTHENING THE SHOULDER TO PREVENT INJURIES
In weight training and athletics, the repetitive movements and daily stresses on the shoulder forces the muscles of the rotator cuff to exert a greater force to stabilize the head of the humerus in the glenoid socket. Because of their inherent laxity in the shoulder, swimmers and water polo players should emphasize preserving the overall stability of the shoulder, by strengthening the stabilizing muscles of the rotator cuff and the scapula.

The strength of these supporting structures is crucial, because as a muscle contracts; tightening of the shoulder capsule occurs, along with the tendons that connect the bones of the joint. This tension in the capsule holds the humeral head in the socket, providing the required stability to the shoulder joint. Excessive stimulation from activity, over a long period of time, can begin a negative cycle that is very common among athletes in sports that stress repetitive arm motions and overhead activities.

The most common shoulder injuries to water polo players are shoulder impingement, rotator cuff tears, bicipital tendonitis and labral injury. The cycle usually starts with shoulder pain and the avoidance of certain movements, which causes atrophy of the involved musculature; and eventually results in instability and possible impingement. Imbalances of strength and coordination occur from this continuous training, and are only reinforced as the athlete continues to perform these exercises.

During the power phase of swimming, when the hand is pulling through the water, it is the major muscles like the pecs (chest), lats (back) and deltoid (shoulder) that are used. These major muscles are strengthened more than the rotator cuff muscles, because they are used for the power phase of swimming; while the rotator cuff muscles are mainly used during the recovery phase in order to lift the arm out of the water and to slow the arm down. These imbalances are often the root of many training injuries and may predispose athletes to a greater risk of injury during further training and competition.

Since rotator cuff strengthening and rotator cuff exercises are not a very common practice among swimmers and water polo players, those muscles are underdeveloped. The larger upper body muscles of the chest and back are strengthened; but the player probably neglects any rotator cuff strength exercises, or any exercises that work on stabilization. The combination of weaker rotator cuff muscles, and over-developed shoulders, chest and arm muscles, causes the muscle imbalances that can increase the likelihood of rotator cuff injury.

Many muscles are involved in shoulder movement, and all work together. Given that the rotator cuff works to stabilize the shoulder joint, it stands to reason that the muscles of the rotator cuff will come into play whenever the larger muscles that work across the shoulder joint are exercised. However, a system is only as strong as its weakest link. In the shoulders. the weakest link is the stabilization system, the rotator cuff. Strengthening the stabilizing muscles surrounding the shoulder, before injuries occur, can help prevent many of the injuries that are common in water polo.

The rotator cuff is the main stabilizer of the shoulder joint during movement of the shoulder. If the ball of the upper arm is not kept centered in the socket of he shoulder, abnormal stress is placed on surrounding tissue, and may cause gradual injury. The preferable way to prevent a shoulder impingement, or muscle tear, is through an exercise program to strengthen the rotator cuff muscles sufficiently; so that the head of the shoulder is held firmly in place and will not slip out of the socket. With no slipping, the tendons will no longer be inflamed or irritated.

If you are regularly involved in activities such as swimming and water polo, that repeatedly put an abnormal amount of stress on the shoulder joint and the muscles of the rotator cuff, then it would definitely be worth your while to do some specific rotator cuff exercises. Doing this will ensure that your shoulder joint stays strong, and decrease the likelihood of incurring an injury.

INVOLMENT OF THE ROTATOR CUFF IN THROWING AND SHOOTING
In addition to the major mover muscles involved in swimming, the rotator cuff muscles also play a part in throwing and shooting a ball. The act of throwing is the most stressful motion on the shoulder and rotator cuff. Water polo players are a perfect example of the importance of proper exercise form, and increased stress from shooting a ball. The arm and the ball (resistance) are thrown forward at a tremendous velocity, anywhere from 30 to 50 miles per hour. In the final phase of shooting the ball, the shooter is basically trying to throw his arm away from his body. The rotator cuff is responsible for decelerating the arm at the end of the shot, and holding the arm in the socket during this stressful action.

Pictures 7-A: Accelerating and decelerating the arm puts tremendous stress on the shoulder muscles. The rotator cuff muscles keep the arm from being "thrown away from the body", as well as keeping the ball of the arm in the shoulder socket when the arm is in the overhead unstable position.

As the muscles in the rotator cuff contract to slow down the arm, a rotator cuff injury (tear) can occur; because more force is produced by accelerating muscles than the decelerating muscles can handle. This happens when the imbalance that is created between these opposing muscle groups, results in overuse of muscles and ultimately injuries of the shoulder. This is another example of the importance of strengthening the stabilizer muscles of the shoulder.

DESIGNING A STRENGTH TRAINING SYSTEM FOR WATER POLO PLAYERS

If we just want water polo players to become bigger and stronger, then we can easily accomplish that by having them perform traditional dry-land exercises in the weight room. Traditional weight training teaches us that more is better, no pain no gain, etc. If the goal is to add muscle and become increasingly defined, then there is indeed some validity to this approach.

However, water polo players are not weightlifters, and they do not need to be traditionally defined in the Arnold Schwarzenegger sense to swim fast. Most water polo muscles are developed doing the sport, not in the weight room. They may not be visible gains, but remember that the idea is to gain swimming and water polo strength, not cosmetic bulk. When initiating dry land training remember that athletes who perform in a water medium might not benefit from the same training as land based athletes.

As a whole, dry land training should create fluidity, momentum and functional strength, while maintaining cardiovascular fitness and range of motion; and at the same time strengthen muscles around the joints that provide stability and prevent injury.
Weights are to be used as a complementary strength-building tool in order for the water polo player to retain range of motion, while gaining applicable strength. The strength gained in the weight room must be applicable to what you are trying to accomplish. Trying to get bigger muscles is not one of the things that we hope to gain from weight lifting.

Observe the bodies of the top water polo players in the world, and you will see that they have a long and lean look. They are strong without being bulky, and they have long limbs to gain leverage in swimming, shooting, shot blocking, etc. Adding extra bulk does not help the water polo player perform better. In fact it can be a detriment in terms of adding drag resistance (from increased frontal area) that the player has to push through the water.

Added bulk in the lower body (legs and hips) is especially detrimental to getting up and down the pool fast. When is the last time that you saw a water polo player with huge legs and butt muscles? Most have slim legs that are light and stream-lined, that don't add too much drag, but are strong in the sense that they can repeatedly apply enough force to increase propulsion.

If water polo players feel that they would like to feel and look stronger, beyond what they get from swimming and playing water polo; and if dry-land resistance training is to become a part of their training, the results of scientific studies, basic scientific principles, and common sense have to be followed for the weight training to be effective.

Along with developing overall body strength, the correct major muscles of the upper body that are used in the game must be strengthened; and in a way that is specific and similar to the movements used in the water. The legs must also be trained to provide the base of support that will allow muscle strength to be applied in the water. The supporting and stabilizing muscles of the body (shoulder) must also be strengthened to prevent injury.

A PROGRAM FOR STRENGTH TRAINING
A variety of strength training methods can be utilized, including dry-land exercises, in-the-water specific resistance training, body-weight exercises, and resistance (stretch) band exercises. A program that will "cover all your bases" and help insure that water polo players are getting the strength that they might need, will include the following:
1. Every day in the water resistance training (sprints, resistance cord exercises, heavy balls, etc)
2. Year around rotator cuff and scapular stabilizer strength training for the shoulders using resistance cords and dumbbells.
3. In season circuit training program that duplicate the movements in the water by utilizing resistance cords, body weight exercises and dumbbells.
4. Off-season dry-land resistance training program utilizing free weight and machine-based moderate-weight exercises that are specific to water polo

HOW MUCH TIME DO YOU HAVE?
In team sports such as water polo, a lot of time must be spent in learning the skills and tactics necessary to play the game, and at the same time train and condition to play the game at the optimal level. There is only so much time for practicing the game; so any time that is spent doing something that does not help performance, is wasted time.

Spending a lot of time doing dry-land training that does not apply to water polo because it is not "specific" enough, can be classified as "wasting time", especially if the time spent is not productive or helpful in improving performance. Consequently, dry-land training must be carefully planned and efficient in order to be effective.

OFF-SEASON STRENGTH TRAINING
Because of the time constraints during the season, some teams will do their dry-land strength training during the off-season, when players are not as active in the water. If players are not playing water polo or swimming during the off-season, or only playing a few days a week, then I can see some value in off-season strength training. Strength training, if nothing else is available, is a good way to keep the bodies muscles in shape during the off-season; and to strengthen the shoulder muscles that help prevent shoulder injuries from occurring.

If I was coaching a team today, I would probably have them do some kind of strength training (2 sets, 8-12 reps, moderate weight) during the off-season; just to keep my players in reasonable muscle shape during that time off, and as a "change of pace" from in the water training.

During the off-season, a coach has a choice of doing resistance exercises that target most muscles in the body, or to do the "Big Ten" program (described below) that targets specific muscles that are used for water polo. Shoulder strengthening exercises should continue to be done year around for injury prevention.

IN-SEASON STRENGTH TRAINING
Once the team starts full-time daily training in the spring, summer and fall, I would modify my training by doing less dry-land weight training, and by doing more circuit training that involves body weight exercises, stretch band exercises and shoulder strengthening exercises. I would also put more emphasis on in-the-water strength training with more sprinting, swimming with stretch bands and heavy balls; and using stretch cords, push downs and explosive jumps for the legs.

Based on the scientific evidence and water propulsion principles that are listed above, I would probably have my team continue only shoulder strengthening exercises and in-the-water strengthening exercises during the prime competitive season; and spend most of the time learning to play water polo. If I only have 2-2 1/2 hours a day of practice time during the season, I would rather spend that valuable time practicing and playing water polo; and not performing dry-land strength training.

The coach can even teach the players how to use a stretch cord, so that they can spend 15 minutes a day at home performing shoulder stabilizing exercises; and not have to spend valuable practice time doing these exercises at the pool. If a coach insists on having his team perform dry-land strength exercises during the season, time can be saved by having the players perform only one set of each exercise instead of the standard 2-3 sets.

In studies that have compared strength achieved from one, two and three sets of the same exercise, it was found that athletes made the same strength gains by doing only one set of each exercise, as they did by doing two or three sets. To be effective, one set of each exercise does require a 2-second lift, and a 3 to 4-second lowering of the weight be performed in order to gain strength during both the eccentric (lowering weight) and concentric (lifting weight) parts of the lift.

RESISTANCE TRAINING PROGRAMS FOR WATER POLO

The following training program for water polo has been designed to utilize the above principals of strength training, and their application to swimming and water polo:

THE "BIG TEN"
(All exercises are 1-2 sets of 8-12 reps unless noted otherwise)

1. Seated rows (hands horizontal)

2. Dips- As many as you can do in one minute with body weight, 15-20 reps on weight assisted machine**

3. Chin-ups- One-set overhand grip (prefer angle grip if available). Do as many as you can with body weight, 15-20 reps on weight assisted machine** (See pictures below of angle grip chin-ups).

⌒ angle grip   ──── straight grip

Angle grip chin-ups

4. Lat pull downs- Wide grip and narrow grip- one set of each

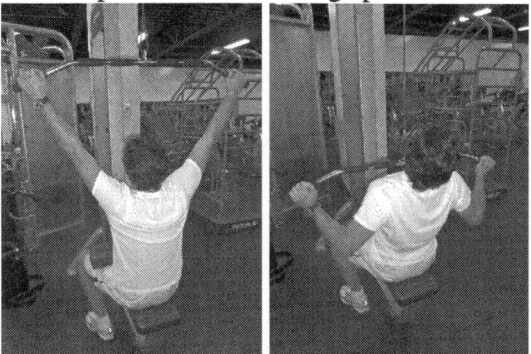

5. Elbow extensions (triceps pull down) with rope or angled bar

6. Straight arm pull downs (kneeling or standing)

7. Bent-arm flys- (machine, 90 degree elbow bend)

8. Deltoid- Side (middle), front (anterior) and bent over (posterior) deltoid exercises with dumbbells- one set each of 12 reps

a) side (middle) deltoid   b) anterior (front) deltoid   c) posterior (back) deltoid

9. Incline bench- Pull-ups (laying face down on incline bench. Pull (lift) weights up to under side of bench), or alternate one arm lat pull.

Incline bench

One arm lat pull

10. Oblique/abdominals- Legs raised above ground, bring knee and opposite elbow together. Hold heavy ball in both hands and move from one side to another. (two sets of 25 reps).

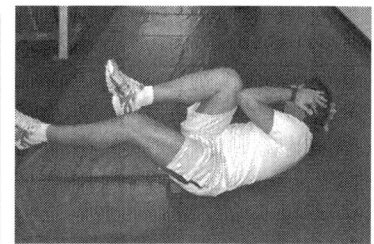

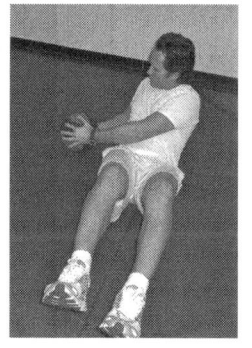

**The weight assisted machine is the best way to do dips and chin-ups without having to lift the athlete's complete body weight, and perhaps increase the stress and cause injuries to the elbow and shoulder joints. This machine also allows you to perform the exercise at a faster pace than if you were lifting your body weight. These kinds of machines are not available at all facilities.

Pick a weight that you can move at normal speed, but at the same time make it difficult enough so that the last repetition is hard to do. You should feel a burning sensation in your muscles, and the weight should be getting difficult to move as you perform the last few repetitions.The weight-training program described above should be followed immediately with 4 to 6 rotator cuff and shoulder stabilizer exercises as described below.

ROTATOR CUFF EXERCISES

In addition to strengthening the major movement muscles of the shoulder, specific exercises that strengthen the rotator cuff muscles can be done with stretch resistance cords, about three days a week, and all year around as an injury preventative.

WHERE AND WHEN TO MAINTAIN THE SHOULDER

Depending on an athlete's training cycle, shoulder maintenance can be done within a strength session, while resting or waiting a turn in practice at the side of the pool, or as a detailed workout that specifically focuses on an athlete's rotator cuff and scapular stabilizers. These workouts can also be designed for off days, travel days, alternate days (not performing strength training), or active rest days as a means of recovery.

To insure that every member of the team strengthens these important muscles, about 10-15 minutes per day of shoulder stabilizer exercises can be added to the team's normal training program. These exercises can also be performed at home by the athletes; although they may lack the discipline, and will not have the watchful eye of the coach. If athletes understand that these exercises can prolong their career, and prevent common shoulder injuries, they might be more inclined to do them at home.

As a coach, you will not be happy when one of the players on your team comes up with a shoulder injury that prevents him from playing, or limits his shooting power and ability. These kinds of injuries are common among water polo players; but can be prevented with proper strengthening of the stabilizer muscles. Do not wait for an injury to occur before you start a rotator cuff strengthening program for your team. The most important concept is to prevent and maintain this unique joint, before the problem becomes an issue that cannot be resolved.

WHAT EQUIPMENT SHOULD I USE?

Strengthening exercise can be performed with light-weights (dumbbells) or stretch-resistance cords that provide resistance when stretched. Unlike heavy weights, stretch-resistance cords are easy to transport and can be used anywhere. Players can take stretch cords with them and perform many of the exercises at home.

Resistance cords come in a variety of thicknesses that provide different levels of resistance, and are usually color-coded. Resistance bands are attached to a door-knob, or other immovable object, or the athlete can stand on the cord to anchor it down. When using resistance bands, increasing the distance you stand away from where the cord is attached increases the resistance.

ENDURANCE WORK- LOW RESISTANCE, HIGH REPETITION

Although the majority of movements in the weight room, and athletic realm, involve short bursts of medium to high intensity strength exercises; endurance is also required to both resist the onset of fatigue, and aid in the recovery between bouts. Doing high-rep, low-resistance exercises with a stretch-resistance cord is the best way to gain endurance in the muscles.

Shoulder instability often occurs when these rotator cuff and scapular muscles become fatigued. The high-volume work associated with endurance is also the best method for improving tendon and ligament strength. The goal of this program is to prepare water polo players for the nature of intense activity that occurs in a water polo game. These high-speed exercises are more sports specific than normal resistance training using weights.

Doing sets of 25-30 repetitions for each exercise is a good place to start to develop both the strength and endurance aspects of the shoulder muscles. The athlete should start feeling fatigue in the muscles as he approaches the last several repetitions. If 25-30 repetitions are too easy, then the athlete should get a heavier resistance cord, increase the resistance by holding the cord closer to where it is attached, or stand further away from the attachment. If the athlete can only do 10 repetitions before fatigue sets in, then he should obtain a lighter resistance cord or stand closer to where the cord is attached.

After several months of performing sets of 25-30 repetitions for each exercise, obtain a band with enough resistance so that the athlete can only perform 10-15 repetitions before tiring. Start the exercise by pulling the hand slowly to the final position, hold that position for several seconds, and then slowly return the hand to the starting position. Perform 10-12 repetitions of each exercise in this manner.

These high repetition sets are also recommended for the larger scapular stabilizers to help delay the onset of fatigue during activity. Therefore, the traditional strength exercises for the scapular stabilizers, such as rows, shrugs, reverse flys and bent over lateral raises, may be also be performed doing high repetition repeats with stretch cords on alternate days. Heavier resistance with weights on one day can be followed by high rep exercises with stretch cords or dumbbells on the next day.

ROTATOR CUFF EXERCISES USING STRETCH CORDS

The most common rotator cuff exercises with stretch cords are internal and external rotation of both arms, arm abduction (moving arm away from mid-line of body), and the internal rotation and horizontal adduction (moving arm toward midline of body) of the arms. Variety is important to insure that all of the rotator cuff muscles are used; so choose one exercise in each category and perform those for several sessions, before switching to another exercise for the next few sessions.

Following are common rotator cuff exercises:

INTERNAL/EXTERNAL ROTATION EXERCISES
1. Internal/External Rotation-Elbow at side

Attach band to a door-knob. Stand sideways to the door. Grab the band with one hand with your elbow pinned to your side. Internal rotation consists of pulling the band towards your body, and external rotation consists of pulling the band away from your body. Remember to keep the elbow tucked into the side during the entire range of motion (See pictures 7-B on the next page).

Picture Sequence 7-B: External Rotation   Internal Rotation

2. 90-degree Internal/External Rotation
For external rotation, attach band in front of you at between waist and chest level. Grab the band with one hand, and raise your arm in the air forming a 90-dregree angle. Internal rotation consists of pulling the band down towards the ground (attach band behind you at shoulder level). (See pictures 7-C below).

Picture sequence 7-C: 90 degeree external rotation   90 degree internal Rotation

3. HORIZONTAL ADDUCTION/ ARM ROTATION EXERCISES
Crossover: Attach the band to something that is a few inches off the ground and directly in front of you. Using your left arm first, start with the band near your right hip. Keeping your arm straight for the whole movement, pull the band across your body until your arm is completely extended above your head on your left side. After completing the prescribed number of repetitions, start the band near your left hip and pull the band across your body until your arm is completely extended on the right side of your head. After completing repetitions with your left arm, perform the same two exercises with your right arm. (See Picture sequence 7-D on the next page).

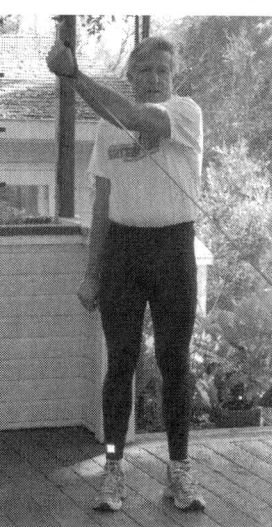

Picture sequence 7-D: Left hand- Crossover right to left and crossover left to right

4. Lateral Raise with Internal Rotation using stretch cord or dumbbell (pouring can of coke): Stand on cord. With arm at side and thumb pointed toward ground (shoulders internally rotated), slowly raise arm to the sides but slightly toward the front (at about a 30 degree angle to the front of the body) until almost shoulder level. See Pictures 7-E below)

Pictures 7-E: Pouring can of coke, thumb down

5. Abduction- Standing Arm Abduction:
Grab elastic tubing with both hands about shoulder width apart. Arms are straight. Begin with the arms at various heights (below waist, above waist, shoulder height,) Pull both hands away from his the midline. Hold for a count of 5 seconds. 15 reps at each height. (See picture sequence 7-F and 7-G on the next page).

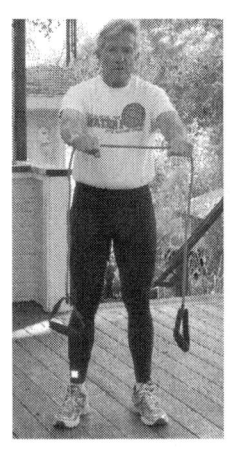

Picture sequence 7-F: Standing Arm Abduction- below waist and above waist

Picture sequence 7-G: Standing Arm Abduction- shoulder height

DRY LAND CIRCUIT TRAINING PROGRAM

Circuit training consists of a series of stations, with a different exercise at each station. The circuit can be set up with as many stations as necessary to accomplish the goals of he team. Stations can be situated around the pool deck or in a weight-room, with two players assigned to each station.

Twelve stations can accommodate 24 players at the same time. When a whistle or horn blows, everyone starts together by performing the particular exercise at that station. After the first player performs the exercise, then the second player also does the exercise. Upon completion of each exercise, a horn or whistle indicates that each pair must rotate to the next station, in a clockwise direction. Once they arrive at the next station, another horn or whistle will indicate the start of the next exercise.

The beauty of circuit training is that everyone on the team can work out at the same time, and it doesn't take a lot of time to complete. A circuit can be set up around the pool deck, utilizing only stretch cords and body weight exercises, or in the water using surgical (teathered) tubing and heavy balls. This is particularly helpful during the competitive season, because it will allow players to maintain specific water polo strength without utilizing heavy weights.

A circuit requires little time to complete, allowing the team to spend more time in the pool preparing for games. During the off-season a circuit can be set up in a weight room, utilizing weight machines and free weights instead of stretch cords. The off-season circuit can also be performed twice in one session, so that each player performs two sets of each exercise.

Following is a circuit that can be set up around a pool deck. The team can do this circuit twice a week, just prior to jumping into the pool for water polo practice:

Station 1- Push-ups: 2 sets x 12-15 reps (body weight)

Station 2- Dips (triceps): 2 sets x 12 reps (body weight)

Station 3- Crunches: 1 set x 40 reps (body weight) Standard crunches (hands folded across chest, lifting shoulder blades off the ground; or abdominal oblique exercises described under the "Big-Ten" above

Station 4- Bent over straight-arm pull or slightly-bent arm pull: 2 sets x 25

Station 5- Bent over triceps extension: 2 sets x 25 reps (stretch cord)

Station 6- Bench leg straddle jump: 2 sets x 12 reps (body weight)

Station 7- Forward and backward shoulder flys: 1 set each @ 25 reps

Station 8- Rowing exercise (seated): 2 sets x 20 reps (stretchcord)

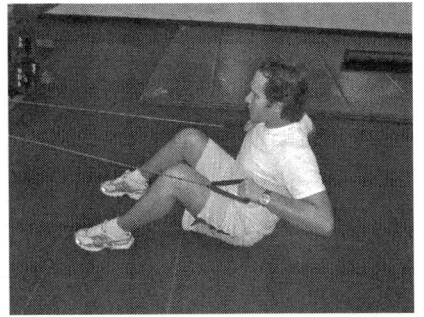

Station 9- Upright row (standing): 2 sets x 20 reps (stretch cord)

Station 10- Pull-ups (pull-up bar) as many as possible, hands forward and backward.

Station 11: Full arm shooting motion- 20 reps each arm

Station 12: Shooting tricep extension-20 reps each arm

Station 13:Bent arm fly- Squeeze elbows and forearms together (2 sets x 15 reps)

Station 14: Rotator cuff exercise- Internal/external rotation with elbow tucked in to side. Perform internal and external rotation on alternate days. 20 reps frp each arm (See rotator cuff exercises above)

Station 15: Rotator cuff exercise- Internal/external rotation with 90 degree arm elevated and out to side. Perform int/ext on alternate days. 20 reps for each arm. (See rotator cuff exercises above)

Station 16: Throwing basketball against wall (standing 3 feet away) 2 minutes each arm

More stations can be added utilizing other muscles or other rotator cuff exercises. If there are more stations than players available, leave the extra stations at the end of the circuit; so each pair of players will always have an open station to rotate to.

Many of these exercises are even more specific to water polo than the above weight room program, because of their reliance on stretch cords, rather than weights. The stretch cords allow for more duplication of the movements utilized in playing water polo; whereas free weights and machine weights are more restrictive. The circuit program also includes exercises for the rotator cuff, shoulder blade stabilizer muscles and shooting exercises.

This circuit can be done in lieu of, or in conjunction with the above weight-room (Top Ten) exercises. Integrating the two together depends on the timing of games; but the ideal program would include two days of the weight-room program interspersed with one or two days of the pool circuit. Because of the high-repetition and lower resistance involved in both of these exercise programs, they can be performed on back-to-back days and players can recover quickly without risk of injury.

IN-WATER (IN-SEASON) STRENGTH TRAINING CIRCUIT
Following is a pool training circuit to gain "applicable" (specific) water polo strength in the water and performed during the competitive season:
1. Tethered swim using surgical tubing or elastic band tied around waist
   Swim out 30 seconds, rest 30 seconds X 10 repeats

2. Weighted ball exercise- passing with 2 hands, both players in water
   One minute passing, 30 seconds rest X 5 sets

3. Wall pull-ups- 2 sets of 10

4. Partner "combative" drills

5. Partner passing with Mikasa light weight ball- one hand

6. Tethered eggbeater- player in vertical position using surgical tubing tied around the waist and eggbeater away from the wall. Eggbeater out to maximum length and hold for 30 seconds x 8 reps

7. Push-ups on pool deck- 2 sets of 12-15 reps

8. Weighted ball exercise- two hands, one player on deck, one in the water
   One minute passing, 30 sec rest X 5 sets

Any number of dry-land exercises as desired, can be added to this in-the-water pool circuit. If a coach does not want to perform in-season dry-land training for his team, then "In-water" training as described above, can be utilized to gain specific water polo strength.

The most obvious in-the-water "water polo specific" strength training is head-up sprint swimming, explosive leg drills, counterattack drills, and simply playing water polo. This kind of training will allow the water polo athlete to achieve exactly the strength needed to play the game of water polo.

WEEKLY PLAN

If a coach decides to do an in-season strength program, the best scenario if the team has Friday and/or Saturday games, is the following:
Monday- The "Big Ten", "Dry-land Circuit" or "In-Water Circuit"
Tuesday- Rotator Cuff execises as described above
Wednesday- Ultra-short sprint training
Thursday- The "Big Ten" , "Dry-land Circuit" or In-Water Circuit"
Friday- Rotator Cuff exercises as described above
Saturday- Game
Sunday- Day off

If games are (mid-week) Wednesday and Saturday, use the following scenario:
Monday- The "Big Ten", "Dry-land Circuit" or In-water Circuit
Tuesday- Rotator cuff exercises
Wednesday- Game
Thursday- The "Big Ten", "Dry-land Circuit" or In-water Circuit
Friday- Rotator Cuff exercises
Saturday- Game
Sunday- Day off

The biggest challenge for the water polo coach when it comes to strength training, is to decide which of the three programs listed above are to be utilized for the team; or whether they should be used at all during the competitive season. Time management is critical when trying to impliment a strength program, especially during the season. A team needs a minimum of two hours a day during the season to work on water polo related activities. Anything less than that would not be fair to the players.

With 2 hours or less available for training, the only option is to gain the strength necessary to perform in games by doing high intensity swim sprints and counterattack training, and weighted ball and explosive leg training in the water. Because of time constraints, any dry land training in this case can be done during the off-season.

If a coach has more than 2 hours of scheduled practice time, then the half hour before practice or a separate morning session can be used for the dry-land circuit training program, and/or the in-water circuit, as described above. These two circuits can be done on alternate days, for a total of four days of circuit training each week.

If a team is going to dry-land strength training like the "Big Ten" during the competitive season, I would suggest that the training be done in a morning session, and not immediately prior to an afternoon practice session. The reason for this is so the players will be fully recovered for their water polo afternoon practice session.

I personally don't believe that a dryland strength program like the "Big Ten" is required or necessary during a competitive water polo season. All of the strength necessary to play water polo can be achieved by in water circuit training and by overloading the muscles with sprint swims and explosive leg drills in the water. It is up to the water polo coach to make this decision. At least consider the research and the physiological and fluid dynamic principles presented in this manual, before going into a heavy duty weight lifting program. I would rather spend the time learning how to play the game.

Note: I don't believe that it is necessary to start youngsters under the age of 14 on a dryland strength program with machines and free weights. This is my own personal opinion, based on observation and experience. Again, coaches can make their own decisions on this; but I don't believe it is necessary while young people's bodies are still growing and developing.

It would be a good idea, though, to get youngsters started on strengthening the shoulder stabilizer muscles with stretch bands, as described above. If you can get young people started on this at a young age, and get them to make it part of their daily routine, we might be able to prevent the injuries to the shoulders that can occur at a later age. I really believe that having youngsters swimming and playing water polo is a great way to develop their bodies, without subjecting them to heavy-duty dry-land strength programs.

CHAPTER 8
EXERCISE MYTHS THAT COACHES NEED TO KNOW THE TRUTH ABOUT

There are a lot of misconceptions in the world of athletics that coaches and athletes just blindly follow without questioning, especially when it comes to training and conditioning. Many fallacies about training for sports have been handed down from generation to generation, without questioning whether they are right or not. They are usually based only on "word of mouth", or "overall success", and have no scientific basis or proof that they really work.

There are so many factors that go into whether a team is successful or not, that it difficult to say whether one particular aspect of training may have been the major contributor to success. In fact, many times a coach with great athletes on his team can achieve success, even if he trains them incorrectly. Great athletes many times can overcome poor coaching. To take any one training method, and say that is the reason for the success of an athlete or a team, is risky, without proof that the method actually was the cause of the success.

The coach of a winning team or a champion athlete may go before a group of coaches at a technical clinic, and espose his methods of training and his tactics as the reasons why the team or athlete was successful. For example, the coach of the champion athlete may state that his champion swimmer swam 20,000 meters a day in training, and that this was the reason for his success. Who is to say that this same athlete could not have achieved success on only 5,000 or 10,000 meters a day of training?

To say that swimming 20,000 meters a day was the reason why that athlete performed well is really a stretch; and doesn't take into consideration all of the things that may also have contributed to his performance, like body type, muscle structure, how hard he worked, how intense was the training, what kind of training it was, experience, technique, etc. Testimony about what one champion athlete did is not a proven scientific study.

The only way to determine if a particular exercise routine or a particular physical attribute is beneficial to better performance in a sport, is to conduct a study in which many people are involved in identical training; and all outside factors are controlled as much as possible. Part of the group will use the method in question, and part of the group will not. To make it even more effective and to overcome the placebo effect, (an athletes performs better because he thinks that what he is doing will make him better) is to have a third group perform a third method, which has been determined ahead of time, has no effect at all on performance.

For instance, in a study on vitamin supplements, hiding a placebo in a pill that looks like all the others is easily done. Using a placebo in training studies, however, is not always possible because of the difficulty of performing a physical skill that the athlete is unaware will help him. Individual differences, ability, and reaction to training stimulus are also difficult to account for. So is the effect of differences in motivational levels from different athletes in regards to training intensity and motivation to perform at the highest level.

MYTHS ABOUT SPORTS HEROS AND THE EFFECTS OF HEREDITY

One of the biggest myths in the world of sport is the perception that if you train like a champion athlete, use the same techniques that he/she does, eat the same foods that he/she eats, wear the same shoes that he/she does, use the same equipment that he/she does, and take the same supplements that he/she does, that you will end up having the same success that he/she has in his sport. This is what the equipment manufactures, supplement companies and even the star athlete himself would like you to believe; especially if the company, or the athlete, are trying to sell you a product, or a book(s) about the super-star.

Athletes should not discount the influence of heredity on the success in all sports. Heredity probably plays more of a factor than athletes think it does; and whether they are successful in their sport or not. The fact of the matter is that the successful super-star in any sport has inherited from his parents the type of body characteristics that make him successful in his/her sport.

There are many characteristics in sports that can be developed with training and practice; but if you don't have the essential characteristics that are absolutely necessary for success in your sport, you will not achieve the same success as the athlete who has those characteristics. Having the necessary physical characteristics does not guarantee success in a sport or activity; but in most cases it is essential to start with those characteristics.

The successful athlete must then train hard, and also have the right mental attitude to add to his physical characteristics. That being said, no matter how hard you train in a particular sport, you will never be as successful as Michael Jordan (basketball), Michael Phelps (swimming), Lance Armstrong (cycling) or Tony Azevedo (water polo), because you may not have started with the same physical characteristics as they have started with.

Athletes tend to gravitate to sports in which the kind of body that they have will allow them to be successful in that particular sport. Every sport has physical attributes that are important to be successful (size, strength, flexibility, different types of muscle fibers, endurance capacity, sprint speed, mental toughness, etc). If you want to be successful in your sport, hope that you have inherited from your parents the characteristics that define success in your sport. The next time you watch the Olympic games on television, notice the similarities of the body types inherent in each sport.

An extreme and obvious example would be to compare the body types in gymnastics and basketball. Physical characteristics in other sport activities are just as obvious (distance runners versus sprinters), and some are hidden inside the body and not so obvious. (Joint structure, flexibility, cardiovascular system, muscle fiber types, etc).

TYPICAL MYTHS IN ATHLETICS
Many myths have developed about how an athlete should train to be successful in their sport. An example of this kind of myth that led to a practice that was commonplace in football in the 50's and 60's, was not providing water to football players in hot weather; because of the idea that it made the athlete mentally tougher. How many football players have died, or have been severely injured, by not drinking water during a two to three hour training session in high heat and humidity; simply because the coach didn't know any better?

It seems absurd now that we know about it; but it is amazing to think that for years a lot of football coaches really believed that withholding water made the player tougher. Who did they learn this from? The coaches before them who did this to them when they were players; or from coaches of championship teams who used this method of training. As long as a team that withheld water won a championship, that was good enough for everybody else. No one even thought about looking in to consequences of dehydration. It was just excepted that this was the way to produce champion teams.

Another technique that is still practiced at some health clubs and wrestling teams is to exercise with full body rubber suits in order to lose weight. This is a dangerous practice that elevates body temperatures to an extreme level, and without any way to cool off. Most of the weight that is lost by doing this comes from water loss; also causing severe dehydration of the body. Any trainer or health instructor with any kind of knowledge about how the body works would not allow this practice. Yet, this was a common practice in gyms and wrestling teams well into the 70's and 80's.

Static stretching before and after exercsie is another of these kind of myths that have been passed down over the years from coach to coach, and exercise teacher to exercise teacher; without ever questioning whether it really works or not. Stretching is so ingrained into the exercise culture around the world, that many professional teams, as well as high school and college teams, and of course health club classes, continue this practice today; in spite of the perponderance of evidence that it doesn't do what it is supposed to do.

It really is amazing to me to see trainers and coaches of professional sports teams still blindly using techniques for training that went out with the dark ages, and are a complete waste of time. How many professional baseball teams have their athletes stretch before a game, thinking that they will prevent injuries by doing so? Probably all of them! The player then sits on the bench or stands in the outfield for several hours on a cold night; and then suddenly is asked to sprint to first base from a standing position, resulting in a hamstring pull.

Why is this happening in baseball and other sports? Because trainers and coaches are creatures of habit, and keep doing things the same way all of the time. How many hundreds of hamstring pulls have to occur every season before baseball trainers figure out what is going on. The answer is simple---they just do not have an understanding of stretching, and that all of the stretching in the world does not warm up the body. Even if they do warm-up properly, the coach will still ask a player to sit in the dugout for eight innings on a cold night, and then tell him to go in as a pinch runner in the ninth. The effects of any warm-up are long gone by then.

"Tradition" (the way things have always been done) is a great way to justify what athletes do; and many coaches and athletes refuse to change what they do, despite negative evidence to the contrary. Despite the indisputable proof that chewing tobacco causes tongue and mouth cancer, countless numbers of professional baseball players chew the vile stuff throughout every game. Why? Because of tradition. How can we expect them to stop the worthless practice of stretching before every game or practice, when they will not stop doing something that they know causes cancer?

Then there are people who spread myths because it is in their best interest to do so. Swim coaches who spread myths about water polo, strength coaches who insist that you have to lift weights to succeed in all sports, trainers and coaches who spread myths to perpetuate their own reputation, and stretching and exercise teachers who gain their livelihood by spreading these myths, all have the same thing in common; they all personally have something to gain by doing so.

Some people spread untruths because they are trying to sell you something from which they will make a lot of money from. You will see a lot of these products in magazines, newspaper ads, and infomercials on television; everything from abdominal machines and twister trainers to vitamins, muscle builders and energy boosters. They all claim that only their product can help you to perform better, build bigger muscles, lose weight, etc, and it can easily be accomplished in just a few minutes a day, or by taking a few pills. Before you rush out and buy one of these products, remember that nothing comes as easy as they say it does. There are no magic pills or magic machines that will substitute for a sensible diet and hard work.

DON'T JUST ACCEPT-QUESTION AND ANALYZE!
I always listened to my coaches and utilized many things that they taught me when I became a coach. However, I constantly analyzed what I was doing, and why I was doing it. If I couldn't answer questions about why we were doing something; or didn't understand something myself, I would find out the answer or change to something different. If you as a coach cannot explain to your team what you are doing, and why you are doing it, then educate yourself by doing research and asking questions. Don't just blindly accept what has "always been done" in the past.

Skepticism is an excellent trait for athletes and coaches to develop when evaluating what they are being told by other people. Question everything that you do or are told by others; instead of just accepting something that you do to your body and take into your body; and what you have others do to their bodies. Make sure that what you are doing has been proven to benefit you or your team, and that it is not just for the benefit (financial or self-promotion) of the people who are telling you these things.

MYTHS ABOUT TRAINING FOR WATER POLO

MYTH: YOU CAN'T COACH SPEED

TRUTH: True sprinters are born with more white (fast twitch) muscle fibers that contribute to speed; and consequently have an advantage over athletes with less white FT fibers. If two swimmers with different proportions of white and red muscle fibers perform the exact same training and use the same techniques, then the swimmer with more white fibers should be able to swim faster in a sprint race.

The good news is that the athlete with less white fibers can be trained to swim faster; although he will never achieve the speed of the athlete with more white fibers. Perhaps the statement "you can't coach speed" should be modified to read "you can't coach the potential for speed". The athlete's potential for swimming fast depends on the amount of fast twitch muscle fibers and the type of body that the person is born with. However, an athlete can't just jump into the water and suddenly just start swimming fast. The player still has to trained with the proper training, and be coached in the proper technique in order to realize that potential.

The same holds true for the water polo athlete who is born with the potential to perform the eggbeater kick. He/she still has to be trained to be able to correctly perform the kick, and apply it to the many water polo skills that utilize the eggbeater kick.

MYTH: THE MORE FLEXIBLE YOU ARE, THE BETTER SWIMMER AND WATER POLO PLAYER YOU WILL BE.

TRUTH: You hear athletes say that "I need to be more flexible", even though they have normal range of motion in every joint. What's this all about? Why are people worried about being more flexible? Probably because someone told them that they could perform better in their sport if they were more flexible. Unless you are an acrobat, a gymnast, a ballet dancer, a yogi, or a martial artist, you probably don't need to be more flexible.

These kinds of activities demand more flexibility because they rely on "extremes of motion" for movement. People who successfully participate in these extreme motion activities are probably born with greater joint flexibility than normal people to begin with. They are successful in those activities because they started out with naturally flexible joints. They did not acquire them later on.

Recent research on swimmer's flexibility suggests there is no indication that extraordinary shoulder joint motion or flexibility is necessary to achieve a fast, efficient stroke. Elite level competitive swimmers are naturally selected to their sport; just as gymnasts are naturally selected for their sport. They are generally flexible and possess loose connective tissue (general joint laxity). Increased flexibility beyond normal range of motion is not required for success in swimming.

The same is true for water polo. There is no research that indicates that a player can swim faster, or throw the ball harder, with a more flexible shoulder. Because of its "ball and socket" arrangement, the shoulder joint already has the most range of motion of any joint in the body. How much more range do you need than the 360 degrees that the shoulder already has?

Many players believe that flexibility is required in the knee, hips and ankles to be able to perform the eggbeater kick. This may be true, because players who have the best eggbeater kick, usually have the joint structure of the knees that gives them the flexibility to turn the foot and leg out to the side.

This is much like breaststrokers in competitive swimming. Water polo players who can position the legs in this manner have the ability to create maximum force and speed when they push down on the water. Good eggbeater kickers, as well as good breaststrokers are born with this ability. While you can train your legs to improve the eggbeater kick, you will never achieve the powerful kick of the player or breaststroker who has the natural kick that he/she was born with.

You certainly cannot improve the flexibility of the joints by stretching them. In fact you can damage the ligaments and tendons of a joint by forced stretching. Once the full range of motion of a joint is reached (as dictated by muscle and bone structure), the only way to go past that point, and increase the range of motion, is to stretch ligaments and tendons that are not made to be stretched.

The joints of the legs depend on the tightness of its ligaments and tendons to hold them together. The range of motion of the knee joint has its limits, and cannot be increased by forced stretching. Unless you were born with the ability to position your legs in the "frog" kick position, no amount of stretching will help put them in that position.

MYTH: YOU DON'T NEED TO WARM-UP BEFORE PRACTICE OR A GAME!
TRUTH: A proper warm-up is not only necessary, but essential to prepare for the intensity and effort required in practice and games. Every joint has a maximum range of motion (ROM) and athletes need to perform at the "full" range possible. However, when the muscles, ligaments and tendons are cold before we use them, their range of motion is limited and we feel tight. Consequently our range of motion is less before we warm up and loosen up the muscles and tendons.

It is actual movement that increases the range of motion of a joint. Only by contracting a muscle will heat be produced in the muscle body. This helps by increasing the active flexibility of the entire muscle, rather than just the passive aspects (static stretching), which only includes the ends of the muscle (i.e. tendons and ligaments), and does nothing to increase the temperature of the muscle.

In other words the warmed up muscle is more easily elongated and contracted, and the increased fluid in the joint, helps increase the range that the muscle can move thru. The same thing hold true for warmed up ligaments and tendons. They become more pliable and easier to bend. This active flexibility is what carries over to sport. The best activity to actively perform in order to warm up for a game or practice, is the sport activity itself. This is called, for lack of a better term, active stretching. However, it is not stretching at all, but "warming up".

MYTH: THE PLAYERS LOOK TIRED AND OUT OF SHAPE, SO WE HAVE TO DO MORE SWIMMING TO GET THEM BACK IN SHAPE
TRUTH: Some coaches, when they see that their players are not trying hard, or look tired in a game, will punish them by making them swim more in practice. The problem is not that players are loafing, but that they are probably exhausted from strenous training sessions; and the coach has failed to rest them to allow for replenishment of necessary energy stores.

Piling on more swimming will not make the problem go away. Not only will it make it worse, but it could possibly result in overtraining the players, bringing on injuries and sickness. There is usually a reason why highly motivated athletes look tired and fatigued. The answer is more rest, not more swimming.

MYTH: IN ORDER TO GET THE TEAM IN SHAPE QUICKLY, THE COACH NEEDS TO PILE ON THE YARDAGE DURING THE FIRST WEEK OF PRACTICE
TRUTH: Actually, the exact opposite is true, especially if the players are coming off a period of inactivity in regards to swimming and leg work. The biggest mistake a coach can make is to pile on the yardage during the first week of training. This happens often during the so-called "hell-week" at the beginning of the season, where coaches often overload the players with excess swimming, weight lifting, running, leg training, etc for up to 6-8 hours a day, thinking that it is going to get the team in shape faster. The result is sick and broken down players with injuries to the shoulders that may take weeks to repair.

The "gradual" approach is much more effective than the "hit em' hard" approach; and it will still get them in shape for the upcoming competitive season. Hard training at the beginning of the season must be gradually introduced to the team, to allow them to adjust their bodies to activities that they many have not performed for a while. Doing a lot of long, slow swimming does not get them in shape any quicker, and does not prepare them for the intense sprint swimming that will be performed later on.

During the first few days of practice, it is best to swim short distances at medium speed and with fairly short recovery periods between each swim. As the player's bodies adjust to the training, then gradually increase the intensity of each swim; and at the same time increase the rest periods, until a one to one ratio of work to rest is achieved.

This is also the time to gradually increase the intensity of the leg training (eggbeater kick), as well as the speed of shooting the ball. Training should not be more than 4 hours a day during this period of time, divided into two sessions, with a good portion of the training going to learning game skills and tactics. More learning goes on when the players are not exhausted from being overtrained. It doesn't take that long to get the players into game shape by using this method of training. It actually takes longer if the coach piles on the intense, long training immediately during the first week(s) of practice. (See "building a base" above)

MYTH: WATER POLO PLAYERS NEED TO JOIN THE SWIM TEAM DURING THE OFF-SEASON IN ORDER TO STAY IN SHAPE FOR WATER POLO
TRUTH: This practice was probably started years ago when coaches would coach both swimming and water polo at both the high school and college levels. We still continue this practice today, especially at the high school level; even though most water polo coaches do not coach swimming anymore. Sometimes it is at the request of the swimming coach, who probably wouldn't have much of a team if it wasn't for water polo players.

The question begs to be answered. Why are our water polo players, especially in high school, required to be on the swim team? Is it really necessary? You don't see basketball, soccer and football players being required to go out for the track or cross-country team. Most players on most Olympic water polo teams around the world did not swim on an organized swim team when they were young. I don't see the Hungarian counterattack suffering because their players did not swim on a competitive swim team.

What do these players (Hungarians, Serbs and Italians) do if they don't swim during the water polo off-season? They play water polo! Or they perform water polo related swimming that is organized by the water polo coach, not the swim coach. Many of them play year around, with a break of several months during the summer.

Swimming longer distances of freestyle, backstroke, breaststroke and butterfly with the head down, and using a wall, does not give an athlete any advantage for water polo; unless a young player doesn't know how to swim at all. All a water polo player needs to learn is how to swim fast with the head up for distances of 5-25 meters. There isn't any need to be on a swim team in order to be able to do this.

Any water polo coach can teach a player how to swim fast for a short distance, and then quickly change directions. You don't have to have a swimming background to do that. I can teach someone how to perform water polo swimming in just a matter of days.

If a coach can provide year around training for water polo players, swimming on the swim team during the off-season is not necessary. The training that a water polo player receives on the swim team is not necessarily beneficial for water polo, unless he specializes in sprint (50, 100) races. A water polo coach can do a much better job of providing water polo specific swim training for the athlete during the off season. Swim coaches are only concerned with training swimmers. They could care less about providing water polo specific training to the swimmers on their team.

What I object to is forcing water polo players, who hate swimming, to be on a swim team. Some water polo players absolutely can't stand having their face in the water and following a black line up and down the pool for 2-3 hours a day. They would rather play water polo. If a player doesn't want to swim, then he shouldn't have to. To me, this is just the way for a "lazy" water polo coach to take time off during the off-season, and have the swim coach do his work for him. Can you imagine a basketball coach telling his players that they all have to be on the cross-country team during the off season. He would have a revolt on his hands.

If a water polo coach wants his players to improve, then he should provide off season water polo for them, instead of requiring that they swim on the swim team. The water polo coach should take responsibility for his own players during the off-season, instead of handing them off to the swim team. It is my understanding that some Southern Calif. high schools are now providing off-season training for their players and not requiring them to be on a swim team. A big plus is that the small amount of swimming (2000 yards, 2-3 days a week) that they do is all water polo related. The rest of the workouts are spent playing and learning water polo.

I am not saying that swimming on a swim team is bad for you. If a player really likes it, and that is what he/ she wants to do it, then they should swim. It is certainly not going to hurt them. Just don't expect it to make them better water polo players. I just think that are better ways to get in shape for water polo, than just swimming. You have to practice water polo to get better at water polo. Learning the skills to play water polo is the most important factor in playing the game, beside having a good eggbeater kick. Swimming is what it is and water polo is what it is!

MYTH: CROSS-TRAINING IN THE OFF SEASON HELPS WATER POLO PLAYERS PERFORM BETTER DURING THE SEASON

TRUTH: The belief that "cross-training" exercises are valuable for specific competitive performances is erroneous, and is not supported by science. If an athlete is going to perform in a certain manner in a competition, then training exercise intensity, duration, and form need to mimic the intended competitive demands. Otherwise, trained fitness will not be employed in the sport competition. This requires that coaches do not waste time training skills and conditioning that does not specifically apply to the skills and physical part of a game. It is ridiculous to think that running during the off-season will help a swimmer during the competitive season. The exact opposite is true! It can actually be detrimental to swimming performance.

But what about triathletes, don't they cross-train? No, they do not. They train for three separate sports (swimming, running and biking), because they are required to perform three different sports in their event. Training for swimming does not necessarily help the triathlete run or bike faster, and vice-versa. Some triathletes are great swimmers who come out of the water in first place; but quickly lose their position and fall well back in the pack in the biking and running phases.

I think it is safe to say that the media and shoe-makers have combined to confuse many young and older athletes about the need for cross-training. Nike, and all the folks who sell exercise equipment would like you to believe that "cross-training" is a key to peak performance. The concept sells more sports shoes and exercise machines, but is it true?

Well, no. Any sport you pursue places highly specific demands on your body, in at least two major ways. First, the exercise will have a very specific pattern of joint and muscle coordination. For a rower, there is absolutely no substitute for rowing. Ditto for swimming. Skills from one sport also do not transfer to another sport, even for similar skills. For instance, throwing a baseball, football and water polo ball require completely different skills, even though the action of throwing the ball is similar.

Second, the exercise will place high metabolic demands on a very specific group of muscles. For example, running and cross-country skiing appear to involve many of the same muscles used in a similar movement pattern. Yet, several research studies have demonstrated that there is NO relationship between VO2 max (maximum oxygen consumption-a measure of aerobic capacity) measured by running, and VO2 max measured by cross-country skiing in a group of elite-trained skiers.

So, what's the harm in training in an activity that is not the same as your sport? For starters, the possibility of a positive transfer of training effects from one sport activity to another are negligible at best. Not only that, but performing a non-specific activity wastes valuable time that you could actually be training for your specific sport activity. There is also the possibility that it would have a negative effect or detract from performance.

If the athlete is performing some other kind of sport activity during the off-season, as a mental relief from the rigors of their primary sport, then by all means go for it. Just don't expect it to have a physical carry over to your sport activity. Definitely forget the running on dry-land for water polo players. Running is not needed or should not be attempted at any time (unless you are a triathlete). It should not be required during the off-season, not during "hell week", and definitely not during the competitive season.

MYTH- GETTING MY BODY STRONGER BY LIFTING WEIGHTS IN THE OFF-SEASON WILL BENEFIT ME DURING THE SEASON

TRUTH- Just as metabolic effects such as aerobic oxygen consumption are not transferred from one aerobic event to another, neither is the overall "general" strength gained from weight-training transferred to increased strength or performance in a specific sport activity.

Weight training will definitely make an athlete stronger when lifting weights; but will that strength be transferred to a specific sport like water polo, and will it improve performance in that sport? Only if the strength training targets specific muscles and movements used in water polo is there a possibility of a transfer effect.

If the activities of strength training do not replicate those of water polo competition, then the value of the increased strength for water polo will be greatly decreased, or be of no value at all. The strength gained will simply serve no purpose in a game or practice. In other words, "overall" or "general" body strength does not translate to the specific strength needed for a particular sports activity.

Only by performing the specific activity of water polo will the necessary strength be achieved to play water polo. Only by overloading the muscles in the water while performing the skills of water polo, namely swimming and eggbeater, will the strength to play water polo be achieved. (See Chapter 7 on "Resistance Training for Water Polo" for more information on strength training).

MYTH: WE NEED TO TEST OUR PLAYERS PHYSICAL ABILITIES IN ORDER TO DETERMINE WHETHER THEY CAN PLAY THE GAME.
TRUTH: Testing a person's physical abilities, like squat strength, vertical water jump, 30-meter swim time, 10 x 200 meters swim test, arm-strength, and any other physical test, really does not tell you a lot about what kind of water polo player that person is. All it really tells you is how good that person is at performing that particular physical test. These kinds of tests can be useful when trying to determine if a particular quality, like arm-strength, translates to speed in the water. This is because you can measure both of these parameters, arm strength and speed in the water.

It is when coaches try to go the next step that they get into trouble. Trying to correlate swimming ability (speed or endurance) to determine whether a person can perform the water polo counterattack, has its drawbacks. That is like saying that someone who swims 20 meters in 12 seconds, will be better on the counterattack than someone who swims 20 meters in 14 seconds. This does not correlate, because swim speed for 20 meters is only one factor in a successful counterattack. Positioning, anticipation, reaction, getting a quick start, holding front position, etc are all critical factors in a successful counterattack.

Several studies on shooting a water polo ball tried to determine if vertical height in the water, and arm strength in the shoulder muscles, correlated to ability to shoot the ball faster. No correlation was found, again because there are so many other factors that go into shooting the ball, than vertical height and shoulder/arm strength. Leg power (not height in water), shoulder rotation, positioning, correct form, follow through, shooting around the defender's arm, beating the goalie, etc are all factors that go into shooting the ball.

Technique then becomes a more important factor in shooting the ball, than arm strength or height in the water. Ability to place the ball into the goal is the ultimate test of shooting a water polo ball; not vertical height in the water and arm strength.

An example of the futility of testing physical parameters to analyze performance, was a classic study conducted by the University of Louisville, Kentucky; in which they examined the famous NFL Combine that tests college football players who enter the draft. The combine consists of a series of drills, exercises, interviews, aptitude tests, and physical exams designed to assess the skills of promising college football players, and to predict their performance in the NFL.

NFL teams rely almost exclusively on the combine in determining how high they should draft a player, and in what order they draft players. Success in the combine can mean millions of dollars to drafted players, while a weak performance can mean the "kiss of death" in terms of draft status and money. In this study, U of L, looked at quarterbacks, running backs and wide-receivers, and how they performed in the combine; and then looked at them again 6 years later to determine their success in the NFL.

Using correlation analysis, the University found no consistent statistical relationship between combine tests and professional football performance, with the notable exception of a sprint test for running backs. The NFL teams who drafted players based on the results of the combine could just as well have based their picks on film analysis of college performance, and completely done away with the combine. They probably would have been more successful basing their draft picks on performance, rather than the results of a battery of physical and mental tests. The Oakland Raiders are a good example of using speed tests to draft wide receivers who cannot catch the ball that is thrown to them.

The same can be said for our US National Junior Water Polo team, that at one time actually selected players for the team based on how they did in a timed 10 x 200 meter swim set. Since that set was at the first practice session of the try-outs, the players were probably so exhausted after that, they could not perform the skills necessary to play water polo. If they applied this swim test to members of the World Champion Hungarian Junior team, most of those players would not have made the US team that placed ninth in those same World Championships. They simply would not have passed the swim test!

The bottom line is that it is NOT necessary to perform numerous physical skill tests in order for a coach to evaluate the ability of his players to play the game of water polo. Simple observation of a player during practice, and in games, will determine whether he/she has the abilities to play the game. Performing successful counterattacks is more a determination of a player's water polo speed, than measuring his ability to swim a set of 10 X 200 yard swims using walls and flip turns. The ability to block a ball, or shoot a ball, is more a determination of water polo leg strength than measuring the height a player can jump out of the water.

MYTHS STARTED BY HEALTH CLUB INSTRUCTORS, ATHLETIC TRAINERS AND STRENGTH COACHES.

Some of the things that we do as coaches come from health club teachers and fitness instructors; who many times have no formal training or degree in their field. They simply pass on to everyone who will listen, what they learned from other health club instructors, who also don't have degrees or formal training. Static stretching before you start to exercise, in order to get you warmed up, is one of the myths perpetuated by many in the so called "health and fitness" field, without any idea why they are doing it; or whether it actually works or not.

Fitness instructors, from so-called "health" clubs, are the same people that for years promoted belt vibrators and wooden rollers that would vibrate or massage the fat away from your body (butt), without having to do any work yourself. I hate to say it, but many professional and some college team trainers fall into this category. Many are not certified, and only have the experience that was passed on to them. Most trainers keep doing the same incorrect things that they learned from the trainers before them. The next time you see a pro or college football or baseball team warm-up, what is the first thing they do before doing anything else? Stretch their cold muscles! Why? In order to warm up and prevent injuries!

STRETCHING THE TRUTH-THE BIGGEST MYTH IN SPORTS!

The United States Centers for Disease Control and Prevention (CDCP) did an in-depth study and summary of hundreds of studies on stretching, and essentially came to the conclusion that "Pre-workout and post-workout static stretching, as it is performed by many teams and athletes, does not do what it is intended to do. Stretching does not prevent injury, muscle soreness, warm up the athlete, or increase flexibility. In fact, there is evidence that stretching can cause injury to muscles and joints, and decrease athletic performance".

Despite a preponderance of evidence to the contrary, there are still coaches and trainers that continue to have their teams practice static stretching prior to and after training and games. This qualifies "stretching" as the biggest myth perpetuated in sports!

STRETCHING MYTH # 1- YOU MUST STRETCH TO WARM-UP BEFORE A WORKOUT OR GAME IN ORDER TO PREVENT INJURIES

TRUTH: The typical warm-up of static stretching that some athletes perform before a practice or game does not prepare muscles for the active contraction-relaxation process that occurs during most sports and activities. The main reason for this is that heat is only produced by a contracting (working) muscle, not by stretching a muscle. Static stretching also decreases the tension in the muscles, which decreases force production.

Body heat is generated by metabolic activity, particularly muscle contraction. The best way to warm-up is to start doing a kinder, gentler version of the activity you have in mind, i.e. walk first, jog and then run. Since static stretching does not "contract" muscles, and since contraction is what draws blood into a muscle and generates metabolic activity to provide a "warm-up", there is no warming up imparted by stretching.

Dynamic (movement) warm-ups, where the athlete actually performs the activity that he/she will participate in, better prepares the body by increasing core and muscle temperature, heart rate and blood flow, range of motion of the limbs involved, and activates the nervous system that recruits muscle fibers to contract.

Numerous research studies by scientists all over the world during the past 10-15 years, have provided conclusive evidence that static stretching before any physical activity does not prevent injuries to the joints and muscles involved. In fact, stretching before your muscles are warmed up can actually increase your chance of injury. Putting a "cold" muscle in its weakest position (fully stretched) and applying a load of body weight or muscular force, is one sure way to injure it.

STRETCHING MYTH # 2- I NEED TO STRETCH SO THAT I CAN BECOME MORE FLEXIBLE
TRUTH: First of all, it has never been proven that most sports activities require increased flexibility beyond a normal range of motion, unless you are an acrobat, gymnast, yogi, contortionist or martial artist. Besides, most of the people that succeed in those activities were naturally selected with joints that are flexible beyond a normal range of motion.

Secondly, and more important, stretching a muscle doesn't make an athlete more flexible either. Muscles have a limited range over which they can be stretched, which as it must be in order for the muscles and joints they serve to be protected. You can stretch only as far as the muscles, and the structure of the joint will allow. Attempting to stretch beyond your limitations can be dangerous, as it results in weakening of the tendons and ligaments.

Most of the problems and derangements in the shoulder joints of swimmers and water polo players, for example, are not a result of "inadequate" flexibility, but of "excessive" flexibility. Over-stretching of the muscles and tendons surrounding the shoulder, caused by overuse and forced static stretching, can result in a so-called "loose" shoulder. Instead, a firm muscle and tendon joint structure is needed to protect and hold the joint in place; especially when movement of the arm above the head (swimming and throwing a ball) puts the joint in a vulnerable position and subject to injury.

Many people confuse flexibility with range of motion. Moving the muscle through its full range of motion is important in most sports activities, and is also helpful in increasing performance and preventing injuries. Range of motion can be increased by performing dynamic (movement) activities to warm up cold and tight muscles and joints, not by performing static stretching.

STRETCHING MYTH # 3- I NEED TO STRETCH AFTER I WORK OUT SO THAT I WON'T BE SORE THE NEXT DAY

TRUTH: Another popular idea about stretching is that it prevents that insidious deep tenderness and pain that follows a hard workout, or a workout that uses different muscles then the athlete is used to using. That soreness is called "delayed onset muscle soreness" or DOMS for short. Some people believe this like it is a religion. Unfortunately, the evidence suggests that they are kidding themselves.

In controlled scientific studies in which athletes performed the same training, and where some stretched and some did not, it was found that the stretched athletes experienced the same soreness and pain as the athletes who did not stretch. All of these studies have shown that nothing short of amputation of the sore limb can prevent DOMS; certainly not static stretching!

STRETCHING MYTH # 4- IT IS BETTER TO STRETCH AFTER A WORKOUT WHEN YOUR MUSCLES ARE WARM

TRUTH: There is absolutely no physiological reason why an athlete should stretch after going through a two hour practice session! As shown above, it certainly doesn't prevent muscle sorness the next day. This myth has been perpetated by stretching gurus, when it was proven beyond a doubt that static stretching a cold muscle before practice has no affect on anything, and can be detrimental to performance. In order to keep selling the hundreds of stretching manuals that are on the market (and they all think that their method is the only one that works), the proponents of stretching had to come up with something.

Since a muscle is not warmed up by stretching before practice, why not stretch after practice, when the muscles are warm? Athletes could even use all of the same exercises that were being promoted in stretching manuals. The only problem with this concept, is that static stretching after exercise, is just as worthless as static stretching before exercise. It doesn't matter when you do it, static stretching doesn't work, and is a complete waste of time and the money you spend on buying a stretching book.

MYTH- COOLING DOWN IS NECESSARY AFTER YOU EXERCISE

TRUTH- The act of cooling down (slow and easy swimming) started at swim meets, when swimmers had to swim two or three events back to back, or in a short period of time. The primary reason for cooling down was to help dissipate any lactic acid that was built-up from swimming a race at all out speed. Swimming slowly helps dissipate the built up lactic acid by allowing the circulatory system to move the lactic acid around the body, and slowly convert it back into energy (ATP).

This practice helped prepare for the next race that might come a half-hour after the first race; so that the swimmer could start the race without high levels of lactic acid in the muscles. Then coaches got carried away and decided that id this worked after a race, then you also had to "cool down" after every practice or exercise session.

This practice slowly spread to running and cycling and other sports. This became a way (so they claim) for athletes to prevent soreness the next day, as well as remove lactic acid from the body. Despite evidence to the contrary that it does not prevent soreness, coaches and players still continue this practice. The baseball world calls it "flush runs", jogging or running the day after pitching, or soaking their elbows in ice to clear the soreness from the day before. Football even goes so far as to immerse their players in a tub of ice after practice to prevent soreness the next day.

It is amazing what people will do because of a little muscle soreness. I don't care how sore I am after practice; there is no way that I would immerse my body in a tub of ice. The cure is worse than the symptoms! Numerous scientific studies have proven that nothing you can do will prevent next day soreness after you perform strenuous physical activity, except completely avoiding the exercise in the first place.

Getting rid of excess lactic acid is also totally unnecessary, unless the lactic acid build up might have an effect on your very next performance or practice session. This can only happen in a swim meet when you have two events close together, a water polo tournament where you have two games very close together, or back to back high intensity practice sessions with little time between sessions.

Other than that, there is no need to cool down after you swim, especially if your next time in the pool is the next day, or much later on the same day. Lactic acid will dissipate completely by itself over a relatively short period of several hours. Most certainly, it will be gone by the next day, or the next practice session.

It is a good idea to perform some mild aerobic swimming between games, if the games are close together. Some easy swimming during half-time of a water polo game is also a good idea. This method of "cooling down" does help dissapate lactic acid much quicker after a tough game or first half of water polo.

THE SECOND BIGGEST MYTH IN SPORTS- YOU HAVE TO LIFT WEIGHTS TO COMPETE IN YOUR SPORT

Is it necessary for water polo players to perform dry-land strength training for increased performance in their sport? What could be wrong with getting stronger? For the general public who wants to lead a healthy and productive life, exercise, along with diet are important parts of that healthy lifestyle. Strength training is one facet of exercise that can be of considerable benefit to everyone. However, there is a difference in lifting weights for health and fitness, and lifting weights to get stronger and improve athletic performance.

Almost every kind of sports program in the country has some kind of strength training program. The current mentality, among coaches in most sports, is that since you need some strength to perform a physical activity, then all you have to do is have your athletes lift weights, get stronger, and thus perform better in their particular sport. Coaches have been conditioned by strength trainers to believe that weight training is necessary for success in all sports, without even knowing if it can even be applied to their sport.

However, the implications derived about strength training from studies by reputable sports medicine experts, doctors and exercise physiologists, goes against this traditional thinking; and probably will not be welcomed by the strength industry. There is no doubt that athletes, and just about everyone who lift heavy objects in a systematic manner, will gain strength. The world of "strength" training (lifting weights), however, is steeped in myth and misconceptions; which ultimately leads to many athletes being exposed to unnecessary and sometimes counter-productive training.

It has been determined that a large number of sporting activities do not require excessive levels of strength. Swimming is one of those activities. Some swim teams will spend as much as one fifth of their training time on resistance training on machines, free weights, and weight racks and resistance tubing in the water. Such an emphasis seems a bit excessive considering that strength is not a big factor in success in competitive swimming.

Sure, you say, you don't need a lot of strength to swim a long distance aerobic swim; you need endurance. But what about sprint swimming and water polo? Don't the sprint swimmer and sprint water polo player require strength to swim faster over a short distance? Not according to studies performed on sprint swimmers by different researchers. In a classic study performed by Costill, Sharpe and Troup is was found that only a minimal level of strength was required for sprint swimmers; and this could be best provided by practicing maximum sprint swims; not with dry-land resistance training.

Another study performed by Tanaka, Costil, et al, compared sprinters who performed dry-land strength training in their swim training; and those that performed the same sprint training, but without additional resistance training. It was found that despite increased strength in the swimmers who utilized resistance training, there was no increase in performance in measured sprint swims over the group that did not do resistance training. In other words, there wasn't a transfer of increased strength to sprint swim performance. Since sprint swimming is required of the water polo player, we can also apply the studies in sprint swimming to water polo. The reasons why additional strength aquired from dry-land exercise does not transfer to faster swimming have been documented in Chapter 7 on "Resistance Training for Water Polo". The findings of the above studies conclude that increasing strength for sprint swimming and water polo is not necessary for optimum performance in those activities.

In order to achieve the necessary strength to perform those activities, it is only necessary to perform the activity itself. In other words, to swim faster in a race, or in a water polo game, only requires that the athlete swim maximum sprint swims in practice. To become a better water polo player, it is better to practice playing water polo, rather than lift weights. Although my own experiences with weight training for my teams does not qualify as a scientific study, I think that I can justify, at least to myself, the need (or not) to lift weights and play water polo successfully.

In 32 years of college coaching, my teams probably lifted weights during 60% of the 32 competitive collegiate seasons. I probably did this because it was the "thing to do" and the players expected it. Although the players did not seem to mind the years that we did not do weights. We produced championship teams in both the years we lifted weights and in the years we did not. I certainly couldn't tell the difference in our play.

One thing we did do every year, however, was to play the rest of the year, including the summer Senior National Championships with doing any weights at all. Neither did most of the other teams that we played against in the summer. We also won Championships at the summer Nationals without doing weights at all. Once again, I could not tell the difference in our play in the summer when we didn't push weights, and in the Fall season when we did push weights. To me, it did not really make a difference in our play.

Years ago when I was coaching, lifting weights for water polo was one of these "things" that coaches did, without actually looking into whether it was necessary or justified. We just assumed that if you were stronger you could swim faster, perform the eggbeater better, and play water polo better. With the aid of scientific analysis, numerous research projects, 32 years of experience, and just plain common sense, I can now safely conclude that lifting weights is NOT necessary to be a successful water polo player.

MYTHS STARTED BY SWIMMING COACHES

First of all let me explain that swim coaches are involved in a sport that is very different from water polo. The only thing the two sports have in common is that the athletes have to swim in the water to perform both of them. However, many of the training techniques that are used in swimming simply do not apply to water polo. The key is to apply the applicable principles of swim sprint training to training the water polo player. It is up to the water polo coach to do this.

Secondly, you have to understand that most swim coaches do not like water polo. The main reason being that they do not want to lose their swimmers to another sport, especially one that involves a ball, and scoring goals, and having fun. Let's see, what would you rather do? Put your face in the water and follow a little black line up and down the pool for hours; or play water polo? No-brainer on this one!

Don't get me wrong. I am all for letting my water polo players join the swim team during the off-season, if they want to swim. I will never force a player to swim unless they really want to. What bothers me is the swim coaches that will not allow their swimmers, who want to play water polo, to be on the water polo team at all, not even for a few months. It would probably help the swimmers mentally to play a team sport for a few months out of the year, and get away from staring at the bottom of the pool. Some of the myths that swim coaches perpetuate are simply to keep their swimmers on the swim team, and off the water polo team.

MYTH: WATER POLO MESSES UP YOUR SWIM STROKE

TRUTH: This is the first myth that swimming coaches try to spread about water polo. While it may be true that the freestyle swimming stroke is different than the water polo freestyle stroke, you are still using similar muscles and using the same muscles and cardiovascular systems.

It would seem that it would be rather simple to change from one to the other. What is the difference between switching from water polo freestyle stroke to swimming freestyle stroke, and switching from butterfly, backstroke and breaststroke to freestyle stroke?

The four competitive swimming strokes are completely different from each other; yet swimmers make that switch all of the time, sometimes during the same event, the individual medley. Actually, the water polo stroke is closer to the freestyle stroke than any of the other three competitive strokes. This argument does not hold water! (Pardon the pun)

MYTH: WATER POLO GETS YOU OUT OF SHAPE FOR SWIMMING

TRUTH: Water polo is definitely different than swimming a 1500-meter swim race, so I would have to somewhat agree with swim coaches there. Water polo is essentially "speed" work for several hours a day. It is certainly more speed work than some swimmers will get in their swim workouts. It might even do some good for the 1500-meter swimmer. It has been proven, in numerous swim studies, that while training for the long distance aerobic swim race like the 1500 will not improve sprint swim speed, the opposite effect is true. Training for anaerobic short sprint events can actually help improve the aerobic capacity of the long distance swimmer. Interval swimming is based on this principle.

But, the simple fact is that swimmers probably do a lot of unnecessary swimming as it is. This statement is coming from the same swim coaches who have their swimmers train for a short 50-yard two lap race by swimming 10,000 yards a day. Most swim races are 100 to 200 yards long and swum at a very fast pace.

Granted, water polo will not get you in shape to swim your fastest 200-yard swim race; but it certainly can't hurt you. I have always believed that swimmers swim more yardage than necessary for the length of the actual race. Maybe they should try a little water polo so they can learn to swim fast? Just kidding, swim coaches!

One of the fastest swimmers in the world played water polo for me at Stanford, Olympic gold medalist Pablo Morales. At the end of the fall water polo season, Pablo would join the swim team and swim in an early season meet. His early-season swim times, coming just off the water polo season, were still the best on the swim team for that time of the year. Of course he would do even faster times at the end of a long swim training season of 4-5 months. After playing water polo in the fall of one year, Pablo broke the world-record in the 100-meter butterfly that next summer. He seems to have recovered pretty well from that "terrible" water polo season that got him out of shape and ruined his stroke.

MYTH: YOU HAVE TO BUILD A BASE AT THE BEGINNING OF THE SEASON BEFORE YOU CAN DO ANY WATER POLO OR SPEED WORK
TRUTH: This is one of the biggest myths in sports, especially in swimming. Some water polo coaches believe that at the beginning of the season, the players need to build an "aerobic base" with long slow swimming, believing it lays a mythical foundation for faster sprint training later on in the season. The whole concept is actually beyond belief. Let's see, swimming a lot of slow, long distances so that you can swim fast later on? On a physiological basis, there is no rational to this concept.

It has been proven in countless studies that slow aerobic swimming does NOT help to improve the fast anaerobic swimming that is required in water polo. A swimming base may be needed for a water polo player, because they need to "swim" to be able to play water polo, and that is only taught by swimming; so I guess that it can be called a "base".

This skill should be taught to the unskilled swimmer, at a slower pace until the motor pattern of swimming is learned. However, the skill of swimming that then has to be learned by a water polo player, is the skill of swimming fast for short distances, with the head out of the water. These are the motor patterns that cannot be learned by swimming slow. That slow paced motor learning has nothing to do with developing the energy systems and fitness to play competitive water polo.

If you want to be fit to play water polo, then swim fast in daily anaerobic sets performed during the training session. If you want to have an aerobic benefit, then continue the anaerobic endurance training. You'll get that "aerobic base" you want for your recovery; but it will come from a meaningful anaerobic fast paced training system.

There is no reason at all why water polo players can't start out the season by swimming fast, as long as you gradually build up the speed at the beginning. Interval training at shorter distances and higher intensities is by far the most efficient and effective way of getting players in shape, because it allows swimmers and water polo players to swim at or near race pace, or game counterattack pace. Why waste time doing a lot a slow swimming that does not carry over at all to the fast sprint swimming that is required to play a game? All that a lot of slow swimming does is decrease your speed, decrease your power, and produce overuse injuries (rotator cuff and shoulder muscle).

MYTH: IF I TAPER (REST) MY PLAYERS TOO MUCH, THEY WILL GET OUT OF SHAPE.
TRUTH: Many swim coaches are afraid to rest their players during the competitive season, thinking that they will get out of shape. Most swim teams will not taper until the end of the season, because mid-season swim times are not that important; nor are the results of dual meets. At the end of the season is when the swimmers have to do their best times. This is not always the case in water polo where a mid-season game may be just as important as an end of the season game.

Some water polo coaches are so worried about their players getting out of shape, that they will still have their team perform two training sessions on the day before a game. That is fine, as long as your team is playing an opponent that you know you can easily beat. However, if you are going to play a game that you know will be a difficult one, don't expect your players to perform well if you don't rest them. If you expect a good performance from your team, you need to have them start the game with a full tank of energy producing carbohydrates (glycogen).

Depending on the length and intensity of the practice sessions, water polo players will use up much of their glycogen (carbohydrate) stores that are utilized by the body to provide energy for muscular contraction. Two-a-day training sessions are especially draining on the water polo athlete. So, even of the athlete eats three fully-loaded carbohydrate meals a day, including snacks, he will probably start the next days practice with a little less glycogen than he had the previous day.

By the end of the week, it is possible that his glycogen stores will be at a very low level. This can severly limit performance, even during moderate intensity activity. No matter how ample your fat stores, after you deplete your muscle glycogen stores, you will experience fatigue to some degree; and be unable to maintain the pace and intensity required in practice and a game.

The coach doesn't have to rest (taper) his athletes for every game. But if his team has an important game that may decide whether they make it to post season competition; he may need to rest his players to help restore their glycogen levels and give them the energy necessary to help win the game. The best way to restore glycogen levels, and still get in the necessary training during the week, is to do a gradual taper.

The team can still have long and strenuous training sessions at the beginning of the week; but the practice sessions at the end of the week should be much shorter, and much less strenuous. In other words, the practice sessions have to be "tapered down" in terms of intensity and length. The best way to accomplish this is to take in more carbohydrates in the diet, and burn off less carbohydrates by training less. As a coach, you can't always control what your athletes eat; but you do control how much rest they get.

If you need to win an important game, the least of your worries as a coach is whether your athletes will get out of shape or not. Going easier on training sessions for a day or two before a game is NOT going to get the players out of shape. The athlete's body takes a long time to get "in shape"; it does not lose conditioning in one or two days.

MYTH: YOU HAVE TO TRAIN 10,000-YARDS A DAY TO SWIM A 50-YARD RACE
TRUTH: Unfortunately this is the kind of mentality that some water polo coaches have when training water polo players. Where did we get it from? From swimming coaches of course! Think about this for a minute and you will get my point. Training for a race that takes around 20 seconds to swim a distance of 50 yards, by swimming 8000-10,000 yards a day of slower paced swimming than the actual race, is the same as having 100 meter sprint runner who runs a 10-second race, training by running 8-10 miles a day at a much slower pace then 10 seconds per 100 meters.

Water polo requires even shorter swims than 50 yards. It is an anaerobic sport that involves a lot a short swims of 5-25 yards, constant changes of direction, and lots of time spent in a vertical position. What is there about swimming a lot of yardage that applies to the way the game of water polo is played? What is there about swimming repeat 500 and 1000 yard swims, or even 100 and 200 repeat swims, that applies to a player who sprints a maximum of 25 yards at a very fast pace?

Swimming at speeds that are slower than game (counterattack) pace and at distances that are much longer than the distances swum in a game (5-22 meters) does nothing to stimulate the muscles and energy systems that will allow the water polo player's body to adapt and improve.

I assume that you are reading this manual because you are a water polo coach. I hope that you get the picture and get away from this swimming mentality. Constantly remind yourself of this, and you shouldn't fall into the "swimming long distance and high volume" trap. A coach can improve his players conditioning for water polo only by increasing the intensity of the swims, not the volume of the swims.

I will give three examples of the fallacy of swimming a lot of yardage to get in shape for water polo:

1) During my 32 years as a collegiate coach, our average swimming yardage per day for my teams was about 1500 yards per day, consisting mostly of short repeat swims of 100 yards or less. That was probably the shortest total distance swum per day for any team at the collegiate level. Yet, we were able to win 80 percent of our games (an NCAA record) and played in 14 NCAA Final Games (Eight NCAA Championships, also an NCAA record). Despite the fact that we did not do a lot of lap swimming, we won many games and championships by out-swimming our opponents and wearing them down with a devistating counterattack.

2) My college team went to Europe in 1986 for a three week period and did absolutely no swim training at all during that time. We only played daily water polo games against various club teams in five different countries. When we returned, we won the USWP Senior National Championships against club teams that had been training all summer, and consisted of the top collegiate players in the country and all of the players from the USA National team. Why? Because we got in shape by playing water polo. We were in water polo "game shape". No swim training was necessary!

3) Every year in the middle of our competitive water polo season, when we are in tip-top shape, we have a game against our older, out of shape, and somewhat heavier alumni players; and every year they beat us. Not only do they not do any swim training, but some of these guys haven't been in a pool for years.

How do they do it? Because they know how to play the game. To me, this underscores the importance of spending as little time as possible swimming laps and spending as much time as possible learning how to play the game.

Made in the USA
Lexington, KY
19 November 2012